THE CAMBRIDGE COMPANION 1

M000252194

Theatre has engaged with science since its intersection of the two disciplines has been ....ᴜ…ₙ ᴜₙₜₑᵣₑₛₜ ₜₒ scholars and students. *The Cambridge Companion to Theatre and Science* gives readers a sense of this dynamic field, using detailed analyses of plays and performances covering a wide range of areas including climate change and the environment, technology, animal studies, disease and contagion, mental health, and performance and cognition. Identifying historical tendencies that have dominated theatre's relationship with science, the volume traces many periods of theatre history across a wide geographical range. It follows a simple and clear structure of pairs and triads of chapters that cluster around a given theme so that readers get a clear sense of the current debates and perspectives.

KIRSTEN E. SHEPHERD-BARR is Professor of English and Theatre Studies at the University of Oxford. Her publications include *Science on Stage: From Doctor Faustus to Copenhagen* (2006), *Theatre and Evolution from Ibsen to Beckett* (2015), *Modern Drama: A Very Short Introduction* (2016), and *Twentieth-Century Approaches to Literature: Late Victorian into Modern* (2016), coedited with Laura Marcus and Michèle Mendelsohn and shortlisted for the Modernist Studies Association book prize.

CAMBRIDGE COMPANIONS TO

THEATRE AND PERFORMANCE

The Cambridge Companions to Theatre and Performance collection publishes specially-commissioned volumes of new essays designed for students at universities and drama schools, and their teachers. Each volume focuses on a key topic, practitioner or form and offers a balanced and wide-ranging overview of its subject. Content includes historical and political contexts, case studies, critical and theoretical approaches, afterlives and guidance on further reading.

Published and forthcoming titles

The Cambridge Companion to Theatre and Science *Edited by Kirsten E. Shepherd-Barr*

The Cambridge Companion to International Theatre Festivals *Edited by Ric Knowles*

The Cambridge Companion to the Circus *Edited by Jim Davis and Gillian Arrighi*

The Cambridge Companion to American Theatre since 1945 *Edited by Julia Listengarten and Stephen Di Benedetto*

The Cambridge Companion to British Theatre since 1945 *Edited by Jen Harvie and Dan Rebellato*

The Cambridge Companion to British Playwriting since 1945 *Edited by Vicky Angelaki and Dan Rebellato*

The Cambridge Companion to British Theatre of the First World War *Edited by Helen E. M. Brooks*

Related Cambridge Companions

The Cambridge Companion to African American Theatre *Edited by Harvey Young*

The Cambridge Companion to the Actress *Edited by Maggie B. Gale and John Stokes*

The Cambridge Companion to British Theatre, 1730-1830 *Edited by Jane Moody and Daniel O'Quinn*

The Cambridge Companion to English Melodrama *Edited by Carolyn Williams*

The Cambridge Companion to English Restoration Theatre *Edited by Deborah Payne Fisk*

The Cambridge Companion to Greek and Roman Theatre *Edited by Marianne McDonald and Michael Walton*

The Cambridge Companion to Greek Comedy *Edited by Martin Revermann*

The Cambridge Companion to Greek Tragedy *Edited by P. E. Easterling*

The Cambridge Companion to Medieval English Theatre, second edition *Edited by Richard Beadle and Alan J. Fletcher*

The Cambridge Companion to Performance Studies *Edited by Tracy C. Davis*

The Cambridge Companion to Theatre History *Edited by David Wiles and Christine Dymkowski*

The Cambridge Companion to Victorian and Edwardian Theatre *Edited by Kerry Powell*

THE CAMBRIDGE
COMPANION TO
THEATRE AND SCIENCE

EDITED BY
KIRSTEN E. SHEPHERD-BARR
University of Oxford

CAMBRIDGE
UNIVERSITY PRESS

CAMBRIDGE
UNIVERSITY PRESS

University Printing House, Cambridge CB2 8BS, United Kingdom

One Liberty Plaza, 20th Floor, New York, NY 10006, USA

477 Williamstown Road, Port Melbourne, VIC 3207, Australia

314–321, 3rd Floor, Plot 3, Splendor Forum, Jasola District Centre, New Delhi – 110025, India

79 Anson Road, #06–04/06, Singapore 079906

Cambridge University Press is part of the University of Cambridge.

It furthers the University's mission by disseminating knowledge in the pursuit of education, learning, and research at the highest international levels of excellence.

www.cambridge.org
Information on this title: www.cambridge.org/9781108476522
DOI: 10.1017/9781108676533

First published 2020

A catalogue record for this publication is available from the British Library.

Library of Congress Cataloging-in-Publication Data
NAMES: Shepherd-Barr, Kirsten, 1966– editor.
TITLE: The Cambridge companion to theatre and science / edited by Kirsten E. Shepherd-Barr.
DESCRIPTION: Cambridge ; New York, NY : Cambridge University Press, 2020. | Series: Cambridge companions to literature | Includes bibliographical references and index.
IDENTIFIERS: LCCN 2020014101 (print) | LCCN 2020014102 (ebook) | ISBN 9781108476522 (hardback) | ISBN 9781108700986 (paperback) | ISBN 9781108676533 (epub)
SUBJECTS: LCSH: Drama–History and criticism. | Science in literature. | Scientists in literature. | Theaters–Stage-setting and scenery. | Literature and science.
CLASSIFICATION: LCC PN1650.S34 C36 2020 (print) | LCC PN1650.S34 (ebook) | DDC 808.2/936–dc23
LC record available at https://lccn.loc.gov/2020014101
LC ebook record available at https://lccn.loc.gov/2020014102

ISBN 978-1-108-47652-2 Hardback
ISBN 978-1-108-70098-6 Paperback

CONTENTS

List of Illustrations   *page* vii
List of Contributors   viii
Acknowledgements   ix

Introduction   1
KIRSTEN E. SHEPHERD-BARR

1   Objectivity and Observation   12
    DAN REBELLATO

2   Staging Consciousness: Metaphor as Thought Experiment in
    McBurney's *Beware of Pity*   26
    JANE R. GOODALL

3   The Experimental/Experiential Stage: Extreme States of Being of and
    Knowing in the Theatre   40
    CARINA BARTLEET

4   A Cave, a Skull, and a Little Piece of Grit: Theatre in the Anthropocene   55
    CARL LAVERY

5   The Play at the End of the World: Deke Weaver's *Unreliable Bestiary*
    and the Theatre of Extinction   70
    UNA CHAUDHURI AND JOSHUA WILLIAMS

6   Bodies of Knowledge: Theatre and Medical Science   85
    STANTON B. GARNER, JR.

7   Pathogenic Performativity: Urban Contagion and Fascist Affect   101
    FINTAN WALSH

8   Theatres of Mental Health   116
     JON VENN

9   Devised Theatre and the Performance of Science   131
     MIKE VANDEN HEUVEL

10   Theatre and Science as Social Intervention   146
     MICHAEL CARKLIN

11   Acting and Science   162
     RHONDA BLAIR

12   Staging Cognition: How Performance Shows Us How We Think   176
     AMY COOK

13   Clouds and Meteors: Recreating Wonder on the Early Modern Stage   188
     FREDERIQUE AIT-TOUATI

14   'The Stage Hand's Lament': Scenography, Technology, and Off-Stage
     Labour   203
     KIRSTEN E. SHEPHERD-BARR

     Index   219

ILLUSTRATIONS

5.1 From Deke Weaver, *The Unreliable Bestiary: Bear* (2016):
Ranger Joe with mask of polar bear expert
Malcolm Ramsay   *page* 76
6.1 Poster for the Federal Theatre's production of *Spirochete* in
Chicago (1938)   89
6.2 Julie Hesmondhalgh as Vivian Bearing in Margaret Edson's
Wit (Manchester Royal Exchange Theatre, 2016).   95
12.1 *Marjana and the Forty Thieves* stages an evolution in our
conceptual system from thinking about individuals telling
stories to stories generating individuals. Anish Roy, black
microphone visible on his forehead, tells a version of the
story to a small group of spectators (Target Margin
Theatre, 2019; directed by David Herskovits)   183
13.1 Fontenelle, *Conversations on the Plurality of Worlds*   190
13.2 Engraving of the last act of *Les Noces de Pélée et Thétis*,
set design by Torelli   190
14.1 Theatrical patent for Loie Fuller's serpentine dance
mechanisms   214
14.2 Theatrical patent for Loie Fuller's invention of simulated
flames   215

CONTRIBUTORS

FREDERIQUE AIT-TOUATI, CNRS/EHESS (National Centre for Scientific Research/ School for Studies in Social Sciences), Paris

CARINA BARTLEET, Oxford Brookes University

RHONDA BLAIR, Southern Methodist University

MICHAEL CARKLIN, University of South Wales

UNA CHAUDHURI, New York University

AMY COOK, Stony Brook University

STANTON B. GARNER, JR., University of Tennessee

JANE R. GOODALL, University of Western Sydney

CARL LAVERY, University of Glasgow

DAN REBELLATO, Royal Holloway University of London

KIRSTEN E. SHEPHERD-BARR, University of Oxford

MIKE VANDEN HEUVEL, University of Wisconsin-Madison

JON VENN, The Royal Central School of Speech and Drama

FINTAN WALSH, Birkbeck University of London

JOSHUA WILLIAMS, New York University

ACKNOWLEDGEMENTS

My thanks go first and foremost to the contributors to this book, with whom it has been a privilege and a pleasure to work and from whom I have learned so much. Their ideas and their commitment are inspiring.

I also wish to thank my editors at Cambridge University Press: Kate Brett, who first suggested this book to me, and Emily Hockley and Eilidh Burrett, who have patiently and expertly guided the book through to completion. I am also grateful to Alexandra Paddock, Katherine Gurnos-Davies, and Niall Summers for their invaluable editorial assistance. Environment is key to any book project, and the Faculty of English and St Catherine's College, Oxford provided unparalleled intellectual as well as physical spaces in which to think, write, and exchange ideas for this book.

Chapter 14 is the result of several stages of testing out ideas: first, in a talk I presented to the American Chemical Society on theatre's engagement with chemistry, specifically stage lighting; then as a presentation on backstage labour to a conference at the University of Warwick on nineteenth-century theatre; finally, as a keynote address I gave at the 2018 British Society for Literature and Science conference, Oxford Brookes University. My thanks to all of these organizations, particularly the BSLS, for the opportunity to explore my ideas. I am also indebted to Jane R. Goodall for her careful reading of the chapter in draft and her suggestions, all of which have strengthened it, and to David Wilmore of **theat**research consultancy for providing high-quality images of the theatrical patents shown here.

Finally, my warmest thanks and gratitude go to my family, near and far, especially Graham, Callum, Gavin, and Alastair. This book is for you.

KIRSTEN E. SHEPHERD-BARR

Introduction

An audience follows a park ranger into the woods looking for wolves ... A young Danish prince contemplates a skull in a dug-up grave ... A wheelchair-bound blind man spars verbally with the carer who is about to leave him ... A woman with a deformed spine is murdered by a fanatical doctor who wants to dissect her corpse ... A bald, cancer-ridden woman recites the poetry of Donne as she lies dying ... Two pairs of couples in Regency dress dance a waltz as the lights gradually fade ...

These moments and images come from memorable plays and performances that, in various ways, engage with scientific ideas. Some of them will be instantly recognizable as 'science plays': Shelagh Stephenson's *An Experiment with an Air Pump*, Tom Stoppard's *Arcadia*, Margaret Edson's *Wit*. Others will be familiar as famous plays, but it might come as a surprise to think about Shakespeare's *Hamlet* or Beckett's *Endgame* as engaging with science. The first example on the list may be unknown to most readers, as it is part of an ongoing series of site-specific performance works about species loss and other impacts of climate change, a relatively new area that theatre is exploring in powerful ways. Most of these examples come from plays written and performed within the past few decades, a period of great activity and interest in putting science on stage. However, that is by no means a recent tendency; theatre and science have a long history of interacting, going back to the ancient Greeks, for example in the playwright Aristophanes' *The Clouds* and (as one of the chapters in this book explores) in Plato's metaphor of the cave. That history has been charted in numerous books and articles defining the field of theatre and science. This book gathers some of the findings that have emerged from this growing discourse and presents new developments and directions of inquiry. Contributions come from many different areas of expertise within the field of theatre and science and demonstrate how far it has expanded since it began to be a 'field'.

And when, exactly, was that? Many of those working in the field would agree that it was Michael Carklin's pioneering conference, 'Theatres of

Science', at the University of Glamorgan (now the University of South Wales) in 2004 that marked out the territory by recognizing that there was more to the engagement of theatre and science than a few scattered plays and articles here and there. Many of the contributors to this volume, including Carklin himself, were at that 2004 conference. *The Cambridge Companion to Theatre and Science* provides a snapshot of the field as it is now, building on seminal works such as Joseph Roach's *The Player's Passion: Studies in the Science of Acting*, Natalie Crohn Schmitt's *Actors and Onlookers: Theatre and Twentieth-Century Scientific Views of Nature*, Allen E. Hye's *The Moral Dilemma of the Scientist in Modern Drama*, William Demastes's *Theatre of Chaos: Beyond Absurdism*, Charles A. Carpenter's *Dramatists and the Bomb: American and British Playwrights Confront the Nuclear Age, 1945–1964*, and Jane R. Goodall's *Performance and Evolution in the Age of Darwin*. In addition, Carl Djerassi's articles and plays proposed a 'science-in-theatre' model that engendered lively discussion, much of it in the journal *Interdisciplinary Science Reviews*, which has regularly featured articles on the relationship between theatre and science. All of this publishing activity coincided with a surge of playwriting and theatre-making on scientific themes, ideas, and figures, accentuated by the excitement and controversy over Michael Frayn's 1998 play *Copenhagen*, which became a watershed moment for theatre and science in raising fundamental questions about what it means when the two domains meet. What responsibility, if any, does the playwright have toward real-life people and actual scientific ideas being depicted? And what defines a successful 'science play'? My book *Science on Stage: From Doctor Faustus to Copenhagen* addressed such questions as it explored the phenomenon of the 'science play', and in the same year (2006) Sue-Ellen Case's *Performing Science and the Virtual* traced the ways in which science has been performed in a variety of modes, from alchemy to the contemporary virtual avatar. These were followed by Eva-Sabine Zehelein's *Science: Dramatic: Science Plays in America and Great Britain, 1990–2007* and Tiffany Watt-Smith's *On Flinching: Theatricality and Scientific Looking from Darwin to Shell Shock*, which was one of the first studies to consider the theatre–science interaction as a two-way street, with scientists often borrowing from performance and incorporating theatrical techniques into their experiments. There has also been greater recognition by historians of science and medicine of the role played by theatre in the cultural dissemination and embeddedness of scientific ideas and medical findings and innovations, for example in Martin Willis's *Staging Science: Scientific Performance on Street, Stage, and Screen* and Bernard Lightman and Bennett Zon's collection *Evolution and Victorian Culture*.

As this brief (and by no means complete) summary indicates, interest in creating theatre works that involve scientific ideas, and in discussing, analyzing, and reviewing them, has continued to build steadily over the past several decades. In 2013 and 2014, two special issues of *Interdisciplinary Science Reviews* on theatre and science (co-edited by Bartleet and Shepherd-Barr) took stock of the field and signalled, through their range of contributors, possible future directions it might take. Many of these directions have been borne out now in books, for example Jenni Halpin's *Contemporary Physics Plays*, Anna Harpin's *Performance, Madness, Psychiatry: Isolated Acts*, and Nicola Shaughnessy's *Applying Performance: Live Art, Socially Engaged Theatre and Affective Practice*. There are also in-depth studies of single areas of science or medicine and theatre, such as disease and contagion (Fintan Walsh's *Theatres of Contagion* addresses this area), psychiatry and 'madness' (Christina Wald's *Hysteria, Trauma, and Melancholia: Performative Maladies in Contemporary Anglophone Drama* pioneered this area), evolutionary thought (my book *Theatre and Evolution from Ibsen to Beckett* and Goodall's *Performance and Evolution in the Age of Darwin*), and the diagnostic gaze (Alex Mermikides and Gianna Bouchard's *Performance and the Medical Body*, which explores this topic transhistorically). Mathematics on stage has received expert analysis from Steve Abbott in particular. One can find whole books devoted to single plays, such as Liliane Campos's *The Dialogue of Art and Science in Tom Stoppard's Arcadia*, and dozens of articles in a wide range of journals attest to the range and variety of the field as it currently stands.

In short, there is no end to the hypertextual resources readers can draw on as they read this companion. In addition, there is a wealth of resources in the field of 'literature and science' that have particular relevance to performance and science. Although it has tended to focus on narrative forms like the novel (and in particular the nineteenth-century novel), the field of 'literature and science' is an important close relative to 'theatre and science' and its common ground is touched upon in the final chapter of this book.

The Cambridge Companion to Theatre and Science aims to provide something different from what is already available on this subject both in print and on the Internet. It is also different from many companions and guides to a field, topic, or theme in the way it is designed to be consumed. The book recognizes that habits of reading have changed because of the accessibility of digital resources; as book historian Leah Price points out in *What We Talk about When We Talk about Books* (2019), we now read in hypertext mode, taking every book or article as a starting point and stopping to look things up as we go along, knowledge gloriously proliferating at every turn or detour. If every statement in a book can be thus explored and probed, how, then, should a book like this one best serve its readers, who have instantaneous access to so much more information than it can provide? The main job is not to duplicate what is already out there. This book therefore is a companion in the truest sense: it guides readers to the key ideas and topics within the growing field of theatre and science and gives a clear picture of what that field is all about, yet leaves readers completely free to develop and pursue their own areas of interest – to look up plays that pique their curiosity as they go along, or performances that they want to know more about, or theatres and theatre companies that are mentioned, or playwrights, scientists, directors, actors, designers, and so on.

Thus, while dozens of individual plays are discussed in the book, it is not a comprehensive guide to 'science plays'. Rather, it is a companion to some of the key developments and ideas within theatre and science: it guides the reader to and through them, using case studies to illustrate points along the way, and it pays attention to performances as well as to texts. This makes it both more interesting and of more lasting value. Without depth of analysis and expert contextualization, the book would just be a list of science plays. Such lists are available elsewhere, as are analyses of individual plays in articles and books, many of which are listed in the Suggested Reading sections that appear at the end of each chapter.

In parallel with the rise of the 'science play' came the development of other ways of engaging with science on stage, notably through devised performance and through theatre as social intervention. The book explores such developments, and also significant new areas such as theatre and the environment, ecology, and animal studies; theatres of mental health; and performance and cognitive science. The place of technology and invention within the study of theatre and science also comes under scrutiny, with case studies from different periods and cultures. The medical sciences are represented in two chapters dealing with contagion and disease as powerful theatrical starting points. An overarching theme is metaphor, explored in several chapters for its explanatory power, yet also robustly interrogated in terms of its cultural role as the dominant mode of telling scientific stories. Observation and experiment unite the scientific method with the theatrical, and their convergence as well as their significant divergences are explored here, with a strong link to diagnosis. Theatre as laboratory emerges as the abiding common ground of the book as it ponders how science and performance interact.

The book is structured in pairs and triads of chapters that consider a particular aspect of theatre and science in different ways. This structure allows the reader to get a sense of the discourse on the given theme or topic, its history, debates, and key areas of investigation, as well as some of its representative plays and productions. Brief synopses of each chapter follow below. One of the book's strengths and innovations is its treatment of period and its balance of earlier and later material. In terms of period coverage, the book is not overwhelmingly focused on the twentieth and twenty-first centuries like many discussions of theatre and science but touches on key moments, plays, and performances across the centuries, from the Greeks through to the medieval and Renaissance theatres, from the eighteenth century to the present. In addition, individual chapters are often transhistorical rather than confined to a specific temporal span. While the emphasis tends to be on Western theatre, there is broad cultural coverage within that framework as well as geographical spread beyond the Anglophone world.

The first three chapters of the book introduce key concepts central to both theatre and science: objectivity, experiment, and metaphor. Dan Rebellato's 'Objectivity and Observation' starts by tracing the development of objectivity in both science and theatre through classical and early modern theatre, in which it was a fairly unimportant epistemic virtue, into the late eighteenth century where objectivity begins to emerge through the idealizations of 'Truth-to-Nature' in biology and in literary and theatrical Romanticism. He shows that although some conceptions of scientific objectivity and observation treat these as virtuous by the extent to which they rise above personal or historical bias, the practice and theory of both objectivity and observation have changed through history. Drawing on the work of Lorraine Daston and others, the chapter goes on to show that the emergence of modern ('mechanical') objectivity, and a new relationship with observation, mark both nineteenth-century science and Naturalist theatre. Making the comparison explains some of the antitheatrical claims of Naturalist authors and the contradictions of Naturalist practice. As nineteenth-century 'objectivity' is superseded, so the theatrical figuration of science gravitates towards areas of ambiguity, chaos, and indeterminacy. In Chapter 2, 'Staging Consciousness: Metaphor as Thought Experiment in McBurney's *Beware of Pity*', Jane R. Goodall begins by observing that the repertoire of science plays is dominated by works in which scientific issues are the subject of the drama, rather than a mode of exploration, in symbiotic relationship with those of the theatre itself. This kind of symbiosis can occur only if the collaborative process is set up at the outset, so that the script evolves in concert with all aspects of staging and enactment – a method pioneered by Theatre de Complicité, under the direction of its founder Simon McBurney. Taking as a case study McBurney's stage adaptation of Stefan Zweig's novel *Beware of Pity*, the chapter explores the question of how consciousness might be staged, rather than talked about. Central to the experiment is the process of working with metaphor, both as literary conceit and as an approach to theatrical realization. In Chapter 3, 'The Experimental/Experiential

Stage: Extreme States of Being of and Knowing in the Theatre', Carina Bartleet charts the intersections between theatre and science and explores how experience and experiment are interlinked in each domain. Looking at three key scientific ideas and theatrical moments, the chapter draws out contextual aspects of the science that reflect the scientific concerns of their moments. Exploring first a play from the early years of the recent resurgence in the interest in theatre and science, the chapter investigates how the biological and medical sciences with their obvious link to genetic testing and human experience are represented, and moves on to consider how science, gender, and life become crystal clear in early twenty-first-century theatre. It concludes by looking at how theatre is shaped by the experience of climate change and its science in the 2010s through two very different plays, one a staged lecture and the other a production whose deliberate excess results in an expansive 'Epic' theatrical form that appears to take precedence over the science.

Two chapters on environmental issues in relation to performance come next. In Chapter 4, 'A Cave, a Skull, and a Little Piece of Grit: Theatre in the Anthropocene', Carl Lavery argues for a new way of thinking about what an ecologically oriented dialogue between theatre and science might give rise to. He does so by reading three canonical western texts – Plato's Cave, Shakespeare's *Hamlet,* and Beckett's *Endgame* – as instances of geology. The aim is to show how Western theatre is not simply a privileged space for human society to reflect on itself, as is often claimed, but a nonhuman medium, a decidedly mineralized practice – the very thing that so troubled Plato and that has caused Western philosophy to remain so suspicious of the stage. Reading Western theatre as geology, moreover, permits a theory of eco-performance criticism appropriate to/for the Anthropocene. Whereas accepted models of eco-theatre tend to run into dangerous contradiction, practically and theoretically, by divorcing themselves from theatre's larger ecology and history, this chapter discloses, by contrast, the extent to which the theatrical medium is always *already* ecological by dint of its occluded mineralogy. In Chapter 5, 'The Play at the End of the World: Deke Weaver's *Unreliable Bestiary* and the Theatre of Extinction', Una Chaudhuri and Joshua Williams situate the American artist Deke Weaver's long-term project *The Unreliable Bestiary* within the ecological politics of the Anthropocene. Weaver aims to create a performance for every letter of the English alphabet, with each letter representing an endangered species or threatened habitat. The performances he has made to date – Monkey (2009), Elephant (2010), Wolf (2013), Bear (2016–17), and Tiger (2019) – address the looming threat of the sixth great extinction by pairing the most fantastic flights of the animalized imagination with the most astonishing facts discovered by animal science. Reactivating and reconfiguring the medieval bestiary in this way allows Weaver to braid together an epistemology derived from the 'squishy science' of performance with an affect he calls 'plain old wonder', producing a new theatrical grammar for being in and with extinction and a new ethical framework for encountering our remaining animal others.

The book then turns to medical science and practice with a triad of chapters on, respectively, the medicalized body in performance, the concept of contagion on stage, and the staging of mental health conditions and their diagnosis. In Chapter 6, 'Bodies of Knowledge: Theatre and Medical Science', Stanton B. Garner, Jr., discusses how, as scientific medicine gained ascendancy in the nineteenth and twentieth centuries, theatre became an important site for the examination of scientific medicine's aspirations, achievements, limitations, and dangers. Early twentieth-century plays celebrated the pioneers of modern disease research and their accomplishments, while later twentieth- and early twenty-first century plays display a growing critique of scientific medicine and its conception of the body as an object of medical knowledge. David Feldshuh's *Miss Evers' Boys* considers the human and ethical stakes of the infamous Tuskegee syphilis study, and Susan-Lori Parks's *Venus* addresses the historical objectification of anomalous bodies. Margaret Edson's *Wit*, given extensive discussion here, explores the conflict between scientism and subjectivity in the context of the modern research hospital. The medium of theatre is central to these dramatic critiques; medical science may formulate the human body as an object of knowledge, but theatre's bodies look back in the midst of their display. Next, in Chapter 7, 'Pathogenic Performativity: Urban Contagion and Fascist Affect', Fintan Walsh looks at two recent performances, Arinzé Kene's *Misty* (2018) and Neil Bartlett's *The Plague* (2017), which depict cities under siege. Contagions, figurative and literal, spread among residents, destroying lives and tearing the fabric of the urban environment. In both productions the city is at war with itself, via the circulation of disease that passes between infrastructure and people. Focusing on these plays and their productions, this chapter explores how ideas of contagion are deployed to capture a sense of intangible danger spreading throughout the city, especially London, and how this formulation finds impetus in contemporary discourse that mobilizes the risk of economic, cultural, and political contagion as part of a divisive rhetoric. The chapter also considers how we might understand these forms of representation and discourse in light of the prevalence of 'pathogenic performativity', in which the language and phantasmagoria of contagion are deployed as tactics of governance, with theatre enabling its exposure or perpetuation. Finally, in Chapter 8, 'Theatres of Mental

Health', Jon Venn analyzes the legacy and influence of the diagnostic gaze in contemporary British theatre, examining how theatre can offer a site to negotiate the complex dynamic between psychiatric institutions and the experiences of patients. Contemporary psychiatry has overseen a vast expansion in the categorization of mental illness. Mental disorders can be identified and ascribed to individual patients in an act of diagnosis that signals mental illness as a 'performative malady'. Alongside reflecting shifts in the etiology of mental disorder (increasingly focused upon a biomedical model), the speech-act of diagnosis has implications for the legal status and care of the patient. Analyzing works such as Joe Penhall's *Some Voices* and Lucy Prebble's *The Effect*, this chapter suggests how theatre can offer a reimagination of diagnosis by situating and troubling the role of the psychiatric user.

The next two chapters recognize the extraordinary diversity and range of types of performances that engage with science and challenge the dominance of the mainstream 'science play'. In Chapter 9, 'Devised Theatre and the Performance of Science', Mike Vanden Heuvel notes that as science has become more interdisciplinary and recognized as a form of contingent knowledge circulated across cultural fields, devising has emerged as a suitable method for creating performances with scientific content and themes. By virtue of its multivocality (involving a number of authors), its multimodal forms of storytelling and address (through language, dance, physicalization, digital media, installation and site-specific environments, and the like), and its presentational modes, devised performance can often render scientific ideas performative, capturing not just what they 'are' but what they 'do' and how they disseminate in the public understanding. Across scientific fields that are increasingly interrelated, devised performance provides new ways to move beyond merely conveying scientific ideas, choosing instead to invite spectators actively to map domains of knowledge and construct ideas that are constantly in transit. One of the most significant areas of interaction between theatre and science is in the application of specific social problems, and in Chapter 10, 'Theatre and Science as Social Intervention', Michael Carklin covers a broad range of practices, from science public engagement events to collaborations between artists and scientists, theatre for young people, drama education initiatives, and global activism projects. He examines several case studies: first, examples of exhibitions, lectures, and demonstrations focusing on Michael Faraday and the Royal Institution Christmas Lectures, and also on public autopsy demonstrations; second, arts–science collaborations, known as 'sci-art', with reference particularly to the work of Y Touring; and third, theatre and activism in relation to climate change, as exemplified by the Climate Change Theatre Action project. His discussion is framed within his own experience as a practitioner working at the boundaries of theatre and science.

Performance and cognition, another key development in the field of theatre and science, is explored in the next pair of chapters. In Chapter 11, 'Acting and Science', Rhonda Blair surveys intersections between views of acting and paradigms of science, and addresses views of the human. The chapter begins with a brief historical overview, starting with Plato and Aristotle and proceeding to early twentieth-century scientists such as Pavlov and Freud. The focus is on late twentieth- and early twenty-first-century cognitive sciences and neuroscience, which provide the actor with concrete, material information about how body and brain work. This helps to eliminate misapprehensions about how different aspects of the self operate and offers insight into imagination, intellect, emotion, memory, and language, among other aspects of our experience. The discussion addresses the fact of actors as complex processes, inextricably connected to each other and their environments, and how the actor might utilize the findings of science. In Chapter 12, 'Staging Cognition: How Performance Shows Us How We Think', Amy Cook shows how theatre operates as a kind of cognitive prosthetic, helping us stage and imagine what we are not yet able to see around us or within us. Committed to embodied and extended theories of cognition, the chapter examines the relationship between the stories told onstage across the centuries and the shifting conceptions of the self and the other. Through a kind of wormhole between *King Lear*, the pageant wagon of the medieval period, and the off-off-Broadway theatre of today, the chapter connects the theatrical innovations around personation, or the taking-on of a character, in these different periods to argue that the theatrical conventions that set up the relationship between character and actor display a changing notion of the self. This shifting of theatrical conventions generates discomfort at first, as spectators learn to consume stories in a new way; and the discomfort unveils what we need to learn next.

The role of technology has received relatively little attention by scholars of theatre and science, who have tended to privilege scientific ideas and subject matter (as well as scientists themselves), following a pattern established by the broader field of 'literature and science'. The oversight is surprising, given the many and varied ways, both contemporary and historical, in which theatre and technology are intertwined, especially the central role technology has played in shaping playwriting norms and audience responses alike. Another way of putting this is that technology usually comes first; thus, electricity gave us modern playwriting, and Ibsen, Chekhov, O'Neill, Glaspell, and everyone else who followed are unimaginable without it. The final pair of chapters in this book explores technology and theatre through transhistorical examples of scenography. In Chapter 13, 'Clouds and Meteors: Recreating Wonder on the Early Modern Stage', Frédérique Aït-Touati traces the *theatrum mundi* (theatre as world) metaphor back to its technical and philosophical roots. By comparing iconographic sources from scientific texts with scenographic ones, the chapter follows the evolution of the notions of machine and wonder in the seventeenth century and argues that the material culture of theatre played an important role in the development of Cartesian physics and the new cosmology, and in particular in the mechanization of the world picture. The chapter focuses on the relationship between Fontenelle, Descartes, and the engineer and architect Giacomo Torelli, whose scenography gained him the name of 'the great sorcerer'. Paradoxically, it is by taking up Torelli's design, combined with Descartes's new definition of meteors, that Fontenelle manages to define a new type of 'wonder', scientific and no longer magical. In Chapter 14, '"The Stage Hand's Lament": Scenography, Technology, and Off-Stage Labour', I explore advances in stage technology from the nineteenth and twentieth centuries that profoundly shaped and influenced both theatrical performance and playwriting, particularly in the domain of stage lighting. Opening with the mid-twentieth-century example of Josef Svoboda, the chapter then goes back to the invention of limelight and its behind-the-scenes manipulation, which leads into a consideration of other kinds of technologically oriented off-stage labour. The discussion then turns to theatrical patents of the late nineteenth century, building on recent scholarship on backstage labour with a view to considering how scientific, technological, and theatrical work merge and often share this status of invisibility. The conclusion proposes a model for approaching and teaching theatre history based on a greater recognition of the role of technology, especially in our understanding of 'science on stage'.

There are some stimulating debates inherent in the way the chapters speak to each other, debates that I hope readers will pursue further. For example, Cook's 'swarm logic' and Goodall's 'force-field' are directly at odds, at least at first glance – and both raise profound questions about how humans will survive in the future. Walsh's focus on two plays that rely on spoken description rather than theatrical depiction sits in direct contrast to Goodall's selection of plays that do the opposite and show rather than tell. Blair's account of the history of cognition complements Garner's history of medicine in intriguing ways that, together, give startling insights into the evolution of our understanding of how the mind and body work. Aït-Touati and I come to very different conclusions about the relationship between stage technology and wonder. To some extent, both of these final chapters are concerned with science and technology in the service of wonder, and with the paradox that the wonder of theatre, just like the wonder of science, relies at least in part on not being able to see the mechanisms that generate it. There is another dimension to wonder now too, in light of climate change, as Chaudhuri and Williams suggest; knowledge of the gradual ebbing away of species and habitats adds sharp poignancy and shame to the wonder they inspire.

Theatre's power lies in its ability to show this all in a moment, through a word, image, or gesture, and in real time before a live audience. But the audience is not simply watching. The gasp of delight one often hears at a play dealing with scientific ideas, or the amazement at how an idea seems effortlessly and brilliantly shown, do not necessarily signal a passive kind of engagement. Rather, as this book shows, theatre's interaction with science enables active audience participation, whether overt or subtly implicit, through its combination of liveness, immediacy, science, and communality. The act of spectating (inadequate though the word may be to describe what an audience does at a performance of any kind) involves cognitive processes that activate the whole body and generate new knowledges. One of the aims of this book is to emphasize the extraordinary wholeness of experience that science on stage allows – an epistemology uniquely enabled by the integration of theatre and scientific concepts.

The ongoing interactions between theatre and science are constantly creating new, enriching configurations that neither domain could generate on its own because of specialist knowledge required to access it or because of the inherently closed nature of certain cultures, whether scientific or theatrical. Access is thus a strong underlying theme throughout this volume, and theatre's engagement with science raises salient questions, such as: Who has access to knowledge and expertise? Who can deploy it? What are the uses of science and theatre, respectively? Together, are they a force for change? What can they do in combination that they cannot do separately? While this volume might not be able to answer all of these questions, it provides the foundation for productively thinking about and pursuing them, as the corpus of performance works dealing with science grows ever larger and richer.

I

DAN REBELLATO

Objectivity and Observation

In Ibsen's *An Enemy of the People* (Christiania Theatre, 1883), Dr Stockmann discovers that the spa, the mainstay of the local town's economy, is harbouring an infection in the water pipes, invisible to the naked eye. His suspicions have been proved by a chemical analysis undertaken at the University, and Stockmann is delighted with his discovery, expecting to be roundly thanked for his efforts. Instead, everywhere he goes, he meets resistance. His report is rejected by the Spa Institute; the Mayor leans on the editor of the local radical newspaper and an independent printer to stop the report being published; and at a public meeting that he calls, Stockmann is prevented from discussing his findings and is goaded into lashing out against the town, its leaders, and eventually its citizens, leading to a riot in which his windows are smashed. In his ruined home, Stockmann doubles down on his words, insisting that his rejection from the town has only reinforced his convictions, because 'the strongest man in the world is he who stands most alone'.[1]

Is Dr Stockmann right? It is plausible to read the play as a defence of scientific truth-telling and a satire of political corruption, inspired by the ferocious response to his previous play *Ghosts*. But equally one might point to Stockmann's cupidity, his inept handling of people, and his movement from solidly grounded scientific claims to unfounded and speculative anti-democratic insults by the end of the play. Even Ibsen himself seemed unsure, echoing Stockmann's radical individualism to Georg Brandes, while expressing contempt for 'all the nonsense [Stockmann] comes up with' to the actor Martinius Nielsen.[2] Perhaps the figure who best represents the play's

---

[1] Henrik Ibsen, *An Enemy of the People in: A Doll's House and Other Plays*, ed. Tore Rem, trans. Deborah Dawkin and Erik Skuggevik, Penguin Classics (London, 2016), 366.

[2] Frode Helland and Julie Holledge, eds., *Ibsen on Theatre*, trans. May-Brit Akerholt (London, 2018), 92, 88.

ambiguities is the drunk at the public meeting who wants to vote both for and against Stockmann.[3]

Ibsen's play raises questions about scientific objectivity. Since the mid-nineteenth century, science had laid special claim to the objectivity of its methods and findings, situating, as we shall see, the scientist as the impersonal conduit for accurate representations of nature. Stockmann's scientific credentials might encourage us to think that his investigation is objectively founded, but there are suggestions in the play that his drive for the truth is motivated by personal ambition, family rivalry, or a political animus against the town's population. His observations are similarly tainted as he 'sees' his fellow citizens as 'mongrels', unfavourably contrasted with the better breeding of the 'noble' few,[4] which now uncomfortably recalls the terrible crimes committed in the name of eugenics. Objectivity has come under fire from feminist and race scholars for trying to pass off particular (white, Western, male) perspectives as universal, even as an expression specifically of male subjectivity. In the 1980s and 1990s, postmodernism offered a vastly influential critique of claims to objectivity and universality, and the 'strong programme' of the sociology of science powerfully argued that objectivity and scientific truth were particular historical events that cannot be detached from the specific context of their emergence.[5] Jill Dolan in the early 1990s noted the value of these critiques of academic objectivity in decentring the white, Western, male construction of theatrical history and practice and admitting a wider plurality of voices.[6]

In scientific method, objectivity and observation are often thought to be complementary, but in fact they are frequently in conflict. Observation seems to tell us that the sun goes around the earth, but objectively we can understand that the reverse is true. Alternatively, what we believe is objectively the case can override the evidence of our eyes, as when a generation of biologists accepted Theophilus S. Painter's (inaccurate) count of twenty-four chromosome pairs in human cells, and discounted their (accurate) observation of twenty-three pairs.[7] It is clear that authority and culture, as well as the structures of human consciousness, shape the apparent neutrality of observation. Indeed, objectivity and observation are shaped profoundly by their historical context, in how they are understood and practised, and how they

---

[3] Ibsen, *An Enemy of the People*, 344.   [4] Ibid., 340.

[5] E.g. David Bloor, *Knowledge and Social Imagery* (London, 1976); Bruno Latour and Steve Woolgar, *Laboratory Life: The Construction of Scientific Facts* (London, 1979).

[6] Jill Dolan, 'Geographies of Learning: Theatre Studies, Performance, and the "Performative"', *Theatre Journal* 45, no. 4 (December 1993): 417–41.

[7] See Matt Ridley, *Genome: The Autobiography of a Species in 23 Chapters* (London, 1999), 22–4.

work together. Sometimes they are happily combined; sometimes one or the other dominates; at other times, they recede in significance compared with other epistemic virtues.

Their relationship to theatre (and other performing, literary, and visual arts) is equally changeable. In contemporary Western mainstream theatre, we might find outlandish the idea that theatre offers opportunities for scientific objectivity or observation; theatre's aesthetic fictions can seem precisely the opposite of science's cool impersonality; the liveness and co-presence of audience and performance can seem an unstable foundation for any kind of scientific observation. That *An Enemy of the People* can give rise to precisely contrary interpretations seems exactly the kind of ambiguity that scientific objectivity is designed to eliminate. And yet both observation and objectivity have been claims made for the theatre at particular times.

This chapter juxtaposes theatre history with the history of objectivity and observation, building to a more extended discussion of nineteenth-century Naturalist theatre in which the claim for theatrical objectivity was made most strongly. The discussion reveals surprising affinities between science and art, extending the reach of our analysis far beyond the narrow genre of 'science plays'.

Before Objectivity and Observation

The word 'objectivity' dates only from the early nineteenth century. The words 'objective' and 'subjective' are much older, but originally had almost the opposite meaning from the ones they later acquired; in the seventeenth century, 'objective' referred to the way an object appeared to consciousness rather than its real existence, denoted by the word 'subjective'.[8]

The emergence of the distinctively modern concept of objectivity has been traced persuasively by Lorraine Daston and Peter Galison in their book *Objectivity* (2010). They argue that although some of the components of what we recognize now as objectivity – freedom from prejudice or bias, for example – were identified and valued beforehand, scientific objectivity was an invention of the nineteenth century. What their study focuses on is how and why, of all the 'epistemic virtues' such as accuracy, precision, replicability, and certainty, objectivity emerged to dominate all the others and 'to swallow up the whole history of epistemology and of science to boot'.[9] They follow the development of the modern conception of objectivity from the

---

[8] See 'objective, adj. and n.', and 'subjective, adj. and n.', *Oxford English Dictionary*, 3rd ed. (Oxford, 2004). www-oed-com.

[9] Lorraine Daston and Peter Galison, *Objectivity*, 2nd ed. (New York, 2010), 33, 35.

early modern to modernity and beyond in a succession of phases, each with its own model of scientific practice.

A similar history can be narrated for observation. It may seem as if observing is a neutral human activity, but who looks, how and why they look, and what they look at are all questions with historically variable answers. In *Histories of Scientific Observation* (2011), Lorraine Daston and Elizabeth Lunbeck gather a team of scholars to explore the historical range of scientific looking from the medieval to the contemporary period. Observation, argues Daston, was reconfigured by the late seventeenth century to become 'an essential aspect of both the theory and practice of natural knowledge'.[10] While in the eighteenth century, observation was paired with experiment, by the nineteenth century, the processes were uncoupled, with observation treated as a passive, nonspecialist activity and experimentation the active, central work of the scientist.

It might seem curious to suggest that objectivity and observation have not always been highly valued, but a look at pre-modern and early modern theatre echoes this claim. Neither Plato nor Aristotle rates observation among the theatre's virtues; in fact, for Plato, mimetic representation was one of the many faults of the theatre, the actor and writer pretending to knowledge they did not have. Though Aristotle values mimesis more highly, tragedy's value lies not in observation but in deduction: what tragedy *is*, for Aristotle, is mimesis of a structure of action with the character of necessity. Tragedy can, contra Plato, provide us with knowledge, but a knowledge of how things *must* be, not how they *are*.[11] In none of this analysis is there a place for observation or objectivity. Of the specific accounts of ancient Greek theatre that have survived, actors are praised (or denounced) for the quality of their voice, their verse-speaking, their capacity to inspire emotion, but never are these abilities described in terms of accurate observation. The Roman author Aulus Gellius wrote about the actor Polus who had himself lost a beloved son; when he played Agememnon in Sophocles' *Electra*, he 'filled everything about him not with representations and imitations, but with real living grief and lamentation'.[12] This may sound like 'realist' acting, but it is a performance fuelled by personal experience, not observation.

In Elizabethan and Jacobean drama, objectivity does not appear to be much prized. The words 'objective' and 'subjective' never appear in

---

[10] Lorraine Daston, 'The Empire of Observation, 1600–1800', in *Histories of Scientific Observation*, ed. Lorraine Daston and Elizabeth Lunbeck (Chicago, 2011), 81–113 (83).

[11] Aristotle, *Poetics*, trans. and ed. Malcolm Heath (Harmondsworth, 1996), 1451a-b.

[12] Aulus Gellius, *Attic Nights*, IV.5, quoted in Eric Csapo and William J. Slater, *The Context of Ancient Drama* (Ann Arbor, 1994), 264.

Shakespeare's works. Indeed, in *The Tempest*, Prospero describes his former life as Duke of Milan spent 'dedicated / To closeness and the bettering of my mind',[13] 'liberal arts ... being all my study',[14] and 'neglecting worldly ends'[15] believing 'my library / Was dukedom large enough'.[16] This detached, unworldly, quasi-objective behaviour was, he realizes, a mistake, leaving the way open for his brother Antonio to usurp the throne. Once Prospero has achieved his revenge, he announces, 'I'll drown my book',[17] suggesting that the elevation of human knowledge above worldly matters is a mistake to be corrected rather than a state to be admired.

This is not to say that Shakespeare or other writers repudiated science. It would be more accurate to say that art and science shared a relative lack of concern for objectivity as we now understand it. Indeed, several historians have observed the numerous overlaps in Renaissance Europe between art and science. Elizabeth Spiller argues that in the years between the decline of Aristotelian scholasticism and the rise of modern scientific method, drama and poetry were considered 'knowledge practices' and that 'the act of creation was understood to both require and express knowledge'.[18] Indeed, in *Defence of Poesie* (1595), Sir Philip Sidney could even declare 'of all Sciences ... is our Poet the Monarch'.[19] Henry S. Turner has shown the numerous connections between the spatial sciences and the English Renaissance stage, giving as one example the origins of the literary and dramatic term 'plot' in geometry and noting the continuing significance of spatial thinking in the conceptual apparatus of the early seventeenth-century stage.[20] Meanwhile, numerous seventeenth-century works are both scientific and literary; Mary Campbell cites several, including Johannes Kepler's *Somnium* (1621) and John Donne's *Ignatius His Conclave* (1611); we might also note the persistence of scientific ideas being presented in the dramatic form of a dialogue, most famously Galileo Galilei's *Dialogue on the Two Chief World Systems* (1632) and *Two New Sciences* (1638).

To call a theatre 'The Globe' might hint at objectivity in the form of a universal perspective or a promise to allow the observation of everything, but the three-sided Elizabethan outdoor playhouse was hardly designed for

---

[13] William Shakespeare, *The Tempest*, ed. Stephen Orgel. (Oxford, 1987), 1.2.89–90.
[14] Ibid., 1.2.73–4. [15] Ibid., 1.2.89. [16] Ibid., 1.2.109–10. [17] Ibid., 5.1.57.
[18] Elizabeth Spiller, 'Shakespeare and the Making of Early Modern Science: Resituating Prospero's Art', *South Central Review* 26, nos. 1–2 (Summer 2009): 24–41 (24).
[19] Quoted in Mary Campbell, 'Literature', in *The Cambridge History of Science: vol. 3: Early Modern Science*, ed. Katharine Park and Lorraine Daston (Cambridge, 2006), 756–72 (757).
[20] Henry S. Turner, *The English Renaissance Stage: Geometry, Poetics, and the Practical Spatial Arts 1580–1630* (Oxford, 2006), 21–4.

scientific observation. This began to change in the Jacobean period as the experiments in Italian scenic design entered England through the Court Masque, marking a profound shift in status of the visual and therefore of observation. While the outdoor playhouse gave words the primary responsibility to populate the world, create the scenes and surroundings, and generate whatever knowledge the performance could provide, Inigo Jones's new use of perspective promised to make vision a source of knowledge in itself that rivalled speech. As John Peacock puts it, this was 'a new conception of art itself, and of how it worked; which in turn led to a new way of looking at the world'.[21]

'Truth-to-Nature'

Observation was never considered a wholly sufficient practice for the scientist. When Hamlet urges Ophelia that, before she doubt his love, she should 'Doubt thou the stars are fire, / Doubt that the sun doth move',[22] he evokes both trust and mistrust of observation: trust, in that these cosmological observations are implicitly solid, and mistrust in that they implicitly can be proved false, unlike his love. Shakespeare lived his entire life between Copernicus's *On the Revolutions of the Heavenly Spheres* (1543) and Galileo's condemnation (1633), which reminds us that astronomers had started doubting this view of stars and the plausibility of a geocentric universe as Shakespeare wrote those words. Every assertion of epistemological certainty seems to open up a space for doubt, just as the technology that brought true perspective to the stage simultaneously opened up the possibility of stage illusion and trickery.

Observation could be unsystematic and misleading. Daston and Galison argue that seventeenth-century naturalists were often drawn to 'anomalies and singularities' of nature,[23] in part as a means to forestall premature generalization. But, as the contents of various 'cabinets of curiosities' suggest, there were often no distinctions made between the typical and the atypical, and boundaries between species might be obscured or confounded by a poorly chosen specimen.

Instead arose a new approach to the representation of the natural world that Daston and Galison call 'Truth-to-Nature', a precursor to objectivity. This new principle argued that the scientist must learn 'to see the essential

---

[21] John Peacock, *The Stage Designs of Inigo Jones: The European Context* (Cambridge, 1995), 43.

[22] William Shakespeare, *Hamlet*, ed. G. R. Hibbard (Oxford, 1987), 2.2.115–16.

[23] Daston and Galison, *Objectivity*, 67.

and overlook the incidental', to observe not a particular specimen but the 'regularities glimpsed behind, beneath, or beyond the accidental, the variant, the aberrant in nature'.[24] The practical manifestation of this principle was that an atlas of botany, for example, would contain idealized illustrations of each species, the illustrator composing a perfect version from the botanist's numerous observations.

The literary impact of this approach can be clearly felt in Romanticism. When John Keats suggests in 'Ode on a Grecian Urn' (1819) that 'Beauty is truth, truth beauty', he echoes the new scientific belief that the most beautiful representation of a flower is also the most true and vice versa. A key aesthetic experience for the Romantics was that mixture of terror and beauty found in the sublime; just as eighteenth-century naturalists conquered 'the untamed variability, even monstrosity of nature' by idealizing and ordering it, so the sublime, in Kant's influential formulation, involved a fearful apprehension of nature's power and scale, followed by pleasurable recognition of the still greater power of human mental capacity.[25]

Truth-to-Nature is also reflected in theatrical Romanticism. Daston and Galison describe two variants of the principle, the 'ideal' and the 'characteristic': 'The "ideal" image purports to render not merely the typical but the perfect, while the "characteristic" image locates the typical in an individual.'[26] These are reflected in the apparently contradictory impulses in stage Romanticism. The 'ideal' is visible in its metaphysical aspirations and its presentation of great, extraordinary individuals, such as Hugo's Hernani, Musset's Lorenzo, or Pushkin's Boris Godunov; meanwhile, the characteristic is reflected in its determination to represent ordinary, even working-class characters: drawing on Shakespeare for their model, the Romantics put ordinary people into the action (notably in *Lorenzaccio* and *Boris Godunov*), even, in Büchner's *Woyzeck*, as protagonists.

Despite these overlaps, art and science had, by the turn of the nineteenth century, started to occupy separate cultural realms. In the Romantic period, writers were exhorted 'to express, even flaunt, their subjectivity, at the same time that scientists were admonished to restrain theirs'.[27] As Mary Campbell explains, the literary forms in which scientific discoveries were written up changed and became highly restricted and much more impersonal: the passive voice became standard; the first-person plural replaced the individual avowal; so as not to distract from logic purity, details of personality and

---

[24] Ibid., 26, 67.
[25] See 'The Analytic of the Sublime' section of Kant's *Critique of the Power of Judgment*, ed. Paul Guyer, trans. Paul Guyer and Eric Matthews (Cambridge, 2000), Ak. 5:245–71.
[26] Daston and Galison, *Objectivity*, 70.   [27] Ibid., 37.

history were progressively stripped away, in favour of lucidity and clarity.[28] The way was being prepared for objectivity.

Mechanical Objectivity

There had always been tensions between science and art, and with the new requirement for beautiful renderings of ideal flora and fauna, scientists needed artists to complete their work. Sometimes these relationships were very successful, as in the partnership of the French naturalist René-Antoine Ferchault de Réamur with his illustrator Hélène Dumoustier de Marsilly, whom the naturalist so prized that he left his entire estate to her in his will. More common, and reminiscent of the conflicts between Ben Jonson and Inigo Jones over text and image, were the 'battles of wills, eyes, and status ... when the naturalist peered over the shoulder of the artist'.[29]

Just as a writer's personality was carefully eliminated from scientific writing, so aesthetics began to be excluded from scientific representation. The idealizations of Truth-to-Nature were replaced by what Daston and Galison call 'mechanical objectivity'. It involved 'the reproduction of individual items – rather than types or ideals. The working objects would be gathered into systematic visual compendiums that were supposed to preserve form from the world onto the page, not to part the curtains of experience to reveal an ur-form.'[30] It was 'mechanical' because, where possible, the means of representation would be automatic and require little or no intervention by the fallible human scientist. With its abstraction from individual perspective, this was the first full appearance of objectivity in scientific discourse.

Mechanical objectivity has its equivalent in Naturalist theatre. This is not merely analogous but direct; Naturalism modelled itself explicitly on a science (hence calling itself 'Naturalism'), and the movement's most articulate theorist, Émile Zola, was an enthusiastic reader of scientific writing, in particular of a key text of the new scientific movement, Claude Bernard's *An Introduction to the Study of Experimental Medicine* (1865). As a result, the influence was immediate, with almost no latency. When Daston and Galison suggest that the new movement of mechanical objectivity started to become prominent in the 1860s and 1870s and by the 1880s and 1890s 'could be found almost everywhere',[31] they might just as easily be describing the timeline of Naturalism.

Zola was an unusually faithful devotee of this new science. In parallel with the new restrictions on scientific writing, Zola's prescription for Naturalist

---

[28] Campbell, 'Literature', 759–60.   [29] Daston and Galison, *Objectivity*, 88.
[30] Ibid., 121.   [31] Ibid., 49, 124.

writers is that 'the best style is built on logic and clarity'.[32] This is not mere stylistic minimalism but a direct rejection of aesthetics in the name of science; if you wallow in sentiment, he tells his fellow novelists, and do not 'test your ideas out against reason and verify them through experiment, you are a poet', and he does not mean this as a compliment.[33] Elsewhere, Zola rejects rhetoric (which 'has no role here'[34]) and is sceptical about the significance of literary form (to which, he says, 'we pay disproportionate attention'[35]). Instead, the role of creativity is to generate hypotheses that the novel or play will test; the greater your genius, the more successful your hypotheses: 'in our scientific century, experiment must provide the proof of genius'.[36]

Zola is by far the most programmatic of the Naturalist writers, but there are echoes of his ideas elsewhere. Ibsen described his work as a kind of scientific experiment, remarking, 'I can be likened to a chemist, who has familiarity with substances and awaits the result.'[37] For Chekhov, a practising doctor, 'the writer must be just as objective as the chemist', adding, of his writing, 'I have tried, wherever possible, to take account of scientific fact; and where it has been impossible, I have preferred not to write at all.'[38]

In all three writers, one sees evidence of mechanical objectivity's refusal of idealization. Ibsen denied that Nora in *A Doll's House* was intended to represent a type, denying his intention to lay down 'a hard and fast rule that all women in a similar position to Nora should or must act like Nora'.[39] Toril Moi has argued compellingly that it is Ibsen's abandonment of idealism (and implicitly Truth-to-Nature's idealizations) that marks him out as the first great Modernist.[40] Chekhov scorned the idea that art's purpose was to retrieve the 'pearl' from the 'dung heap'[41] and, describing the writer as a journalist, asked: '[W]hat would you say if a newspaper reporter, out of squeamishness or a desire to give pleasure to his readers, were to describe only honest town prefects, high-minded young ladies, and virtuous railway employees?'[42] Zola scorned 'idealistic novelists [who] cling obstinately to the

---

[32] Émile Zola, *Le Roman Experimental*, in *Oeuvres Complètes: Tome 9: Nana (1880)*, ed. Henri Mitterand and Chantal Pierre-Gnassounou (Paris, 2004), 345. I refer most extensively to Zola's *The Experimental Novel* rather than to *Naturalism in the Theatre* because the former offers a much more systematic exposition of how Bernard's experimental method can be applied to art. All translations from this and other books in French are my own.

[33] Ibid., 339.   [34] Ibid., 345.   [35] Ibid.   [36] Ibid., 339.

[37] Helland and Holledge, eds., *Ibsen on Theatre*, 89.

[38] Jutta Hercher et al., eds., *Chekhov on Theatre*, trans. Stephen Mulrine (London, 2012), 59, 95.

[39] Helland and Holledge, eds., *Ibsen on Theatre*, 95.

[40] Toril Moi, *Henrik Ibsen and the Birth of Modernism* (Oxford, 2006).

[41] Hercher et al., eds. *Chekhov on Theatre*, 58.   [42] Ibid., 59.

unknown'[43] and urged 'displacing idealist hypotheses with the slow conquest of the unknown'.[44]

Mechanical objectivity rests on two distinct moments of observation: the observation (and automatic recording) of nature and then the subsequent observation of the reader (through the multiple dissemination of these images), both processes without the willed intervention of the scientist.[45] Similarly, Naturalism offers the gathering of data (the Naturalist writer's observation of the world) and then the presentation of the results (the Naturalist audience's observation of the play). Zola was, however, insistent that Naturalism was not just 'photography',[46] because between the two moments of observation lay the truly distinctive feature of Naturalism and of nineteenth-century science: the experiment, that is, the arrangement of the facts according to a hypothesis and the writing of the novel as the working-through of the experiment. To the obvious objection that a novel cannot be an experiment because it is composed of fiction rather than reality, Zola notes that scientists always create artificial abstractions of reality – pure substances in laboratory conditions – in order to test it: 'experiment is fundamentally just induced observation'.[47]

But these two moments of observation and reproduction function in complicated ways for the Naturalist writer. It is not clear that a play can be created automatically or mechanically, or can be neutrally and exactly reproduced in performance, so it is instructive to see how these apparent problems were solved or minimized. Daston and Lunbeck note the de-professionalization of scientific observation in the mid-nineteenth century. Concerned that a skilled scientist might be too knowledgeable to observe impartially, it was recommended that the task be handed to amateurs or to machines.[48] Certainly, field observation is widespread in Naturalism: Ibsen affirmed that his plays were drawn 'from life' and once remarked, 'I have constantly studied people and observed their inner lives. I have often walked with Hedda Gabler through the arcades of Munich.'[49]

Zola conducted extensive fieldwork to write his novels. The Zola scholar Henri Mitterand, in the introduction to a collection of Zola's field notes, describes 'his determination to see everything with his own eyes, to hear everything with his own ears. There is no intermediary between the world

[43] Zola, *Le Roman Experimental*, 335.   [44] Ibid., 333.
[45] Daston and Galison, *Objectivity*, 135.   [46] Ibid., 329.
[47] Zola, *Le Roman Experimental*, 324. This is actually a quotation from Claude Bernard, *An Introduction to the Study of Experimental Medicine* (1865), trans. Henry Copley Greene (New York, 1957), 19.
[48] Daston and Lunbeck, eds., *Histories of Scientific Observation*, 3–4.
[49] Helland and Holledge, eds., *Ibsen on Theatre*, 66, 112.

and the text.'[50] This curious phrase reduces Zola himself to nothing ('no intermediary'), but reflects the self-negation of the late nineteenth-century scientist. The watchword of this science was: 'let nature speak for itself'.[51] This entailed the elimination of anything in the scientist that would mediate the world and its objective representation, and 'where human self-discipline flagged, machines or humans acting as will-less machines would take over'.[52] The scientist now 'aspired to waxlike receptivity'.[53]

Zola went to considerable lengths to transform himself into a machine-like data recorder and processor. In 1896, discussing how he wrote his books, he allocated himself a minimal role. Describing his memory, he writes: 'it would load itself up quickly, eagerly; then it would unload. It is a sponge that fills up and empties; it is a river that drags everything with it whose waters soon disappear into the sandbanks'.[54] Zola's mind is a mere sponge or perhaps a clear, soon-disappearing waterway that transports reality straight into his novels. The experiment, the processing, is equally neutral: 'I invent nothing; the novel writes itself, emerging from the material all by itself.'[55] Describing the effect of recalling items from his memory, he insists '*It is a materialisation to excess*. The sunlight that illuminated them almost dazzles me; the smell chokes me; the details cling to me and prevent me from seeing the whole picture.'[56] Zola seems to be describing his mind as a piece of photographic paper, an automatic recorder of sense impressions.

Few other Naturalist figures went as far, but there are echoes of this self-negation everywhere. Chekhov's insistence that 'the artist shouldn't be the judge of his characters and what they say, but simply a disinterested obser-ver'[57] is borne out by the ironic distance of his plays, their lack of evident authorial commentary. Ibsen insisted that to write plays 'the author must to a certain extent kill and submerge his own personality'[58] and said that 'in none of my plays is the author so much of an outsider, so utterly absent' as in *Ghosts*.[59] Daston and Galison describe these efforts of self-discipline as 'technologies of the self' and one can see a certain disciplinary automatism in Zola's continual production of a certain number of words every single day or Ibsen's inflexibly invariant daily routines.[60]

---

[50] Émile Zola, *Carnets d'Enquêtes: Une Ethnographie Inédite de la France*, ed. Henri Mitterand (Paris, 1993), 13–14.
[51] Daston and Galison, *Objectivity*, 120.   [52] Ibid., 120–1.   [53] Ibid., 95.
[54] Émile Zola, 'Enquête sur le Langage Intérieur', *Archives d'anthropologie criminelle 9* (1894): 102–5 (102).
[55] Ibid., 104.   [56] Ibid., 103.   [57] Hercher et al., eds., *Chekhov on Theatre*, 62.
[58] Helland and Holledge, eds., *Ibsen on Theatre*, 131.   [59] Ibid., 83. See also 87, 95.
[60] See ibid., 11.

The second moment, the Naturalist audience's observation of the results of the experiment, gives rise to complex contradictions. Ibsen wished for complete transparency, insisting frequently that the audience should feel they are watching reality itself.[61] André Antoine's deployment of the invisible 'fourth wall' in his staging has a complex relationship to observation. Most obviously, it provides voyeuristic access to a hidden reality and thus situates the theatre as a kind of observational prosthesis, like the telescope or microscope.[62] However, it often situates the audience at an impossible angle, suspended in the air outside the first floor of an apartment, for instance. In addition, Antoine's Naturalistic habit of acting with his back to the audience as one would stand in a real room both enables and frustrates the audience's gaze; and finally, his practice of rehearsing a play without any consideration of the audience and deciding only at the last minute, almost arbitrarily, which angle to show implies that the scene is not intended for any particular perspective at all and is instead to be understood as a view from nowhere. The fourth wall suggests an ambivalence between the priority of observation and objectivity in the Naturalist project.

The Limits of Objectivity

Zola's description of details clinging to his text and preventing appreciation of the whole marks an emerging tension between restraint and excess in mechanical objectivity. The scientist is required to repeatedly record their observations of a given object in minute detail but in so doing risks losing it in a 'swarm of sensations'.[63] For Zola, this swarm manifests itself in great lists of details in his novels that seem to overwhelm the ability of any reader to mentally populate the imagined world. The pared-down style of scientific writing, the 'logic and clarity' that Zola required, set the scene for what Barthes calls the 'reality effect': the production of a sense of realism through the excess of detail over narrative function.[64]

In 1886, the British doctor William Anderson, writing about a seventeenth-century anatomist, lamented his tendency to reach for pictorial allegory, despite being 'almost Zolaesque in his superfluous realism'.[65] Zola is being invoked both approvingly, as someone with a contemporary

---

[61] Ibid., 91, 93, 82, 150.

[62] See Dan Rebellato, 'Sightlines: Foucault and Naturalist Theatre', in *Foucault's Theatres*, ed. Tony Fisher and Kélina Gotman (Manchester, 2019), 147–59, 231–5 (233n63).

[63] Daston and Galison, *Objectivity*, 238.

[64] Roland Barthes, 'The Reality Effect' (1968), in *The Rustle of Language*, trans. Richard Howard (Oxford, 1986), 141–8.

[65] Quoted in Daston and Galison, *Objectivity*, 146.

aversion to allegory, and disapprovingly, as someone whose realism is excessive. In part, Zola's problem is that his attempt to create a union between art and science, if only by subsuming literature within the scientific project, runs up against science's own abolition of aesthetics. In *The Experimental Novel*, he is forced to concede that Claude Bernard has already ruled out the possibility of literature making a contribution to science and that a Naturalist theatre is, by definition, an excess.

Excess would bedevil the project of mechanical objectivity and lead to the development of two successor models of objectivity in the first half of the twentieth century: 'structural objectivity' and 'trained judgment'. In the first, championed by the logical positivists, images were discouraged altogether in favour of the supposedly invariant objects of logical thought. More practically, in the hospital or the laboratory, 'trained judgment' allowed that the scientist needed to select and interpret the image but insisted this ability could be taught and so objectivity was not dependent on personality, genius, or special insight. One might see correlates of 'structural objectivity' in the highly conceptual theatre works of Gertrude Stein where the reader or the audience is required to construct entirely imagined formal unities from the fiercely dislocated and referentially obscure dramatic text. (In addition, is it merely coincidence that the first wholly nonvisual dramatic form, radio drama, emerges at the same time as this radical opposition to sensuous images?) Correlates of 'trained judgment' might be seen in the work of Bertolt Brecht, which shares a suspicion of the neutrality of images and seeks to teach its audience a critical scepticism about representation. We might also look to the Theatre of the Absurd, which characteristically offers recognizable but estranged images of the world: a room full of chairs, a romantic triangle played out in three giant urns, two men waiting by a tree. Although Brecht and the Absurdists are conventionally held to be at opposite ends of European theatre, perhaps, in their different ways, they share a response to the shifting conceptions of objectivity in the mid-century.

Brecht's *Life of Galileo* famously exists in two quite different versions. In the first, written during the Second World War, Galileo's capitulation to the Inquisition is a ruse that affords him the space and time to write yet more radical critiques of papal doctrine that can be smuggled out across Europe. In the second version, written after the atomic bombs were dropped on Hiroshima and Nagasaki, the great scientist's compromise with the Inquisition is presented as the original sin of modern science, a moment of betrayal, where scientific objectivity is sacrificed to power. *Galileo*, in its two versions, marks both the high point and end of a certain theatrical incarnation of the scientist-as-hero, initiated ambivalently by Ibsen's Dr Stockmann sixty years earlier.

It is notable that many of the most successful representations of science and scientists since the war seem to be drawn to areas of science and theatre that mark the limits of objectivity: the ambiguous madness of Dürrenmatt's *The Physicists*, the limits of knowledge marked out by chaos theory in Stoppard's *Arcadia*, the indeterminacy that is both the subject and structure of Frayn's *Copenhagen*, the multiple realities of Nick Payne's multiverse play *Constellations*.

If objectivity might be regarded as being able to see the world other than from your own perspective, it might seem to be incompatible with observation, which must always be from the perspective of the observer. The theatre partakes of this apparent contradiction in productive and complex ways, being both rootedly local and placelessly fictional. But each of these elements – objectivity, observation, and theatre's relationship to each – has a history, and our own perception of theatre's incompatibility with science or drama's unease with objectivity is itself historically produced. It is not beyond imagination that a further series of transformations may once again find value in the notion of theatrical objectivity and see in theatregoing a scientifically valuable methodology for the observation of nature.

Suggested Reading

Axtell, Guy. *Objectivity*. Cambridge, 2016.

Bernard, Claude. *An Introduction to the Study of Experimental Medicine,* trans. Henry Copley Greene. New York, 1957.

Crary, Jonathan. *Techniques of the Observer: On Vision and Modernity in the Nineteenth Century*. Cambridge, MA, 1990.

Daston, Lorraine, and Peter Galison. *Objectivity,* 2nd ed. New York, 2010.

Daston, Lorraine, and Elizabeth Lunbeck, eds. *Histories of Scientific Observation*. Chicago, 2011.

Ekström, Anders. 'Seeing from Above: A Particular History of the General Observer'. *Nineteenth-Century Contexts* 31 (September 2009): 185–207.

Gaukroger, Stephen. *Objectivity: A Very Short Introduction*. Oxford, 2012.

Nagel, Thomas. *The View from Nowhere*. Oxford, 1986.

Peacock, John. *The Stage Designs of Inigo Jones: The European Context*. Cambridge, 1995.

Spiller, Elizabeth. 'Shakespeare and the Making of Early Modern Science: Resituating Prospero's Art'. *South Central Review* 26 (Summer 2009): 24–41.

Turner, Henry S. *The English Renaissance Stage: Geometry, Poetics, and the Practical Spatial Arts 1580–1630*. Oxford, 2006.

Zola, Émile. *Le Roman Experimental*. In *Oeuvres Complètes: Tome 9 Nana 1880,* eds. Henri Mitterand and Chantal Pierre-Gnassounou. Paris, 2004, 315–507.

2

JANE R. GOODALL

Staging Consciousness

Metaphor as Thought Experiment in McBurney's
Beware of Pity

The relationship between theatre and science challenges the limits of language and form. Yet among the repertoire of science plays, there is a predominance of works that address specific scientific questions in an explicit and discursive way. Conflict over ideas is, as Kirsten Shepherd-Barr observes, 'central to the drama'[1] and science is the subject matter, rather than a mode of exploration in symbiotic relationship with those of the theatre itself. Such a symbiosis can occur only if the collaborative process is set up at an earlier stage, so that the script evolves in concert with all aspects of staging and enactment. This is the approach taken by the Theatre de Complicité, which, under the direction of its founder Simon McBurney, has a track record of experimental works exploring consciousness in ways that deploy the resources of theatre in 'complicity' with scientific methods of enquiry. How do you stage consciousness – not just talk about it, as in Tom Stoppard's *The Hard Problem* – but actually stage it, as a medium through which humans experience the world?

Complicité's ongoing collaboration with Marcus du Sautoy, Simonyi Professor for the Public Understanding of Science at the University of Oxford, began with *A Disappearing Number* (2007) and continued in *The Encounter* (2015), which experimented with the use of binaural headphones to enable McBurney 'to beam his thoughts deep into the conscious mind' of audiences during the performance.[2] In 2013, du Sautoy appeared onstage himself in *X&Y*, an attempt to explore the gulf between human consciousness and the infinite reaches of the universe. Framed by glowing geometric structures, Du Sautoy and his co-performer Victoria Gould brought mathematical abstraction into play with biological attraction. The conceptual challenge here was bound up with the performative challenge of portraying

---

[1] Kirsten Shepherd-Barr, 'From Copenhagen to Infinity and Beyond: Science Meets Literature on Stage', *Interdisciplinary Science Reviews* 28 (2003): 193.
[2] Theatre de Complicité, *Encounter*, www.complicite.org/encounterresource/.

different kinds of dynamic, on vastly discrepant scales. This symbolic evocation suggests that engagements between the domains of theatre and science might take a step further from the process of dramatizing scientific subject matter, towards a common venture into realms of cognitive uncertainty.

McBurney's production of *Beware of Pity*, a collaboration with the Berlin Schaübuhne, is not in any topical sense 'about' science. It is a close adaptation of Stefan's Zweig's novel *Ungeduld des Herzens*, written in 1938 as the author, anticipating the outbreak of a second world war, reflects on the atmosphere in his home city of Vienna in the summer of 1914, on the eve of the first. In an article for the *Guardian* to mark the premiere of *Beware of Pity* at the Barbican in February 2017, McBurney tells of finding a translation of the novel in a bookshop and becoming caught up in a world that was 'compulsively alive'.[3] There was, to echo Zweig's own words, a surplus of energy here, a momentum that carried the reader through to the end, as if the tale were told in a single breath. Zweig's narrative draws the reader into the zeitgeist of early twentieth-century Vienna, where an intellectual obsession with nerve force still held sway. Freudian ideas of repression presented a further evolution of nineteenth-century research into the hysterical excesses and deficiencies of psychical energy. But Zweig's narrative has something more nuanced to offer than a view of war as an eruption of collective psychosis. McBurney's production adds sophistication through an awareness of twenty-first-century scientific interest in the interactions between consciousness and environment, and brings a mastery of theatrical metaphor that gives further dimensions of meaning to Zweig's literary images.

The novel is built around an extended conceit: old Europe is represented as a crisis-ridden family whose destiny is bound up with the condition of the daughter, a young woman suffering from alternating phases of hysterical paralysis and nervous paroxysm. Here Zweig is expanding on the metaphoric language he uses in essays and commentaries on the preconditions for the outbreak of war. 'Never since it came into being has the whole world been so communally seized by nervous energy,' he wrote in an article that appeared in the *Neue Freie Presse* on 1 August 1914. 'Until now a war was only an isolated flare-up in the immense organism that is humanity, a suppurating limb that could be cauterized and thus healed.'[4] This was not some psychopathology of the individual, suddenly become contagious, but rather an atmospheric condition transmitted to the biosphere. 'Unremittingly

[3] Simon McBurney, interview for Theatre de Complicité, 2015, www.complicite.org/productions/BewareOfPity (subsequent references are given in the text as '2015 interview').
[4] Stefan Zweig, 'The Sleepless World', reprinted in *Messages from a Lost World*, trans. Will Stone (London, 2016), 45.

the air quivers with secret waves for which science has no name and whose amplitude no seismograph can measure' (42). Are we in the domain of physics, biology, or psychology? Or are all of these in conjunction in an explosive transition phase for which there is no known precedent? He wonders 'if this colossal will, burning from the depths of the soul, can overshoot distances like the vibrations of sound or the convulsions of electricity?' (42).

In *The World of Yesterday*, published in 1942 – the year American troops landed in Europe and the Auschwitz exterminations began – Zweig's specu-lations on the causal factors at work in 1914 had not changed. In the circumstances, he suggests, the very idea of finding any convincing political rationale for war was misguided. Was it, rather, that another way of looking was required? 'It had nothing to do with ideas, and hardly even with petty frontiers; I cannot explain it otherwise than by this surplus of force, a tragic consequence of the internal dynamism that accumulated in those forty years of peace and now sought violent release.'[5] Zweig had scientific interests, but he was essentially a literary writer. A more strictly scientific intelligence might dismiss his hypothesis as nothing more than a well-turned metaphor, but the idea of Europe as a self-generating force field whirling towards catastrophe gains cogency as an extended thought experiment. In *Beware of Pity*, it is employed as a means of pushing at the limits of consciousness through the narration of a story about events in Vienna on the eve of war. McBurney's initial attraction towards it as a theatrical project was, he says, bound up with this apprehension of a recurrent crisis in the *zeitgeist* (2015 interview).

Zweig draws together the antebellum time frames of 1914 and 1938 through two narrative personae. One is a former army officer: Hoffmiller of the Commissariat, decorated for bravery, who recounts a sequence of events in which he was personally involved during the months prior to the outbreak of the last war. The second narrator, an authorial presence 'who has over and over again tried to trace human destinies,' is co-opted as audience to Hoffmiller's reflections after they meet at a Viennese party, where everyone else seems to be engaged in conversations about the immi-nence of a second war. Important metaphors hover in the scene between them, which serves as prelude to the main tale. The coffeehouses and house parties of Vienna are places of cultural convergence where people seem compelled to give vent to 'the storm-laden atmosphere of the times', even as they strive to assure themselves that the catastrophe is not going to

---

[5] Stefan Zweig, *The World of Yesterday*, trans. Eden Paul and Cedar Paul (London, 1987), 154–5.

happen. Unable to participate in the exercise of collective denial, the authorial narrator offers a stoic view: 'The grain of dust that was man no longer counted today as a creature of volition.'[6]

Is there an allusion here to the notion of 'dust mind' to which William James devotes such meticulous attention in his 1909 lectures series, *A Pluralistic Universe*? As James explains it, he encountered the idea in the work of 'the more biologically inclined psychologists' who were concerned with how complex mental capacities might have evolved from 'primordial units of mind-stuff or mind-dust' becoming 'compounded and re-compounded in the modern human brain'. Those propounding the theory invoked an analogy with chemical compounds, but here James had a problem with their reasoning. Compounds in chemistry produce chemical change so that 'they affect surrounding bodies differently'. They belong to 'a reality where things happen'.[7] Nineteenth-century evolutionists also got the metaphor wrong in another way. Dust does not compound; it is associated with disintegration or fragmentation, which is how Zweig was seeing it. Hoffmiller echoes this image as he embarks on his story, which is prefaced by a repudiation of the hero role that has been assigned to him. Individual courage, he says, is a myth. Those who fought in the war 'had been whirled into it like a cloud of dust and simply found themselves caught up in the vast vortex'.[8] Zweig has sought to reflect a reality where collision, disintegration, and transformation were occurring in an intensifying force field. This is what McBurney evokes in his production.

To neuroscientists, the 'hard problem' is that of how the neural activities of consciousness are related to mental states and the sense of self. As du Sautoy explains it in his recent book *What We Cannot Know*, the problem of consciousness raises the essential question of 'what makes me me?'[9] This has been one of the driving questions behind McBurney's work in the theatre. The actor in the centre of the 'wooden O' expresses the centrality of the human subject in the world. The Complicité approach is to disrupt this convention by mobilizing the stage environment so that it takes on a dynamic role not just in the action but in the emotional landscape of the drama and its psychological perspectives.

---

[6] Stefan Zweig, *Beware of Pity*, trans. Phyllis Blewitt and Trevor Blewitt (New York, 2006), xxxi.

[7] William James, 'The Compounding of Consciousness'. In *A Pluralistic Universe*. Hibbert Lectures at Manchester College on the Present Situation in Philosophy, lecture 5 (1909) (Project Gutenberg e-book, 2004).

[8] Zweig, *Beware of Pity*, xxxi.

[9] Marcus du Sautoy, *What We Cannot Know: From Consciousness to the Cosmos, the Cutting Edge of Science Explained* (London, 2017, Kindle edition), chapter 11.

In his 2018 production of Stravinsky's opera *A Rake's Progress* (a collaboration with the Dutch National Opera), McBurney takes the eighteenth-century story of a young man drawn into dissolution and ruin and interprets it as a twenty-first-century psychodrama in which the stage itself becomes an image of consciousness. Michael Levine's set, a paper box onto which changing scenes are projected, alludes to the origins of the story in a set of engravings by William Hogarth. Tom Rakewell, brilliantly portrayed by Paul Appleby, remains at the centre of the picture while the box itself is continuously invaded by the forces of the zeitgeist. The pimps, brokers, and image-makers who begin to control his destiny tear through the walls as they make their entrances and exits. Later, as the rake's journey descends into psychosis, grasping hands rip through the floor. The stage becomes a medium through which external and internal worlds impact upon each other with increasing turbulence. In *Beware of Pity*, this pattern of confusion is one in which collective rather than individual destiny is at stake. McBurney was explicit about the decision to focus on Hoffmiller as a figure embodying 'the consciousness of anybody'. The novel draws him as a project for theatrical interpretation, McBurney suggests, because it is a vehicle for exploring how 'the way an entire generation might be conscious can result in a set of actions leading to disaster' (2015 interview). Here he echoes the words Zweig uses in the preface to *The World of Yesterday*: 'it is not so much the course of my own destiny that I relate but that of an entire generation, which was loaded down with a burden of fate'.[10]

If, from the point of view of scientific method, the 'hard problem' is that of how we can 'know' an individual experience of consciousness, theatre has multilateral ways of approaching it, central to which are the paths of metaphor, one of the foundational elements of stage representation. Metaphor enables thought experiment by allowing one thing to stand for another, or one pattern of things to correspond with another, in order to test a hypothesis without being locked into a definite order of meaning. Metaphor in literary language also allows these virtual equations as a mental exercise, but in theatre, metaphors have sound and motion; they can evolve and mutate through the deployment of objects on stage, behavioural language, choreography. As Shepherd-Barr observes in *Science on Stage*, the semiotics of theatrical performance introduce another order of complexity: 'on stage, "something happens" to objects whose meaning in everyday life might seem straightforward and clear'.[11] They acquire metaphorical possibilities by the very fact that they are there.

[10] Zweig, *The World of Yesterday*, 5.
[11] Kirsten Shepherd-Barr, *Science on Stage: From Doctor Faustus to Copenhagen* (Princeton, 2006), 190.

In contrast to the design of *The Rake's Progress*, the set of *Beware of Pity* has no clear spatial parameters. The performance arena, with its simple chairs and tables, desk lamps, microphones, and lecterns, resembles a rehearsal studio, a place in which the components of a performance are still in the process of coming together. There is vacant space around the horizontal expanse of screen across the back. Pieces of costume hang from wires, and the simple chairs and tables serve as beds, platforms, carriages, steps. A glass booth upstage creates a secondary spatial dimension; actors enter it to make transitions across space and time. The performance itself opens as if the cast are at an early stage of rehearsal, just 'doing a reading' and experimenting with some simple mimed enactments. An actor at a lectern reads verbatim from the novel, in German. Translations appear on screens set above the stage on either side of the auditorium, and the audience themselves must do a great deal of reading to keep up. Zweig's text is a dense convergence of narrative voices: Hoffmiller as the primary voice takes us into the events of his own past, but that too has a pre-history, told to him in extensive detail by others. Why does McBurney choose to keep all this in the production? To do so contravenes basic dramaturgical principles, and certainly goes against the spirit of experimental theatre, which has always been to break up narrative lines, and subordinate language to action. As Artaud put it, 'To break through language in order to touch life is to create or recreate the theatre.'[12]

Hoffmiller's story starts with an incident that would seem to be crying out (perhaps literally) for this kind of breakthrough. He is a dinner guest in the house of a local dignitary, where, after the meal, he invites his host's daughter to dance. What happens next shatters the smooth narrative line and tests all Zweig's powers of verbal expression. The young woman, Edith, responds with a series of convulsions culminating in 'a storm of sobbing, wild, elemental, like a stifled scream'. Hoffmiller himself is stunned: 'I stood rooted to the spot,' he says, 'an icy coldness in my limbs, my collar choking me as though it were a burning rope' (13). Then, as if the surge of extreme nerve force manifested in Edith's fit transfers itself to his own nervous system, the room starts reeling around him so violently he has to hold onto the door frame for balance.

Surely actors trained to be expressive physical performers should at this point break free of the discursive account and take over, communicating the physiological and psychological turmoil of the scene in entirely behavioural terms? Instead, the narrative voice continues to steer, while the actors

---

[12] Antonin Artaud, preface to *The Theatre and Its Double*, trans. Mary Caroline Richards (New York, 1958), 12.

provide a rather cursory and toned-down rendition of what is described. Having myself engaged in some dramaturgical experiments with movement artists, I am aware that they are strongly averse to any approach in which physical performance is relegated to the role of mimesis, so that they are effectively 'illustrating' narrative text. One of their guiding principles is that action should be the primary means of communication. Why would a director of McBurney's virtuosity make such a counterintuitive artistic decision?

It is actually a very subtle decision, born of deep imaginative engagement with Zweig's literary experiment. Is not human consciousness, especially in moments of life crisis, typically manifested as a voice in the head? Configurations of thought and imagined action are 'voiced' to ourselves as accounts of events in the exterior world. In a social milieu, do we not often act out pre-imagined scenarios, and retrospectively tell ourselves versions of what has taken place? The voice of the narrator here is not an accompaniment to the action, but a fully fledged dramatic element in its own right, infused with the psychical energies that are in play. Words themselves spray like shrapnel as the explosion of nerve force is evoked. Here and in the recurring scenes of hysterical outburst, Zweig releases an onslaught of language that, in performance, takes on the quality of a virtuoso recital.

Edith's crises are presaged by arrhythmic disorders of voice and movement – tremor, shudder, palpitation, quivering, stumbling, clutching, jerking – and escalate into full-blown seizure, spasm, fit, fever, frenzy, contortion, paroxysm. In performance, we see her as a seated figure in a white dress with shining hair. But when she speaks, 'in jerky, staccato tones,' in Zweig's description without pausing for breath, her voice is that of another actor, delivering the words at breakneck speed and at heightened volume through a microphone at the side of the stage. The broken rhythms of voice and movement, coordinated with uncanny precision by the two performers, create a jarring effect that transmits to the auditorium. It is always unnerving to be in the presence of hysteria.

Through the course of the action, there are several of these points of cataclysm, referred to as 'nerve storms' metaphorically correlated with electrical storms breaking in the outside world. As a shrewd reader of Freud, Zweig makes it evident, without saying so, that Edith is suffering from a hysterical paralysis. Those around her – and her father in particular – participate in the crisis by interpreting her condition in catastrophic terms. McBurney is offering his own metaphoric interpretation. 'She is Austria,' he says, '... the Austro-Hungarian Empire which at that time was atrophied – it was in a sense crippled' (2015 interview). There is a clear dramaturgical challenge here: How far is this metaphor to be taken? As the figure of Edith is central to the dynamic course of events, and the nerve force she generates is ultimately what determines the destinies of all who are drawn into her crisis, this might convert the whole drama into a form of allegory. Hoffmiller, representing the military, is tasked with saving her. He must sacrifice his personal destiny to her needs, demands, and passions, so that, in another image explored in the production, she becomes like the mythological djinn who takes on the guise of frail, helpless creature and asks to be carried, then becomes a heavier, more grasping burden with every step. The traditional mansion occupied by her family, with its feudal history and its odd, flat-roofed turret, where Edith likes to sit surveying the landscape, might be the seat of empire.

Allegory, though, is a controlling form, a highly structured symbolic pattern of equivalences with no extraneous or inconsistent aspects. That is not the mode of *Beware of Pity*, where the approach is more akin to scientific enquiry: open-ended and fundamentally experimental. The metaphors themselves serve as means of testing perspectives, rather than locking in any overarching conceptual design. McBurney is interested not in creating an arrangement of symbols but in exploring the dynamics of the situation. Hoffmiller as narrator, the speaking consciousness through which it is all communicated, reflects on his own experience through language drawn from the domains of physics and chemistry. Observing that between himself and Edith there was 'none of the galvanic tension' usually present between young people of opposite sexes, he nevertheless finds himself leaving the house in a state of sensory excitement. Aware that some passion has possessed him, he diagnoses it as 'pity,' a condition with acute biochemical symptoms. 'It seemed to me as though a toxin had found its way into my blood and had made it run warmer, redder, faster, pulsate and throb more vigorously' (47). As a passion, pity is both celibate and sterile – another kind of hysterical pathology, perhaps. It cannot respond to Edith's overtly sexual passion, instead sequestering the energies it generates with ultimately catastrophic results.

One of the central questions the drama asks is: What is pity? At one stage, Edith's physician, a Freudian figure called Doctor Condor, gives Hoffmiller a definition. There are two kinds, he says. One is weak and sentimental, a reaction born of the 'heart's impatience' and 'an instinctive desire to fortify one's own soul against the sufferings of another' (176). Its antithesis is compassion, which draws on an inexhaustible fund of patience to reach a point where it is possible to offer true help to one's fellow-beings. Torn between these forms of pity, Hoffmiller experiences the dilemma as a crisis of both conscience and consciousness. McBurney describes it as 'a horrible confusion of emotional states' and 'a kind of biochemical soup' (2015 interview).

The nerve force with which it is infused has a centrifugal dynamic, causing a heightening and enlargement of consciousness. On the mood spectrum, Hoffmiller veers between the extremes of exhilaration and sickening anxiety. On stage, the military jacket and Edith's white dress serve as emblems of the two poles of consciousness between which he is trying to steer a course. Each seems to have a life of its own, the jacket in its glass booth at the back, and the dress floating in space above the action, sometimes sweeping down to engulf the actress who plays Edith as she moves into position centre stage.

From the moment Hoffmiller first experiences pity, the realization hits him 'like a pistol-shot' that it means the loss of psychical boundaries. Compassion, like nerve force, refuses the containment of the individual body. There is no longer any protection from awareness that at every moment someone is approaching death's door, and in every street there are scenes of misery and distress. There are resonances here with Strindberg's *A Dream Play* (1907), with its evocation of human suffering as a tangible quality that eats into the walls and is knitted up into the white shawl that becomes the burden of Indra's daughter, bodhisattva of compassion. But Hoffmiller is entirely mortal, and there is no metaphysical dimension to his story in this dramatization. Rather, the performance is choreographed to evoke a state of psychical agoraphobia. Actors cross the stage in all directions. Storms break around them. A massive image of shattering glass is projected at moments of emotional impact.

Yet for all the emotional hold on the audience – this is, on one level, melodrama – we remain in the domain of a thought experiment. Questions are held in focus throughout. Principal among them is that of human agency, and the degree to which it is at issue in the coming of war. One of the few interpellations to Zweig's text occurs at the start of the performance, with a voice-over announcement that the jacket Archduke Ferdinand was wearing when he was shot has been acquired by the Austrian Military Museum in Vienna. Defaced by the bullet hole and surrounding bloodstain, the jacket is brought on stage and exhibited in the glass booth, which at this point represents the vitrine in the museum. At the end of the performance, after we hear the fatal gunshot ring out, and the announcement of the assassination, Hoffmiller enters the booth to strip, then reappears in a bloodied undershirt. There is no suggestion here that Hoffmiller 'is' Archduke Ferdinand, but rather that the single shot seals his destiny, as one of a vast body of men sent into the maelstrom. He 'wears' the rent in the time/space continuum that sends the train of events on track to war.

In the age of the machine, human consciousness crosses time and distance at speeds that challenge the perceptual frameworks of biological beings. The train is a recurring metaphor in Complicité productions, allowing for virtual transitions as the action moves from one place to another, but also serving as a location in itself, a compartment in which the experience of travel is evoked. In *Beware of Pity*, the glass booth becomes a train carriage, but also a time capsule, linking the twenty-first-century present (when the Archduke's jacket is placed on display as a historical exhibit) with the moment in 1914 when Hoffmiller first assumes his military role. Trains are also metaphors for inevitability. When a course of events is in train, or we enter a train to undertake a journey, the destination is set. Things are 'on track' to a determined outcome, though a train wreck is always on the cards.

There is a mechanistic aspect to the build-up of war on this new global scale, a scale that confounds human cognition. As Erwin Piscator wrote in *The Political Theatre*:

My calendar begins on August 4, 1914.
From that point the barometer registered 13 million dead
11 million crippled
50 million soldiers in combat
6 billion shells exploded
50 billion cubic meters of poison gas
Where is the personal development in all this? No young man develops in
a personal way. Something else develops him.[13]

And what of the fatal moment in which all this is about to happen? Here the 'hard problem' of consciousness must be confronted in a way that is better explored in the laboratories of theatre than of science. To adapt Artaud's formulation, perhaps it is not language itself that we must break through in order to touch life, but a repertoire of cognitive models through which we filter the complexities of experience. That is what it means to create, or recreate, theatre, and in doing so, to keep the frameworks of scientific enquiry open to the immediacy of lived experience.

In the novel, Zweig excels at storm scenes. A sky churns itself into a 'compact metallic mass' that is fractured by a vein of blue light as the clouds 'clatter against one another like heavy black chests' (137). All this is evoked in the staging so that the personal and the elemental are impossible to tell apart, not least for those who are caught up in the breaking cataclysm. It is as if consciousness, the swing door between inner and outer worlds, is being forced off its hinges. The combination of voice-over narrative with the shuttling figures of the actors in the surrounding chaos produces a level of

---

[13] Erwin Piscator, *The Political Theatre*, trans. Hugh Rorrison (London, 2007), 11.

intensity for which the earlier, more halting stages of the action leave an audience unprepared. Historically, psychologically, and theatrically, something is happening that is beyond anticipation – but what is it?

There is no science without a scientific observer. Piscator, especially through his collaborations with Brecht, saw the theatre as a means of situating an observer-consciousness in the auditorium. The audience became a detached spectator, presented with the challenges of cognitive processing and moral appraisal. In mediating between the time frames of 1938 and 1914, Zweig attempts through the distance of retrospect to gain some coherent perspective on chaos. Across the time frames, we observe the resurgence of a massive crisis, a crisis on a scale that, as Piscator so powerfully states, blows individual consciousness from its moorings, but at each of these points, meaning and interpretation take on new parameters.

Matthew Wilson Smith's 2017 book *The Nervous Stage* provides a valuable account of pre-twentieth-century theatrical engagements with the question, 'How did we come to think of ourselves not as souls but as nerves?'[14] He tracks the cultural evolution of the neural subject from the romantic era to the early twentieth century, focusing on key examples that include Büchner's *Woyzeck* and the oeuvre of Strindberg. *Woyzeck*, based on real-life events that took place in the 1820s, dramatizes the causal elements behind a domestic murder committed by someone in a state of psychosis. While Büchner was working on the script in the mid-1830s, he was also conducting medical research on the nervous system. As Smith observes, this was at a time when the mind–body problem was being tackled with a new level of sophistication. Büchner's particular interest was in studies of the skull as an extension of the vertebrae, a hypothesis with the implication that mind–body sensations and impressions are on a continuum. In the drama, though, scientific ideas themselves become demented. The maddest personage in *Woyzeck* is the physician who administers treatments to his patient based on obsessive fixations of his own. Between these and the compulsive disciplines enforced through the regimes of military training that subject Woyzeck's every movement to stringent control, there arises a sense of the whole milieu as psychotic. As a proto-Expressionist work, Büchner's play conjures a world in which there are no stabilizing perspectives; animate beings and inanimate things are alike dragged into force fields that make a mockery of individual will. Following on from Büchner, Strindberg was well versed in the growing literature on

---

[14] Matthew Wilson Smith, *The Nervous Stage: Nineteenth-Century Neuroscience and the Birth of Modern Theatre* (Oxford, 2017), 1.

neuropsychology, including works on neuropathology by Henry Maudsley, Théodule Ribot, and Max Nordau. His dramatic world, like Büchner's, is one in which nerve force flows through the material environment, rendering it unstable and crisis-prone for those who inhabit it. Smith sees *A Dream Play* as 'a passionate, and increasingly desperate, attempt to unify chemistry and the psyche' (180).

One of the common elements in the dramas Smith analyzes is a breakdown of language. He views this through the lens of Artaud, observing how the fault lines run through speech 'to play directly on the nerves of spectators through nonrepresentational and sensorial means' in which the audience becomes a 'sensorium' (11). Here Zweig's approach presents a departure from the traditions of the 'nervous stage' and their evolution in the Expressionist movement of his own time. However violent and pervasive the force fields he is portraying, language retains its hold as a means of translating crisis into narrative. While the course of events may lose coherence, spinning out in increasingly chaotic trajectories, the language itself remains cohesive and logical.

McBurney's decision to make the actual process of reading Zweig's text a central element in the dramaturgy thus indicates a sure instinct for one of the most significant aspects of *Beware of Pity* as an experiment in cognition. This is not Expressionist theatre. As nervous theatre, it has some characteristics that reflect the rationalist ethos of the Vienna Circle more than the psycho-dramatic modes of Expressionism, in which there is no accommodation for coherent understanding of any kind: not through language, nor through sensory information. There is, therefore, no place for the scientific observer, as the audience are drawn in to share the perceptual crises of the hysterical subject.

Zweig's own interests during the Weimar years were situated somewhere between the anarchic experimentalism and the rigorous intellectual commitments of the Vienna Circle. He was not directly involved in either. As he was living in Salzburg in the early 1920s, when the Vienna Circle was in its formative phase, this may account for his lack of association with it. But the enquiries into consciousness pursued by its members are in some respects highly relevant to his concerns in the novel. They were scientifically trained philosophers, strongly influenced by the pragmatism of William James and committed to the principles of logic and mathematics as a stable foundation for human cognition. This commitment underpinned Bertrand Russell's theory of logical atomism, a view of the world as consisting of microcomponents that combined to make more complex objects. 'Russell's solution to the empiricist problem of knowledge,' says Cheryl Misak, is to argue that physical objects 'are logical constructions from the immediately given entities of sensation'.[15] In Russell's own words, 'you can get down in theory, if not in practice, to ultimate simples, out of which the world is built ... those simples have a kind of reality not belonging to anything else'.[16] Here we have a counterpoint to the nineteenth-century image of 'dust mind.' Instead of seeing consciousness as an aggregation of particles, Russell proposed a model of cognition as an aggregate of sensory impressions derived from the logical atoms of the world itself.

This restores the possibility of the scientific observer, even in a world that, in holistic terms, is flying apart in all directions. It brings with it, though, some stringent embargoes on thought experiment. The Vienna circle took an adversarial view of metaphysics, and many of them were also averse to hypothesis: a proposition can be verified, but a hypothesis cannot. Metaphor is closely related to hypothesis, sparked as it is by speculative thinking and the question 'what if?' Given that the stage is always a zone of figurative representation, is theatre even possible without metaphor? There is no poetry without metaphor, and no metaphor without hypothesis and the uncertainty of 'what if?'

Few scientists of the twenty-first century would seek the degree of cognitive certainty that the Vienna circle considered prerequisite to reliable scientific observation. As signalled in the title of his book *What We Cannot Know*, du Sautoy seeks to promote the public understanding of science with an acknowledgement that uncertainty is core business and the 'big open questions' are a necessary challenge. Yet the 'edges' of uncertainty can be reached through dependence on what we *can* know (420). Du Sautoy cites the Newtonian laws of motion as an example of what we can know, and what can be extrapolated from it. The third law states: 'When one body exerts a force on a second body, the second body simultaneously exerts a force equal in magnitude and opposite in direction to that of the first body' (34). The interaction between Hoffmiller and Edith might be an illustration of this law. By metaphorical association, so might the chain of actions and reactions leading to the war.

If, as du Sautoy asserts, 'science has given us our best weapon in our fight against fate', might this insight assist in an understanding of Zweig's question about the causes of war, and thus, by implication, the means of averting fatal consequences? A theatrical performance of Zweig's work enables an

---

[15] Cheryl Misak, 'The Subterranean Influence of Pragmatism on the Vienna Circle', *Journal of the History of Analytic Philosophy* 4, no. 5 (2016): 2.

[16] Bertrand Russell, 'The Philosophy of Logical Atomism', in *The Collected Papers of Bertrand Russell, vol. 8: The Philosophy of Logical Atomism and Other Essays 1914–1919*, ed. John G. Slater (London, 1986), 234. Quoted in Misak, 'The Subterranean Influence', 2.

attendant question to be raised: Was there even the possibility of an observer position, beyond the event horizon, from which a scientific understanding might be reached? That is, at least, a known unknown.

Suggested Reading

Artaud, Antonin. *The Theatre and Its Double*, trans. Mary Caroline Richards. New York, 1958.

du Sautoy, Marcus. *What We Cannot Know: From Consciousness to the Cosmos, the Cutting Edge of Science Explained*. London, 2017. Kindle edition.

James, William. 'The Compounding of Consciousness'. In *A Pluralistic Universe*. Hibbert Lectures at Manchester College on the Present Situation in Philosophy, lecture 5 (1909). Project Gutenberg e-book, 2004.

Misak, Cheryl. 'The Subterranean Influence of Pragmatism on the Vienna Circle'. *Journal of the History of Analytic Philosophy*, 4 (2016): 5.

Piscator, Erwin. *The Political Theatre*, trans. Hugh Rorrison. London, 2007.

Russell, Bertrand. 'The Philosophy of Logical Atomism'. In J. G. Slater, ed., *The Collected Papers of Bertrand Russell, vol. 8: The Philosophy of Logical Atomism and Other Essays, 1914–1919*. London, 1986.

Shepherd-Barr, Kirsten. 'From Copenhagen to Infinity and Beyond: Science Meets Literature on Stage'. *Interdisciplinary Science Reviews* 28 (2003): 193–9.

Science on Stage: From Doctor Faustus to Copenhagen. Princeton, 2006.

Smith, M. Wilson. *The Nervous Stage: Nineteenth-Century Neuroscience and the Birth of Modern Theatre*. Oxford, 2017.

Theatre de Complicité. www.complicite.org.

Zweig, Stefan. *The World of Yesterday*, trans. Eden Paul and Cedar Paul. London, 1987.

Beware of Pity, trans. Phyllis Blewitt and Trevor Blewitt. New York, 2006.

'The Sleepless World – 1914'. In *Messages from a Lost World: Europe on the Brink*, trans. Will Stone. London, 2016, 39–49.

3

CARINA BARTLEET

The Experimental/Experiential Stage

Extreme States of Being of and Knowing in the Theatre

The theatre and the branches of knowledge that the umbrella term 'science' subsumes share common ground. In both there is a commitment to the observable and the repeatable as human activities of knowledge. Wedded to these activities of creating new theatre, or science, is a sense that the experimental or novel brings knowledge that is reproducible or 'rehearsable'. The pairing of drama and science itself is not new, however: Christopher Marlowe's alchemical *Doctor Faustus* and the melancholia of Shakespeare's Hamlet, grounded in humoral theory, suggest that theatre has a history of fascination with knowing about the physical world, and together, theatre and science have the potential to create fresh ways to communicate novel ideas.[1]

Theatre's preoccupation with science is significant in the twentieth century when it and technological change shaped the world. Modernism's distorted, subjective representational theatrical worlds reflected the pace of change through fetishization by the Italian Futurists, the irregular and distinctly unnatural lighting states of German Expressionism, and in Soviet Russia, the systemized actor training of Meyerhold's biomechanics. Moreover, Bertolt Brecht, arguably the most influential theatre modernist, theorized a 'theatre for a scientific age'.[2] These theatricalized engagements explored how the scientific can shape human experience. Towards the end of the twentieth century, theatre showed a marked concern for scientific ideas, for doing science, and for scientists. This chapter traces theatre's preoccupation with science through three of the more pressing topics of the time: molecular structure, genetic testing in medicine, and climate change. It draws together widely discussed plays in theatre and science with newer and

---

[1] See Kirsten Shepherd-Barr, *Science on Stage: From Doctor Faustus to Copenhagen* (Princeton, 2006).
[2] Bertolt Brecht, *Brecht on Theatre: The Development of an Aesthetic*, ed. John Willett (London, 1964), 183–6.

little-analyzed pieces to investigate how theatre has explored science through the experience of doing it or living it. How this relates to the ideas of experimentation and the experimental (including experiential aspects of performance), in the theatre at the end of the twentieth and beginning of the twenty-first centuries, links these pieces and is significant as an analytical focus. In this act of exploration, the chapter interrogates notions of the experimental beyond coupling it purely with notions of avant-garde or novel art into an understanding that adds to it the sense, more familiar in science, of a procedure carried out to discover something or to test a hypothesis.

Millennial Dis/ease

As the turn of the millennium approached, Shelagh Stephenson's *An Experiment with an Air Pump* (1998) explored some of the moral aspects of genetic and reproductive technologies that were a preoccupation of the moment, extending the scrutiny to a metaphor for the theatrical event itself. Stephenson's striking drama adopts a technique common to several British science plays of the 1990s, including Tom Stoppard's *Arcadia* (1993) and Timberlake Wertenbaker's *After Darwin* (1998), in which action is split between two time frames (in Stephenson's play, 1799 and 1999) in a manner that Gyllian Raby has described as 'a simple technique of epic theatre that has been popular among socially aware writers in England for the last half century'.[3] Similarly, Claudia Barnett styles the play a 'moral dialectic' that is founded upon oppositional pairings.[4] Barnett and Raby allude to the play's indebtedness to Bertolt Brecht's notions of dialectical and epic theatre and, hence, to its political dimension, through nonlinear structure and plot founded on a dialogue between the two centuries it opts to stage. The title of the play refers to Joseph Wright of Derby's 1768 painting *An Experiment on a Bird with an Air Pump*, which hangs in the National Gallery in London, and Stephenson's play opens with a tableau vivant of the painting. Wright was a noted artist associated with the famous philosophical circle the Lunar Society, whose members included Charles Darwin's grandfather, Erasmus Darwin, and Joseph Priestley, and was thus at the centre of the scientific advances of the Enlightenment. In an article contemporaneous with the play, Sandra Harding warns that 'the Enlightenment entrenches a faulty

---

[3] Gyllian Raby, 'From Pre-Luddites to the Human Genome Project: Smashing Frames in Shelagh Stephenson's *An Experiment with an Air Pump*', in *Images and Imagery: Frames, Borders, Limits: Interdisciplinary Perspectives* (Peter Lang Publishing, 2005), xv, 293.

[4] Claudia Barnett, 'A Moral Dialectic: Shelagh Stephenson's *An Experiment with an Air Pump*', *Modern Drama* 49, no. 2 (2006): 206–7.

philosophy of nature. Nature is not a cornucopia, available to satisfy limit-less desires.... Moreover, sciences and philosophies of nature, like all other human creations, are *in* nature, not autonomous from it.'[5] The play similarly draws out what Harding terms a 'faulty philosophy' and presents a contemporary view of Enlightenment as a contested and problematized term to make a comparison between science in the period and the questionable benefits of late twentieth-century scientific knowledge and technology.

An Experiment with an Air Pump creates comparisons through those oppositional pairings between the experiences and experiments of 1799 and 1999. Stephenson constructs this through doubling roles in specific combinations, allowing associations to be made between characters and situations across the centuries. For instance, the main characters in 1799, the scientist Joseph Fenwick and his wife Susannah, are doubled by the performers cast in the central roles in 1999, the geneticist Ellen and her husband Tom, thereby highlighting the changing roles of women in the public sphere in the intervening period. The integration of role doubling is a significant facet of the opening:

> *Chiaroscuro lighting up slow revolve tableau involving the whole cast (except Susannah/Ellen), which suggests* An Experiment on a Bird in the Air Pump.... *Strategically placed over the audience are four large projections of Wright's painting.* Ellen, *dressed casually in loose trousers, T-shirt, deck shoes, is looking up at them. Two dressers come on with her costume, wig, shoes etc for the part of* Susannah.[6]

It is Ellen who introduces the play. Tellingly, she observes, 'it has a scientist at the heart of it ... where you *would usually find God'*.[7] With the assistance of the two dressers, the performer playing Ellen transforms into Susannah and steps into the frame of the tableau vivant, theatrically achieving what Brecht termed the *Verfremdungseffekt* by drawing attention to the live reproduction of the painting as constructed and mutable. In addition, Ellen's potential status as an objective observer is negated by this technique, which implicates her in the spectacle.

Stephenson's placement of the scientist centre stage is an equivocal one: the stage directions suggest that Ellen's perspective should not be taken at face value. As Eva-Sabine Zehelein suggests, 'Ellen's version seems to be a

[5] Sandra Harding, 'Gender, Development and Post-Enlightenment Philosophies of Science', *Hypatia* 13, no. 3 (Summer 1998): 153.
[6] Shelagh Stephenson. *An Experiment with an Air Pump* (London, 1998), 3.
[7] Ibid.; emphasis added.

very idiosyncratic reading of [Wright of] Derby's painting.'[8] The tetradic projection of Wright's painting makes it difficult for an audience to miss what is not immediately apparent from the play's text: that the painting does not place the scientist at its centre. Instead, a pool of light focuses the attention away from the experimenter to the reactions of the observers and in particular to the girls (Maria and Harriet are Stephenson's counterparts), one of whom is looking away while the other has a fearful expression on her face. Susan L. Siegfried has argued of the painting that Wright 'used women to explore this area of ethical uncertainty. The two girls at the center of the *Air Pump* are conspicuously distraught at the prospect of their pet bird dying.'[9] This is true of Stephenson's play, which anticipates just such a reading of the painting when she dramatizes this moment as one of 'ethical uncertainty' in the opening sections:

MARIA: Will he die, Papa?
FENWICK: We'll see, won't we?
MARIA: I don't want him to die.
ARMSTRONG: It's only a bird.
HARRIET: It's Maria's pet.
ARMSTRONG: The world is bursting with birds, she can get another –
MARIA: *bursts into tears.*[10]

In the play as in the painting, the girls provide the moment of experiential dis-ease: an ethical fulcrum to the action in contrast to the men of science, Fenwick and Armstrong. Maria and Harriet's concerns for the bird's welfare present an emotional and moral perspective at counterpoint to scientific knowledge and experimental method.

Stephenson resolves her scene with the bird fluttering out, unharmed. Wright's painting does not offer such closure, letting its viewers dwell in the moment of terror, apprehension, and uncertainty over the bird's fate. The play draws on Brecht's practice, but it is not completely indebted to his ideas as Raby notes. According to her, Stephenson's 'suspense, climax and audience identification with the tragic fate of Isobel's rebellion all place her in a tradition more cathartic than epic': the form of theatre associated with Brecht.[11] The scene is also remarkable because it shares with the painting the Baconian separation between knowing and the knowable as described by

---

[8] Eva-Sabine Zehelein, *Science: Dramatic: Science Plays in America and Great Britain, 1990–2007* (Heidelberg, 2009), 150.
[9] Susan L. Siegfried, 'Engaging the Audience: Sexual Economies of Vision in Joseph Wright', *Representations* 68 (1999): 45.
[10] Stephenson, *An Experiment with an Air Pump*, 4.
[11] Raby, *From Pre-Luddites to the Human Genome Project*, 143.

Evelyn Fox Keller in relation to scientific thought.[12] These two aspects point to a play that contains tensions between a classically constructed drama and its political content. The object of the artistic enquiry is not the scientist or his discovery but the reactions of those around him. Furthermore, they respect the paradigm's gendered organization of the knower as masculine and the knowable as feminine, as the inscrutability of the male scientist in Wright's painting is, to risk an anachronism, readable by Stephenson's late twentieth-century audiences. The use of chiaroscuro heightens the sense of mystery: Wright's scientist is mysterious and morally ambiguous. Ellen steps into the frame presenting the perspective of the scientist and, by extension, her own actions as questionable right from the start, since the performer playing her is absorbed into Susannah's role of the passive observer. This questioning of Ellen as a contemporary scientist becomes especially significant to the 1999 strand of the plot, which is driven by her professional dilemma over whether to take a job that risks her work being misused for commercial ends.

If Stephenson's scientist is not at the physical centre of the stage, (s)he is at the core of the moral ambiguities. Ellen is only wrong in her reading of the scene in visual terms: the scientist takes the place of the absent, unknowable God, who decides whether the bird lives or dies. The opportunity to map Ellen onto the masculine template of Baconian science is partially resisted by Stephenson's questioning narrative, but staging science as an equivocal and morally uncertain enterprise is not. In 1799 and 1999, Stephenson presents scientists compromising their ethical standpoints for scientific advantage. In so doing, the events she depicts reveal scientists in both eras at the centre of moral dilemmas in God's stead. In 1999, Ellen develops a test for foetal abnormalities and is offered a lucrative job in industry, and after much deliberation about the pros and cons, in the penultimate scene, she decides to take it. The job means greater opportunities and more money but the company are likely to exploit her findings for profit. Since the information gained from the tests might be of interest to employers and insurance companies, as the other twentieth-century characters point out, Ellen's work could become yet another way of discriminating against people rather than helping them. Ellen herself recognizes the moral aspect to science and her choice to take the job when she reflects, 'I don't think science is value free, I don't think its morally neutral.'[13]

The moral quandary presented in the 1799 strand of the plot is even more disturbing. Young scientist Armstrong feigns love with the Fenwicks' maid,

---

[12] Evelyn Fox Keller, *Reflections on Gender and Science* (New Haven, 1985), 79.
[13] Stephenson, *An Experiment with an Air Pump*, 88.

Isobel Bridie, hoping to get close enough to her to study her pronounced spinal deformity. In a counterpoint, Isobel believes that he loves her in spite of her deformity, and, in the penultimate scene (the same one in which Ellen takes the job), she hangs herself in despair after discovering his heinous deceit. Maria discovers Isobel, her pulse weak. Stage directions and dialogue work in tandem to suggest Armstrong's shockingly dispassionate behaviour. With Maria safely offstage he calls 'Isobel? Can you hear me?'[14] On receiving no response, Armstrong 'hesitates. Then puts his hand over her nose and mouth, and presses down. Her heels flutter almost imperceptibly. In a second it is over. He feels her pulse again.'[15] In this final scene, Armstrong's words are stripped away and devalued as he murders her.

The final act of the play offers comparison between Armstrong's immoral behaviour and those of the characters from the 1990s through several strategies. The first of these is through plotting that allows characters from 1799 and 1999 to share the same stage, and the second is through dialogue and action applicable to both contexts and centuries. The stage directions at this juncture request 'Music, distant sounds of what could be celebrations, or could be riots suggest both the New Year's celebrations in each century and the riots taking place in 1799'.[16] Second, Isobel is present in both time frames: as the servant who falls in love and attempts suicide in 1799 and as the partial skeleton of a woman discovered in the house by Tom in 1999. Finally, the parallels between the scientists are brought into sharper relief in Act 2, Scene 4, when Tom tells Ellen's colleague, Kate, that she is 'unscrupulous, ambitious, and you'd dissect your own mother if you thought it might give you the answer to something'.[17] Rather than stark dialectic there are subtle differences and near parallels drawn between the unscrupulous Armstrong and his 1999 counterpart, Kate, Ellen's friend and colleague. Kate is not entirely lacking in morality; as Barnett pithily puts it, 'she would not kill, so unlike the immoral Armstrong, she is merely amoral'.[18] A scene later, at the play's close, Armstrong pushes this amorality to its extreme in his final act of betrayal: his dissection of Isobel. Her value to Armstrong as an object of scientific enquiry is enhanced by her death. Stephenson links this personal betrayal with the immorality implicit in Armstrong's lack of restraint towards his own scientific curiosity by placing Isobel's body in a coffin so that the final tableau becomes a re-vision of the painting, placing her in the bird's stead as the scientists subject her body to dissection. This mutated tableau theatricalizes the gendered dynamic of Baconian science identified by Keller. At this moment, the play's critique of science and scientists is at its strongest.

---

[14] Ibid., 92.   [15] Ibid.   [16] Ibid., 95.   [17] Ibid., 88.
[18] Barnett, 'A Moral Dialectic', 213.

Thus, the final, gendered image is a reproduction of the painting with a difference: it places the experiential, human, and female cost of scientific discovery and its attendant objectification centre stage.

Life Story as Experiment

Deborah Gearing's 2006 play *Rosalind: A Question of Life* takes its audiences right back to the fundamentals of the gene by exploring the discovery of the structure of DNA. Her play is one of a number of twenty-first-century theatre pieces featuring twentieth-century women crystallographers, including Georgina Ferry's *Hidden Glory* about Dorothy Hodgkin, Anna Ziegler's *Photograph 51* about Rosalind Franklin, and Esther Shanson and Curved Experience Theatre Company's part-scripted, part dance, and part devised *The Nature of Things*, which interweaves the scientific lives of Franklin, Hodgkin, and Kathryn Lonsdale. Franklin's X-ray images of DNA crystals were a significant part of how the molecule's structure was elucidated in 1953. Franklin died of ovarian cancer in 1958 while she was still in her thirties, and her role in the discovery of DNA has only recently begun to be more acknowledged, though she has yet to receive formal posthumous recognition.

On the page, *Rosalind* looks dramaturgically conventional: a series of scenes with speeches given to clearly demarcated characters. Yet Gearing plots her onstage actions by drawing on theatrical techniques that are features of other science plays like Wertenbaker's *After Darwin* (1998), Stoppard's *Arcadia* (1993), and Stephenson's play discussed above. All of these utilize scenes to make distinctions between narratives of past and present characters. Gearing's play is introduced through twenty-first-century characters, the genetics undergraduate Esther and her brother Joe. The performer playing Rosalind is onstage during this sequence, but she has no part other than observer. In the subsequent scene, Rosalind has a monologue, at which point, Esther, the present-day scientist, remains onstage but unaware of her, mirroring the previous scene's conventions. The dialogue immediately contextualizes the difference, giving Esther's birth date as the 1980s: nearly thirty years after the death of Franklin. Rosalind, the character, is foregrounded by this monologue's content: she tells the audience that she was Esther's age (approximately nineteen) when World War II broke out. Thus, although Gearing makes it evident that the two women were born at opposite ends of the twentieth century, she complicates matters by questioning whether the onstage action is a representation of reality at all:

A life begins at the beginning and ends when it must.
Afterwards: what remains? What remains of me?

With a story you begin at the beginning but, this isn't a story.
Let's say it's an experiment.
The idea with an experiment, is that afterwards you know a little more than before. You are on your way to finding the truth.[19]

This speech is central to understanding the play's subtitle, 'a question of life'. Its deictic language draws attention to the life being more than how DNA replicates, for which understanding its structure is pivotal (and by extension also crucial for the audience). Gearing's play asks what remains of this iconic heroine. Is she reachable only through the work she carried out on the molecule's structure? The speech illuminates the artifice of performance through Rosalind as a representation and the possibility that, as a fiction, the story is a thought experiment. Here, in Gearing's version, Rosalind is like Schrödinger's cat: existing an uncertain state of being because onstage she is both alive and dead. Gearing opts not to resolve the issue of which century Rosalind the character exists in, a postmodern move that treats Franklin's time as one of the ludic aspects of the performance. Within the stage world of *Rosalind*, characters signal themselves as fictional representations: as dead, or alive, or both. Moreover, it stages past and present as occurring simultaneously or in juxtaposition, depending on the situation. Thus, Gearing's play-world, for all its experimental feel, is an experiential, fictional realm; it is a temporality in which consciousness, perception, and history collide.

One of the striking features about this work, originally aimed at a young adult audience, is its approach to Franklin's scientific practice. Gearing's thought-experiment technique combines instruction in scientific ideas and methodologies with a simple role play. The economy of the writing means that, in order to retell the scenes from Franklin's life, the performers playing Esther and Joe have to enact the roles of Watson, Crick, and Franklin's lab mate Wilkins. This is effectively achieved by the performers staying in their initial characters but adding a signifying item of costume (e.g., a coat for Wilkins and a lab coat for Watson) and role-playing the characters in Rosalind's scientific life. Through this simple device, the play delivers scientific information to the audience as instruction on how to role-play the other scientists. For instance, Joe says: 'I thought you were taking x-ray photographs of crystals. What are you doing with them?'[20] To which Rosalind replies:

You have to obtain a good crystal before you can even begin to take the photograph.... The X-ray beam is shone into the vacuum and channelled

---

[19] Deborah Gearing, *Rosalind: A Question of Life*, in *Burn and Rosalind* (London, 2006), 74.
[20] Ibid., 87.

through the crystal. The atoms of the crystal diffract the beam ... so the flecks of light on the photographic plate are not a true image – the scientist's job is to interpret those flecks, to reconstruct the molecule.... You have to apply equations.... You have to be able to think in three dimensions.... Our results suggest a helical structure ... containing probably two, three or four co-axial nucleic chains per helical unit, and having the phosphate groups near the outside.[21]

The speech, ostensibly an instruction to someone playing the role, imparts clear information about DNA and the skills and techniques required by Franklin to complete her work. It draws on stage properties that might be found in a school or university teaching laboratory and consists of replicas of two models built by Watson and Crick and Franklin's photograph 51, which has a significant role during a scene in which the characters enact Wilkins's high-handed disregard for Franklin by showing it to Watson without her prior knowledge and facilitating the building of the correct model 2. Gearing underlines this betrayal by having her Rosalind remain unaware of this fact until the scene unfolds before her in a deftly knowing, postmodern articulation of the construction of knowledge. Gearing's fictional play-world documents the life and material conditions under which one of the twentieth century's significant woman scientists worked. What is made crystal clear is the experiential aspects of science: the dedication and painstaking lab practices that made Franklin's work possible and the sociopolitical dimension of its undertaking.

The Anthroposcene: Staging Climate Change

As the 2010s approached, British playwrights rather belatedly turned their attentions to one of the most pressing issues of the day: climate change. In a brief discussion of the topic in the epilogue to her *Theatre and Evolution from Ibsen to Beckett*, Shepherd-Barr observes that these plays give 'new meaning to the vexed issue of how individuals relate to their environments'.[22] In the face of increasing evidence that the effects of climate change were being felt on a global scale, Steve Waters wrote the diptych *The Contingency Plan* (2009); Moira Buffini, Matt Charman, Penelope Skinner, and Jack Thorne presented their combined vision, *Greenland* (2011); Mike Bartlett's 2010 *Earthquakes in London* pitted a climate change scientist against his fragile family dealing with the daily reality of global warming's

---

[21] Ibid., 87–8.
[22] Kirsten E. Shepherd-Barr, *Theatre and Evolution from Ibsen to Beckett* (New York, 2015), 284.

effects; and Duncan Macmillan's *Lungs* (2011) was similarly bleak in its staging of climate change as a deliberation between a couple about whether to have a child. In 2014, Macmillan teamed up with a climate change scientist, Chris Rapley, to create *2071*, which was staged at the Royal Court Theatre in London.

In three respects, *2071* is singular as a theatrical performance: the degree to which its subject matter is scientific in content, its subordination of theatricality to narrative, and its textual afterlife. As Vicky Angelaki observes in her study of twenty-first-century political theatre:

> It is telling that two of the most notable examples of how nature and our universe became a pivot for new writing, *Ten Billion* and *2071*, took on the economic form of the performance lecture. As these works examined how the planet has been led to a combustion point with mathematical precision, the directness of the titles was reflected in their style and content.[23]

Though presented in London, *2071*'s afterlife is a global one: its text is available to download free on open access as well as in a print edition.[24]

What *2071* replicates in theatrical terms is the approach of plays such as Gearing's *Rosalind*, Michael Frayn's *Copenhagen* (1998), and Peter Parnell's *Q.E.D.* (2002) in which a real-life scientist is placed centre stage, as Rapley participates as an onstage incarnation of himself. Where it differs is that Rapley, the scientist, takes the place of the actor in performing the role. His opening lines – 'I've been thinking a lot about the future. As a climate scientist it is part of my job' – introduce the topic by telling the audience what he has done and seen, foregrounding the science in his personal, subjective, lived experience.[25] Furthermore, he asserts, 'I have been head of the British Antarctic Survey, and in that role have been to the Antarctic and the Southern Ocean many times.'[26] The piece proclaims Rapley's experiential qualification to judge: 'My work has enabled me to travel to parts of the planet visited by only a few and to meet experts from all over the world. This has allowed me to see and assess things for myself.'[27] In other words, the journey through climate change starts with Rapley's authority on it: 'A lot has changed in my lifetime.... Major advances ... made in oceanography, meteorology, magnetism'.[28]

---

[23] Vicky Angelaki, *Social and Political Theatre in 21st-Century Britain: Staging Crisis* (London, 2017), 110.
[24] The text of *2071* is available at www.researchgate.net/publication/272086982_2071_Playtext/download. The print edition is the version referenced throughout this chapter.
[25] Chris Rapley and Duncan Macmillan, *2071: The World We'll Leave Our Children* (London, 2015), 3.
[26] Ibid., 5.   [27] Ibid., 6.   [28] Ibid., 15, 20.

The play *2071* is less about science or scientists, however, than using scientific discourse and the figure of the scientist to communicate one of the vital issues of the day. The piece only draws attention to scientific ideas when the arguments about climate change require a precise understanding of the processes that underpin the reasoning behind them. There are two specific areas in which the onstage Rapley explains some of the science: (1) the carbon cycle and, related to it, (2) dynamic balance. The play *2071* explains the carbon cycle in simple terms and how it relates to climate change. It:

> consists of large annual exchanges between the carbon reservoirs of the atmosphere, the land biosphere, the lithosphere and the ocean.. . .
>
> For example, as plants grow on land and in the sea in the spring, they draw down carbon dioxide from the atmosphere, which is later released as the green matter dies and decays.. . .
>
> Physical exchanges take place between the atmosphere and the ocean as carbon dioxide is absorbed into cold dense waters that sink to depths, and is released from areas where warmer water upwells.
>
> These exchanges are much greater in magnitude than our own carbon emissions – but prior to industrialization they were in dynamic balance.[29]

Of dynamic balance, Rapley pronounces:

> Dynamic balance applies to many features of the system, such as the balance of the carbon between the atmosphere, ocean, land and vegetation.. . .
>
> But it especially applies to the energy balance of the planet – meaning that, over time, the amount of energy leaving the planet is equal to the amount entering it.[30]

He concludes that 'we are currently burning 10,000 million tonnes of carbon per year – a figure that has been increasing at a rate of 2 per cent per year'.[31] Textually, the arguments raise alarm in relation to climate change and the wholly experiential assertion of humanity's influence: 'Human impact on the planetary system has been so profound that *many feel* we have irreversibly brought the climatic stability of the Holocene to an end and entered a new epoch. The "Anthropocene".'[32] Crucially, this lecture communicates not exclusively to other scientists but to theatre audiences, whoever they may be. The Anthropocene, the era in which humanity shapes the earth, becomes the Anthropo*scene* in which all humans are actors in this drama.

The play *2071* poses a conundrum for the theatre. Unlike Bartlett's play with its arrogant professor and his three daughters whose lives are shaped by

---

[29] Ibid., 112–14.　　[30] Ibid., 40–1.　　[31] Ibid., 117.　　[32] Ibid., 120–1. My emphasis.

climate change, or Macmillan's own *Lungs* where the couple's personal life and the effects of climate change are completely merged, *2071* uses the subject as its story. The urgency of its tale relies not on onstage action but on its message: in exhorting its audiences to action. In intertextual terms, *2071* is striking in its permutation of texts: the scientist and the message take precedence over dramatic discourse to the point that they are merged.[33]

Equally interested in the experiential, but more theatrically experimental than *2071*, Bartlett's *Earthquakes in London* premiered at the National Theatre in London in August 2010, in conjunction with Headlong. *Earthquakes in London* relates how climate change brings about metaphorical and literal seismic shifts in human existence. The earthquakes of the title symbolize the disruption to human civilization from climate change and the organizational structure of the play itself. The story interweaves the lives of climate change scientist Robert Crannock and his three daughters: Sarah, a government minister overseeing the response to climate change; pregnant Freya; and Jasmine, a student. Ultimately, Freya's daughter, Emily, is presented as a Christ-like figure, who can lead humanity to salvation; her grandfather, Robert, is presented as a complicated and flawed scientist.

Bartlett's work is expansive and ranges between locations and moments in time. In contrast to *2071*, *Earthquakes in London*'s theatricality is deliberately intense, mirroring the climate crisis it comments upon. As Julie Hudson notes, the opening stage directions demand excess.[34] Bartlett instructs the director to employ 'as much set, props and costume as possible. The stage should overflow with scenery, backdrops, lighting projection etc.... The play is about excess, and we should feel that.'[35] Furthermore, the first two scenes mix into each other in a fluid manner that does not respect dramatic conventions or signal changes in scenery. As Hudson observes, the 'constantly shifting episodic structure comes across to the audience as chaotic, and this is quite deliberate'.[36] Throughout, the five acts move seamlessly between locations without clearly demarcated scene changes, creating the theatrical equivalent of a jump cut because, like this form of film editing, the play's simple shifts draw attention to changes in space and time rather than conforming to conventional rules. The effect is rather to create a hybrid

---

[33] Julia Kristeva, 'The Bounded Text', trans. Thomas Gora, Alice Jardine, and Leon S. Roudiez, in *Desire in Language: A Semiotic Approach to Art and Literature*, ed. Leon S. Roudiez (New York, 1980), 36. Intertextuality is characterized as being 'a permutation of texts'.

[34] Julie Hudson, '"If You Want to Be Green Hold Your Breath": Climate Change in British Theatre', *New Theatre Quarterly* 28, no. 3 (August 2012): 265.

[35] Mike Bartlett, *Earthquakes in London* (London, 2010), 5.

[36] Hudson, 'If You Want to Be Green', 265.

form: a supercharged version of Brecht's epic theatre. In the original production, this mingling of the action was reinforced by a twisty thrust stage that snaked around the auditorium as if to mimic Bartlett's dramaturgical choices.

This dystopian, but ultimately redemptive, vision of Britain is set across a number of different time periods: 1967, the 1970s, the play's own near future during the Conservative-Liberal Democrat government 2010–15, and the year 2525. Each act up until, and including, Act 4 features a sequence taking place in the play's past as a prologue to it (1967 in Act 1, 1973 in Acts 2 and 3, and 1991 in Act 4) with an epilogue set sixteen years in the future. Bartlett's choices in plotting his play from the beginnings of climate change science to beyond the present day point his audiences towards seeing causality in the decisions made in the 1960s and 1970s and their consequences for present-day characters. Furthermore, its extrapolation to the future suggests how action in the play's present might have consequences for humanity's future. Its speculative 'what if' breaks up the linear inevitability of determinism to invite questioning of those actions.

Whereas in 2071 the scientist conveys an important message because of the legacy he owes to his grandchild, *Earthquakes in London* has its fictional scientist betray his field and perhaps the planet for personal gain, only for it to be saved by his granddaughter. Act 2 opens with a prologue set in 1973 in which Robert meets with two airline industry men who commission him to study the effects of air travel and the burning of aviation fuel. They intimate that Robert's research needs to be useful if they are to continue their funding.[37] The nonlinear plotting of this consciously Brechtian play means that this segment of Robert's story in 1973 is not returned to until the opening of Act 3.[38] Robert is sure of his results, but the airline men are concerned that the findings are 'not meaningful'.[39] Robert's reply is one of the few passages in which the science is explicit: 'it's clear releasing huge quantities of carbon dioxide into the atmosphere at such a high altitude will cause heat to be reflected ... potentially causing rising temperatures'.[40] Rather than present a conflict of interest, Bartlett – in keeping with the play's indebtedness to Epic Theatre form, and perhaps to Brecht's *Life of Galileo* – presents a moral dilemma for the scientist as he is passed a piece of paper and is urged to 'keep going' and 'There's six months before the final report ...

[37] Bartlett, *Earthquakes in London*, 42.
[38] Mike Bartlett, 'Interview', in T. King and Headlong Theatre Company, *Earthquakes in London: Education Pack* (London, 2011), 7.
[39] Bartlett, *Earthquakes in London*, 66.   [40] Ibid., 67.

Anything could happen.'[41] Bartlett leaves his audience wondering if Robert has succumbed to temptation at the expense of his science.

There is a family secret at the core of *Earthquakes in London*: Freya is pregnant but is behaving in a manner that suggests the child (Emily) is unwanted. At the beginning of the play her husband travels to see Robert to ask him why Freya also visited. The conversation between the two men unravels slowly over the course of the play. It is only in Act 3 that the reason for Freya's distress is revealed in a long exchange that ranges over the Gaia theory, disruption to Earth's dynamic balance, and climate change. Musing on the topic of human overpopulation, Robert suggests that there will be a correction that would result in 'Five billion people wiped from the Earth in a single lifetime. Mass migration away from the equator, world wars, starvation' and reveals that he told Freya that 'her child will regret she was ever born'.[42] Robert's message is proximal to the pretext of Macmillan's *Lungs* a year later. Where *2071* is urgent and apocalyptic in its reach, Bartlett's work is hopeful and less concerned with the scientific message than its urgent human implications.

Theatre's connections with science help create a rich thematic mixture of ideas in all of these pieces. Theatrical daring, too, is a feature. Each draws on the idea of experiment and explores the human dimensions to science by documenting the experiential. Often, as these pieces demonstrate, that means reshaping dramatic form in experimental ways or turning over the theatre to science or experimentation directly, as with *2071* or *Rosalind*. These works look to the scientific concerns of their day to explore humanity at extremes or through crisis and dilemma and, in the case of the climate change plays, to ask, 'What next?' Theatre's mimicry of form is a common characteristic here: these pieces inhabit their theatrical ideas pairing and coiling historical periods around each other like a double helix of DNA or the inflamed structures of the Anthropo(s)cene.

Suggested Reading

Angelaki, Vicky. *Social and Political Theatre in 21st-Century Britain*. London, 2017.

Barnett, Claudia. 'A Moral Dialectic: Shelagh Stephenson's *An Experiment with an Air Pump*'. *Modern Drama* 49, no. 2 (2006): 206–22.

Harding, Sandra. 'Gender, Development and Post-Enlightenment Philosophies of Science'. *Hypatia* 13, no. 3 (1998): 146–67.

Hudson, Julie. '"If You Want to Be Green Hold Your Breath": Climate Change in British Theatre'. *New Theatre Quarterly* 28, no. 3 (2012): 260–71.

Keller, Evelyn Fox. *Reflections on Gender and Science*. New Haven, 1985.

[41] Ibid., 68.   [42] Ibid., 96.

King, T., and Headlong Theatre Company. *Earthquakes in London: Education Pack*, 2011. https://headlong.co.uk/media/media/downloads/Earthquakes_in_London_-_Education_Pack.pdf.

Raby, Gyllian. 'From Pre-Luddites to the Human Genome Project: Smashing Frames in Shelagh Stephenson's *An Experiment with an Air Pump*'. In *Studies on Themes and Motifs in Literature*, ed. Leslie Boldt-Irons, Corrado Fdeerici, and Ernesto Virgulti. New York, 2005. Available at http://spartan.ac.brocku.ca/~graby/pdfs/airpumppaper.pdf http://spartan.ac.brocku.ca/~graby/pdfs/airpumppaper.pdf.

Rapley, C., and Duncan Macmillan. *2071: The World We'll Leave Our Children*. London, 2015.

Shepherd-Barr, Kirsten. *Science on Stage: From Doctor Faustus to Copenhagen*. Princeton, 2006.

Theatre and Evolution from Ibsen to Beckett. New York, 2015.

Siegfried, Susan L. 'Engaging the Audience: Sexual Economies of Vision in Joseph Wright'. *Representations* 68 (1999): 34–58.

Zehelein, Eva-Sabine. *Science: Dramatic. Science Plays in America and Great Britain, 1990–2007*. Heidelberg, 2009.

4

CARL LAVERY

A Cave, a Skull, and a Little Piece of Grit

Theatre in the Anthropocene

Like many disciplines in the arts and humanities, there has been an important 'ecological turn' in theatre and performance studies in the past decade or so. This has led to a radical expansion in the scope and direction of theatre theory, with scholars now producing work that disturbs the unhelpful binary that, for too long, has separated the arts from the sciences, nature, and culture. In this move beyond the human, many of these new publications resonate with Dipesh Chakrabarty's calls for an expanded historiography for the Anthropocene that would perturb rigid borders between history and the natural world.[1] This is because, as Paul J. Crutzen has noted, the Anthropocene is the moment when, for the first time, the human is identified as a 'geological agent, a being that has left its mark in the stratigraphy of the earth and thrown its atmospheric systems off-kilter'.[2] Some of these texts have concentrated on interpretative readings of 'nature' in dramatic works; others on theatre's site-specificity; others still on new materialist discourses. In the latter two cases, theatre is thought to be particularly germane to the production of a new ecological way of thinking and feeling because, on the one hand, it is a physical medium that affects and is affected by its site; and, on the other, because it deals with organic and nonorganic bodies that are subject to the transformative forces of gravity and time.

In an age of species loss, climate change, and poisoned air, there is much to be commended in this shift to ecology and environment by theatre and performance scholars. Nevertheless, one should not remain blind to the possibility that it also harbours a dangerous contradiction: by focusing on the natural environment, the field of theatre studies may end by creating a niche genre that would go by the names of, say, green criticism or eco-performance. Not only would such a move overlook the fact that ecology

---

[1] Dipesh Chakrabarty, '"The Climate of History": Four Theses', *Critical Inquiry* 35, no. 2 (2009): 197–222.
[2] Paul J. Crutzen, 'Geology of Mankind', *Nature* 415 (2002): 23.

is a connected and entangled way of thinking, opposed to all disciplines and genres, but it would also risk transforming eco-performance into a fixed category that, by conforming to a prescriptive set of ideas and forms, might – perversely – prevent serious engagement with ecological issues at all.

In order, then, to argue for a more expansive and radical 'theatrical ecology', this chapter looks to advance two theses. First, it seeks to unfold the forgotten ecological potential that *all forms* of theatre have long possessed by concentrating on the medium's relationship with the earth (in particular, rock and mineral); and second, it extols theatre as offering a *particular* mode of representation that prevents 'nature' from being reduced to a mere concept or idea that can be easily consumed and managed. The overarching ambition is to learn how to live differently on a dynamic, uncontrollable planet of ever-shifting strata.

I achieve these ends by revisiting three familiar 'moments' from the Western theatrical canon in a more or less linear fashion: Plato's cave, Hamlet's skull, and Hamm's little piece of grit in Beckett's *Endgame* (1957). Familiarity, though, should not be equated with recognition in this telluric history. Rather, it is a catalyst for taking theatre in a different direction, one in which geology comes to the forefront – both in the sense that I am concerned with 'shards' of text and, thematically, in that I trace a movement of erosion whereby rock and mineral are reduced first to bone, then to dust. My focus is on Western theatre, since most commentators continue to think of it as being the art form par excellence of the *anthropos*, the medium whose narratives centre exclusively on the historical concerns of human subjects alone.

Importantly, my attempt to decentre Western theatre is not based on a historiographical paradigm that would limit my findings to a specific environmentalist context, as many studies of green Shakespeare do, for instance, by concentrating on the early modern period.[3] Conversely, I experiment with a methodology that 'theatricalizes geology' and 'geologizes theatre' in such a way that the significance of the texts I refer to continue to resonate in the present, taking on meaning in the same, iterative way that a play does when it is staged in a new place and time.

But what does such a double methodology entail? And upon what logic does it rest?

To grasp the relationship between theatre and geology that I am advancing, it is helpful to distinguish between *metaphorical* and *isotropic* similitude. Where metaphors tend to reduce differences between diverse phenomena in a search for unity, isotropes, by contrast, are predicated upon

---

[3] See Gabriel Egan, *Green Shakespeare from Ecopolitics to Ecocriticism* (London, 2006).

the looser idea of equivalence. Unlike metaphorical thinking, isotropism allows for both difference and sameness to exist at the same time, the point being to discover similarities at the level of process, not to produce identity or synthesis. Just as contemporary post-gradualist geology realizes that the strata of the earth are not eternally fixed in some inert, vertical order but always in dynamic movement, so theatre, too, participates in a mode of temporality that emphasizes both duration *and* immediacy, immutability *and* flux. To stage *Hamlet* – indeed any play – is always to excavate latent meanings that have been in operation from the beginning but have not yet been actualized. Isotropically, then, and despite differences, both theatre and geology are predicated on temporal schemas that stress the simultaneity of past, present, and future, the sense in which there is no stable origin to which to return. The fact that the climate in the late Holocene (or early Anthropocene) has been changed due to the rapid burning of hydrocarbon fuels that date back to the Carboniferous epoch highlights the necessity of paying close attention to the alternative temporalities that geology and theatre offer. Anything else today feels like a dereliction of duty, irrespective of what some might critique as the 'rashness' of my approach – a term I borrow from Simon Critchley and Jamieson Webster, who, in turn, take it from Virginia Woolf.[4] As I practice it, a rash approach is one that affirms the possibilities generated by the interpretations of a nonexpert reader, who, because they are not weighed down by the sheer volume of scholarly commentary, may provide unexpected insights. In theatrical terms, a rash reader is like an actor who refuses to 'take direction' and instead invents their own relationship with a role.

The Cave

To date, most readings of Plato's cave have concentrated on its philosophical content.[5] However, in the Anthropocene, the moment when humanity has become geological, more attention needs to be placed on what generally goes unnoticed in Socrates' dialogue with Glaucon in *The Republic*, Book VII: the mineral substance of the theatrical medium itself. For as Plato has it, theatre's origin is located underground, in the very heart of the earth:

> Behold! Human being living in an underground den, which has a mouth open towards the light and reaching all along the den; here they have been from their

---

[4] Simon Critchley and Jamieson Webster, *The Hamlet Doctrine* (London, 2013), 3–4.
[5] A recent exception is Nicolás Salazar Sutil's *Matter Transmission: Mediation in a Paleocyber Age* (London, 2018), a text that concentrates on the cave as a materialist medium, and not as a metaphor in a drama of ideas.

childhood, and have their legs and necks chained so that they cannot move, and can only see before them, being prevented by the chains from turning round their heads. Above and behind them a fire is blazing at a distance, and between the fire and the prisoners there is a raised way; and you will see, if you look, a low wall built along the way, like the screen which marionette players have in front of them, over which they show the puppets.[6]

Plato figures theatre as a first but inferior 'home', or *oikos*. In his primitive scenography, the cave and low wall are made of rock; the shadows produced by fire; the puppets manufactured from 'wood' and 'stone'; the cave a place of childhood. Equally, one should not forget that the spectators/prisoners are creatures of ligament and bone, animals of calcium phosphate. While these subjects can certainly see, they have not yet attained insight, the higher faculty that discerns spiritual substance from elemental shadow.

In the trajectory of liberation that he traces, Plato plots a course from illusion to confusion, until finally the emancipated subject is able to gaze, without mediation, into the very heart of the sun – the source of light and truth. There is, then, in Plato's antitheatricality, a journey from the depths to the heights, a 'steep and rugged ascent' that allows 'mature' humans to transcend the earth and gaze down upon it from without.[7] In this exiting of the earth, this search for certainty, the subject is no longer a spectator confronted only with shadows that mutate. Rather, the subject is now all spirit and transcendentally positioned, able to intuit, intellectually, the unchanging reality of forms and ideas, the source of all science and philosophy. Plato concludes:

> Our argument indicates that this is a capacity which is innate in each man's mind, and that the organ by which he learns is like an eye which cannot be turned from darkness to light unless the whole body is turned.[8]

In comparison to the sun ('the brightest of all realities'), theatre is a dark art, disturbing the clarity of enlightened and immediate knowledge that characterizes 'solar thinking'. Where Plato's proper subject is whole, unmoving, and unchanging, the theatre spectator, by contrast, is confronted with shadowy images that appear and disappear and transform space and time in the most material of ways. Ultimately, then, theatre is discounted by Plato because it is engaged in a continual and clandestine process of becoming different from itself, in ways that parallel the findings of contemporary postgradualist geologists for whom the earth is a multiplicity in constant

---

[6] Plato, *The Republic*, 2nd revised ed., trans. Desmond Lee (London, 1974), 317.
[7] Ibid., 318.   [8] Ibid., 322.

reformation and becoming.[9] Like the rock, from which it is hewn, the base materiality of theatre is not suffused with the abstract spirituality of the idea; rather, it is formed of material that de-territorializes and ungrounds and so thwarts all possibilities of reaching the eternal realm of transcendent being.

It is tempting to see Plato's desire to exit the theatrical cave – and, by extension, the earth – as laying the conceptual foundations for the environmental destruction that Western philosophy, in its diverse articulations, has helped to legitimate and excuse. However, there is an unexpected possibility in Plato's thinking. For the primacy that Plato attaches to unmediated knowledge highlights his own blindness to the fact that without the earth as medium, the so-called higher faculties of the human species would not exist. As John Durham Peters has recently argued, there can be no communication without matter, no way of signifying that does not depend on what he terms our 'elemental legacy'.[10] To use Plato's own allegory against him, there is always a need for a 'cave' for transmission to take place, a medium in which human *technē*, or skill, is able to display itself. Without the rock and mud of the earth to support them, humans would not be able to signify, let alone speak.

This deconstruction of Plato's text is only a first step in its ecological rehabilitation; the more radical leap is to highlight its therapeutic potential, its capacity to transform the violence of Western metaphysics towards the earth – precisely what Plato appears to be actively supporting. To activate this potential, it is necessary to give up on transcendence and to embrace the shadowy stuff that so horrifies Plato – the base materialism of the theatrical medium.

Plato's cave is *both* a mineral surface that allows things to appear and a barrier to proper thought, a paradoxical site of looking that blinds us to 'light of truth'. To attend the theatre, Plato tells us, is to be confronted with an opaqueness, a shadowy limit that is both constitutive and restrictive. In its unfathomability and emptiness (for a cave is a hollow space as well as a lithic or stony one), Plato's conception of theatre reappears in the philosophy of Martin Heidegger and Gilles Deleuze and Félix Guattari, albeit with a very different emphasis. For these thinkers, each of whom has proved influential for the development of ecocritical theory, the earth is not a metaphor that provides a solid ground – an origin or foundation – for thought. Rather, as both base material and dynamic process, it ungrounds thought, showing it to

---

[9] See Nigel Clark and Kathyrn Yusoff's 'Introduction: Geosocial Formations and the Anthropocene', *Theory, Culture & Society* 34, nos. 2–3 (2017): 3–23.

[10] John Durham Peters, *The Marvelous Clouds: Towards a Philosophy of Elemental Media* (Chicago, 2015), 2.

be fissured by a fault line, a crack, or abyss that never enters, fully, into representation and thus human consciousness. In the geophilosophies of Heidegger, and of Deleuze and Guattari, there is always something about the earth that remains enigmatic – a hidden backstage that, paradoxically, refuses to recede from view. Where Heidegger explains how any attempt to create human history (the 'world') is always dependent on the forgetting of the natural world (the 'earth'),[11] Deleuze and Guattari posit the earth as the source of all becoming, the original iteration of 'the body without organs',[12] an energetic entity or nonhuman force field that refuses to sit still or be organized for human ends.[13]

Approached through Heidegger and Deleuze and Guattari, and with its original meaning reversed, Plato's allegory of the cave now unwittingly highlights theatre's ecological potential. At its most basic, this is found in its troubling ability to contest the violence inherent in Western philosophy's will to truth. By the very fact of 'taking place', theatre 'unfixes' and deforms all claims to absolute knowledge. In the most immediate of ways, it teaches us how to approach the earth as an autonomous, affective agent on some perpetual line of flight.

The Skull

One of the most earthly moments in Western theatre is found in Act 5, Scene 1, of *Hamlet*, a scene that famously opens with two rustic sextons or clowns discussing the mores of Christian burial in a graveyard. As the exchange develops, the gallows humour of the episode is interrupted by the appearance of Horatio and Hamlet. Initially, Hamlet appears to be in good spirits, serene even. He reflects with a certain degree of equanimity on the skulls that appear from the 'clay' and engages in some dark jesting with one of the gravediggers about the time-scale for the putrefaction of a corpse:

HAMLET : How long will a man lie i'th' earth ere he rot?

GRAVEDIGGER : Faith, if'a be not rotten before a' die (as we have many pocky corses that will scarce hold the laying in) 'a will last you some eight year – or nine year – a tanner will last you nine year.

HAMLET : Why he more than another?

---

[11] Martin Heidegger, 'The Origin of the Work of Art', in *Off the Beaten Track*, trans. Julian Young and Kenneth Haynes (Cambridge, 2002), 27.

[12] Gilles Deleuze and Félix Guattari, *A Thousand Plateaus: Capitalism and Schizophrenia*, trans. Brian Massumi (Minneapolis, 1987), 149–66.

[13] Gilles Deleuze and Félix Guattari, *What Is Philosophy?*, trans. Graham Burchell and Hugh Tomlinson (London, 1994), 85.

GRAVEDIGGER : Why, sir, his hide is so tanned with his trade that a' will keep out water a great while. And your water is a sore decayer of your whoreson dead body.[14]

However, the mood abruptly changes when Hamlet asks about the provenance of a particular skull, and finds that it belongs to his old playmate Yorick, the court jester:

HAMLET : Alas poor Yorick. I knew him, Horatio. A fellow of infinite jest, of most excellent fancy. He hath borne me on his back a thousand times.[15]

Hamlet's intimate knowledge of Yorick personalizes the skull and plunges him, once again, into the melancholic dark (the cave) that characterized his condition in the early soliloquies – the sadness or 'creatureliness' that, for Walter Benjamin, makes him such an interstitial hero, caught between tragedy and the *Trauerspiel*, or mourning play.[16] In the ensuing conversation with Horatio, Hamlet articulates a deep-rooted sense of existential anxiety, although not, it must be said, without a sense of humour:

HAMLET : To what base uses we may return, Horatio! Why may not imagination trace the noble dust of Alexander, tell a' find it stopping a bung-hole? ... Alexander died, Alexander was buried, Alexander returneth to dust, the dust is earth, of earth we make loam, and why of that loam whereto he was converted might they not stop a beer-barrel.
Imperious Caesar, dead and turned to clay,
Might stop a hole to keep the wind away.
O, that that earth, which kept the world in awe
Should patch a wall to expel the winter's flaw.[17]

In line with Elizabethan and Baroque aesthetics, the skull in Hamlet appears to function as *memento mori*, a reminder that human beings, even great kings and emperors, are fated to return to dust. But in the Anthropocene, and keeping the rashness of my approach firmly in mind, I want to propose that a very different kind of remembrance is being articulated in this scene, one that is intimated in Hamlet's reference both to the 'bung hole' and to the patch in the 'wall'. Hamlet's thinking of the skull here restores a link to

---

[14] William Shakespeare, *Hamlet*, revised ed., ed. Ann Thompson and Neil Taylor (London, 2016), 450–1.
[15] Ibid., 452.
[16] Walter Benjamin, *The Origin of German Tragic Drama*, trans. John Osborne (London, 2003), 135–42.
[17] *Hamlet*, 453–4.

Plato, and thus to the theatre as a vehicle for showing. Only now, the elemental matter or mineral quality of the cave and the shadows that move across it are not so easily dismissed. On the contrary, the shadows – or the skull – are brought into full view, and theatre posited as an irrevocably earthy medium, an art that imposes limitations on knowing and which, as Critchley and Webster claim, brings forth 'a reality that is as mute as rock'.

In Critchley and Webster's historicist reading, the 'mute rock' underpinning *Hamlet* relates to the dissolution of the House of Stuart. Yet for us today, the inarticulacy of rock is neither allegorical nor confined to human history alone. In the Anthropocene, when Hamlet lifts the skull and talks to it as if it were alive, addressing the absent Yorick, a new, more contemporary way of thinking about theatre comes into view. Against the background of a grave – yet another hole in the ground – the human cranium becomes a metonym for theatre's relationship with the earth. While the skull, like the dust of Alexander and Caesar, plugs a hole in being, it does so in such a way that the signifying system it makes use of is troubled. And in that troubling what is disclosed is nothing less than the opacity of the lithic realm itself, our dependence on and entanglement with a prehistoric, mineral world that we are part of but whose secrets we can never penetrate, despite our attempts to measure and 'read' it.

To understand better the parallels I am drawing between Hamlet's skull, theatre, and the earth, it is useful to consider Samuel Weber's deconstructionist take on theatre and theatricality. According to Weber, theatre always 'takes place' in a double sense:

> Its happenings never take place once and for all but are ongoing. This in turn suggests that they can neither be contained within the place where they unfold nor entirely separated from it. They can be said, then, in a quite literal sense to *come to pass*. They take place, which means in a particular place, and yet simultaneously also *pass away* – not simply to disappear but to happen somewhere *else*.[18]

Weber's understanding of theatre as an art that comes to *pass* but does not completely *pass away* positions the skull in *Hamlet* as an uncanny, ruinous mnemonic that remembers and forgets at the same time, bone on its way to dust. Temporalized and mineralized in this way, the skull is haunted not only by the past but also by a future that it can never attain. As a miniature representation of both theatre and the earth, the skull shows that the stillness required for self-presence is impossible. Like the earth, theatre is always

---

[18] Samuel Weber, *Theatre and Theatricality* (New York, 2004), 7; original emphasis and modified citation.

transforming, a parallel that is underscored by Alfred Wegener's theory of continental drift, which postulated that the once unified continent (Pangea) was broken apart by the violent motion or drifting of tectonic plates. For Wegener – and here we see the similarity with Weber's take on theatre – the earth is in perpetual motion, an entity that always 'takes place' and which transforms its identity in the process.

My geological reading of the skull marks a significant departure from extant readings of the function of theatre in *Hamlet*, a play that, from the ambivalent performativity of Hamlet's 'antic disposition' to the metatheatricality of the 'Mousetrap' (Act 2, Scene 2), has long been recognized as having much to say about the complex relation between appearance and reality. In a scene saturated with theatricality, Hamlet quips to the skull: 'Now get you to my lady's table and tell her, let her paint an inch thick, to this favour she must come. Make her laugh at that'.[19] In his critique of cosmetics, Hamlet, like an early Brechtian, appears to use the skull to unveil the social comedy that hides the truth of things. However, in the Anthropocene, such unveiling does not result in transcendence or redemption, and neither does it gesture toward some regulated and consoling *theatrum mundi* organized by a director God. On the contrary, the theatre of the skull, as Plato recognized, shatters all transcendence, all hope of exiting the ground for the sky. The 'favour of the skull' is ironic and disruptive: it reveals the omnipresence of the rock, the fact that we are born from and destined to return to an earth that is constantly splitting and shows no concern for the humans who inhabit it. In the twenty-first century, the ecological stakes of Shakespeare's theatre of the skull revolve around a distressing question: How to affirm our lives as mineral creatures on an unpredictable and violent planet engaged in a process of continual destruction, of becoming through dissolution?

A Little Piece of Grit

There is a moment towards the middle of *Endgame*, Samuel Beckett's second published play, when the blind, incapacitated Hamm – whose abbreviated half-name establishes his kinship with Hamlet – says to Clov, his carer:

> HAMM : In my house *[Pause. With prophetic relish.]* One day you'll be blind, like me. You'll be sitting there, a speck in the void, in the dark, forever, like me.... Infinite emptiness will be all around you, all the

---

[19] *Hamlet*, 453.

resurrected dead of all the ages wouldn't fill it, and there you'll be like a little bit of grit in the middle of the steppe.[20]

Hamm's prophecy pulsates with ecological meaning, but to understand its purchase for this argument, it is necessary to contextualize it historically and textually. Unlike Plato and Shakespeare, Beckett is writing at the dawn of the Anthropocene, in particular that moment in the 1950s when, as a consequence of the wide-scale testing of the atom and hydrogen bombs, the militarized superpowers of the Cold War left the indelible marks of their humanity in the lithosphere and atmosphere. Within the context of the play, the primary point to note is how the image arises in a conversation about the perilous state of the earth, a planet that, if we can believe Hamm's theatricalized grandiloquence, has been subjected to some unspoken environmental catastrophe. Roughly contemporaneous with Rachel Carson's best-selling eco-text *Silent Spring* (1962), *Endgame* depicts a world where no seeds sprout, 'the light has sunk', and food and medicine – painkiller, lozenges, and pap – are running out. In this poisoned landscape, a handful of decrepit survivors huddle together in a shelter, two of whom – Nag and Nell – have been consigned, literally and metaphorically, to the dustbins of 'natural history'. There is nowhere to go in this world. The outside, if it exists, is deadly. One is rooted to the spot, all faith in humanity exhausted:

CLOV : I have a flea!
HAMM : A flea! Are there still fleas?
CLOV : On me there's one. [*Scratching*]. Unless it's a crablouse.
HAMM : [*Very perturbed*]. But humanity might start from there all over again! Catch him for the love of God.[21]

In this sterile place, Hamm's piece of grit points prophetically to a 'world without us', in same way as the ant ferrying the eggs in the desert(-ed) landscape of *Happy Days* (1961). In both cases, this is a near future in which human beings, like the organic matter they are, will be exposed to the erosions and lesions of deep time, subjected to temporal scales and planetary revolutions that are impossible to countenance and always beyond equilibrium.

Faced with such a future, the *anthropos* is humiliated, all its achievements placed in doubt. As conjured by Hamm's image, the little piece of grit is a fragmentary reminder – the very last sign, perhaps – of humanity's terrestrial adventure. Indeed, what the image appears to present us with, in mineral

[20] Samuel Beckett, *The Complete Dramatic Works* (London, 1986), 109–10.
[21] Ibid., 108.

form, is something that obsesses Beckett throughout his career: that is, the unsettling presence of what land artist Robert Smithson (a Beckett enthusiast) would come to call 'entropology' – the gradual but unpredictable loss of heat and energy caused by entropic decline, the collapse of form and shape.[22] There are many erosive tropes in *Endgame*, but the one that resonates most with the 'little piece of grit on the steppe' is found when Hamm expresses a desire to rest his head on a heap of sand at the edge of the shore:

> HAMM : If I could drag myself down to the sea? I'd make a pillow of sand for my head and the tide would come.[23]

As with the image of grit, there are two competing dynamics in operation here: on the one hand, the seeming passivity of the inorganic (sand as eroded rock) and, on the other hand, the active play of the sea, washing the sand away, creating oblivion. Foreshadowing Michel Foucault's celebrated image of the human face being erased by waves at the end of *The Order of Things* (1966), but also pointing beyond that to the Anthropocene, Beckett's play stages the moment when the human realizes that rock, as Jeffrey Jerome Cohen has claimed, is an intimate 'companion', a substance whose fate we share.[24] Or, as Manuel De Landa puts it, a mineral to which we owe a debt:

> In the organic world, for instance, soft tissue (gels and aerosols, muscle and nerve) reigned supreme until 500 million years ago. At that point, some of the conglomerations of fleshy matter-energy that made up life underwent a sudden mineralisation, and a new material for constructing living materials emerged: bone.[25]

In Beckett's universe, we are geolithic creatures, carriers of calcium phosphate. Stone is simultaneously what we inherit and what we become; it evolves and takes different forms. Despite the surface nihilism of *Endgame*, its sheer exhaustion of any kind of transcendence, the point is not to deny our mineral being but to embrace it, admitting in the process that we are born from and return to an earth of erosion and erratic shifting. As Hamm reminds the anonymous protagonist of his interrupted story that may or may not explain Clov's presence in his shelter, 'You're on earth, there's no cure for that.'[26]

Through its disenchanted affirmation of the earth, *Endgame* inherits and expands the mineral quality of *Hamlet*. In it, the wholeness of the skull is

---

[22] Robert Smithson, *The Collected Writings*, ed. Jack Flam (Berkeley, 1996), 323.
[23] Beckett, *The Complete Dramatic Works*, 122.
[24] Jeffrey Jerome Cohen, *Stone: An Ecology of the Inhuman* (Minneapolis, 2015), 8.
[25] Manuel De Landa, *A Thousand Years of Non-Linear History* (New York, 1997), 26.
[26] Beckett, *The Complete Dramatic Works*, 118.

exposed to time, caught up in the process of becoming fossil and grit. A fact that explains, perhaps, Clov's refusal to bury Hamm, his realization that by leaving the excarnated body to decompose and decay, it will reveal the gleaming whiteness of bone:

> HAMM : But you'll bury me.
> CLOV : No I shan't bury you.
> HAMM : She was bonny once, like a flower of the field [*With reminiscent leer*]. And a great one for the men!
> CLOV : We too were bonny – once. It's a rare thing not to have been bonny – once.[27]

In this shift from bonny to bony, Beckett's theatre transforms from being a theatre of the flesh to a theatre of the earth.[28] The goal, as Beckett intimated in his description of the play as being more 'inhuman than *Godot*', is to reveal what, for Plato, always haunts theatre: its dependence on the elemental, on planetary materialities and temporalities.[29] Beckett, moreover, is not content to render our entanglements with the nonhuman dramatic, to keep it as a fictional theme. Beckett achieves his aim by transforming dramatic space into a more expansive mimetic or 'hyper theatrical stage'.[30] Here the locus of conflict – the *agon* that a more traditional dramaturgy contains within a fictional universe of the play and ascribes to human actors alone – spills over from the stage into the auditorium. To provoke this spillage, Beckett constantly undermines the fictional world of the play by having Hamm and Clov highlight the performative nature of their actions and exchanges. At one point, Hamm taps the wall of the set with his knuckles and says, 'Do you hear that? Do you hear? Hollow bricks. All that's hollow.'[31] Such overt metatheatricality produces a theatrical time-space that is simultaneously present and absent, abstract and concrete, here and there. By deconstructing the 'footlights' and extending the theatrical situation outwards, Beckett seeks to implicate spectators in the same entropic process of decline and erosion to which the characters are subjected, all of whom are falling to bits in some way or another.

---

[27] Ibid., 113.

[28] For more on skulls in Beckett, see James Knowlson and John Pilling's *Frescoes of the Skull: The Later Prose and Drama of Samuel Beckett* (New York, 1980).

[29] Samuel Beckett in Maurice Harmon, ed., *No Author Better Served: The Correspondence of Samuel Beckett and Alan Schneider* (Cambridge, 2000), 11.

[30] Les Essif, 'Introducing the "Hyper" Theatrical Subject: The *Mise en Abyme* of Empty Space', *Journal of Dramatic Theory and Criticism* 9 (1994): 67–88 (74).

[31] Beckett, *The Complete Dramatic Works*, 104.

In the face of this impersonal collapse, the one thing that Hamm and Clov can agree on is that 'something is taking its course',[32] an anonymous temporal stream ruining the integrity and identity of every person and thing. Speculating on his own erosion by time, Clov, like Hamm, has recourse, once again, to a mineral image, showing the bones of his body crumbling into black dust:

> CLOV : But I feel too old, and too far, to form new habits.... I am so bowed I only see my feet, if I open my eyes, and between my legs a little trail of black dust. I say myself the earth is extinguished, though I never saw it lit.[33]

On this extinguished earth, this planet where bodies collapse into trails of dust, the timescale that *Endgame* ultimately discloses so palpably is geologic, the time of stone. This is a nonhuman temporality that brings together the mineral theatres of Plato and Shakespeare and which, through its axiomatic self-consciousness, subjects spectators to elemental becomings. As something impossible to stop or control, this anonymous 'something' exposes all in the theatre to cosmic temporalities that will ground their bodies down, leaving them as 'little bits of grit' in the middle of some endless, empty steppe.

Conclusion

Theatre is not just a fleshy art but a mineral one, a medium of stone and bone.[34] To make progressive ecological sense of theatre's unrecognized minerality, it is important to reject nineteenth-century geology's obsession with fixing and 'stilling' the earth. Instead, and in keeping with the findings of modern geology, we are compelled to recognize that we now live on a planet in continual motion, a matter of plate tectonics and continental drift. Like the theatre itself, the earth is never complete; it is a multiple and multistate entity constantly remoulding its original material and diverging from itself as it becomes different in time and space. Drawing remarkably close to Samuel Weber's deconstructionist notions of theatre and theatricality, the geographers Nigel Clark and Kathryn Yusoff caution:

> Theorising a dynamic planet – no less than other aspects of its inhabitation – tends to be as much a matter of working with an inheritance as it is of tangling with the novel or emergent.[35]

---

[32] Ibid., 107.   [33] Ibid., 132.

[34] For a related essay, see Rebecca Schneider, 'Theatre of Bone', in *Experiencing Liveness in Contemporary Performance: Interdisciplinary Perspectives*, ed. Matthew Reason and Anja Mølle Lindelof (New York, 2016), 147–55.

[35] Clark and Yusoff, 'Introduction: Geosocial Formations and the Anthropocene', 11.

In theatrical terms, such an inheritance contests the onus that much eco-theatre places on narrative, on telling stories about the destruction of nature. Rather, it simply asks audience to pay attention to the 'nature' placed in front of them – namely, to the fleshy and stony materialities of human and nonhuman bodies being eroded in the here and now of the theatrical event. Taking heed of the current realization that increased information is doing little to prevent a 'bad' or eco-fascistic Anthropocene from occurring, there is little to be gained for the field of theatre studies, theoretically and practically, in trying to raise consciousness about something that we already know. Perhaps a more effective mode of operating is for theatre practitioners and scholars to relinquish their obsession with constructing and deciphering narratives and to pay attention instead to the earthiness of the medium, thereby allowing us to participate in a new ontology of spectatorship. In the Anthropocene, it is incumbent upon us to approach this theatrical ontology as something geological, a way of being terrestrial that binds us to an earth caught up in a process of perpetual fissuring, and which places serious limits on the human capacity to know and exploit it without consequence. The point, in other words, is to understand spectating as an activity that emerges from and ties us to an unpredictable earth, the recognition of which *may* leave us better prepared to face future dangers that are already here, working away beneath our feet.

Suggested Reading

Beckett, Samuel. *The Complete Dramatic Works*. London, 1986.

Chakrabarty, Dipesh. '"The Climate of History": Four Theses'. *Critical Inquiry* 35, no. 2 (2009): 197–222.

Clark, Nigel, and Kathryn Yusoff. 'Introduction: Geosocial Formations and the Anthropocene'. *Theory, Culture & Society* 34, nos. 2–3 (2017): 3–23.

Cohen, Jeffrey Jerome. *Stone: An Ecology of the Inhuman*. Minneapolis, 2015.

Critchely, Simon, and Jamieson Webster. *The Hamlet Doctrine*. London, 2013.

Deleuze, Gilles, and Félix Guattari. *A Thousand Plateaus: Capitalism and Schizo-phrenia*, trans. Brian Massumi. Minneapolis, 1987.

Durham Peters, John. *The Marvelous Clouds: Towards a Philosophy of Elemental Media*. Chicago, 2015.

Egan, Gabriel. *Green Shakespeare from Ecopolitics to Ecocriticism*. London, 2006.

Essif, Les. 'Introducing the "Hyper" Theatrical Subject: The *Mise en Abyme* of Empty Space'. *Journal of Dramatic Theory and Criticism* 9 (1994): 67–88.

Harmon, Maurice, ed. *No Author Better Served: The Correspondence of Samuel Beckett and Alan Schneider*. Cambridge, 2000.

Heidegger, Martin. 'The Origin of the Work of Art'. In *Off the Beaten Track*, trans. Julian Young and Kenneth Haynes. Cambridge, 2002, 1–56.

Knowlson, James, and John Pilling. *Frescoes of the Skull: The Later Prose and Drama of Samuel Beckett*. New York, 1980.

Salazar Sutil, Nicolás. *Matter Transmission: Mediation in a Paleocyber Age.* London, 2018.

Schneider, Rebecca. 'Theatre of Bone'. In *Experiencing Liveness in Contemporary Performance: Interdisciplinary Perspectives*, ed. Matthew Reason and Anja Mølle Lindelof. New York, 2016, 147–55.

Weber, Samuel. *Theatre and Theatricality.* New York, 2004.

5

UNA CHAUDHURI AND JOSHUA WILLIAMS

The Play at the End of the World

Deke Weaver's *Unreliable Bestiary* and the Theatre of Extinction

The play begins with extinction.

> *One at a time, the MONKEY-MAN writes the names of primate species on the chalkboards. After each primate is listed, an educational voice reads the name that was just written over the PA. Periodically, the MONKEY-MAN looks the chalkboards over, picks up an eraser, and erases one of the species (the most critically endangered primates). A bell sounds with each erasure.[1]*

This sequence functions as part of the pre-show that the US artist Deke Weaver created for his 2009 performance *Monkey*, occupying our attention – or not – as we take our seats. Once the performance proper begins, the fate of the primate species the world has lost or is about to lose is scarcely mentioned again.

Why has Weaver taken such an understated approach? We are accustomed to thinking of the extinction of charismatic animals like monkeys and apes as deeply affecting, even heartbreaking – and yet all that Weaver provides is a name in chalk, a swift stroke with an eraser, a bell. The clinical economy of this sequence is especially notable because Weaver's overarching purpose in creating *Monkey* – along with the other pieces that make up his long-term performance project, *The Unreliable Bestiary* – is to alert his audiences to the unfolding disaster of the sixth great extinction the world has seen:[2]

---

[1] With *Monkey* and *Elephant*, we refer to the performance texts as they have been published in Chaudhuri and Hughes's *Animal Acts*. Our analysis of *Wolf* and *Bear* relies on unpublished materials shared with us by the artist and – in the case of *Wolf* – Chaudhuri's experiences of seeing the show live. See Deke Weaver, 'MONKEY', in *Animal Acts: Performing Species Today*, ed. Una Chaudhuri and Holly Hughes (Ann Arbor, 2014), 141–2.

[2] The term 'the sixth extinction' has been popularized by Elizabeth Kolbert, *The Sixth Extinction: An Unnatural History* (New York, 2014).

It's been said that by 2050, climate change, rapacious resource extraction, and our exploding population will push half the species on the planet into extinction. The lions and tigers and bears of our ancient stories will be long gone. Central to our myths, embedded in our language, rooted in our imaginations – what will we do when our dreams disappear?[3]

Clearly, Weaver has chosen to eschew sentimentalism of the lone-polar-bear-on-the-tiny-patch-of-ice variety as he explores the harrowing ecological realities of the Anthropocene. He has also turned away from the aesthetic and political model of Aristotelian tragedy, which many contemporary theatre, film, and television makers consider ready-made to tackle calamities of almost every type. For Weaver, the constraints of tragedy – its focus on emblematic individuals, its cultivation of well-worn emotions, its tendency to moralize – are too limiting. In order to help audiences understand what it will be like when beloved animal species are 'long gone', he must impress upon us that mass extinction means a profound dislocation of 'our myths', 'our language', 'our imaginations', and 'our dreams'. Rather than individualizing extinction and positioning it within the inexorable, agonistic unfolding of a linear plot, he has chosen to present a canvas that is as 'incomprehensibly vast' as the crisis itself.[4] He makes performances capable of taking in entire species and what we have taken them to mean. And rather than moralizing about extinction by endeavouring to engender the same feelings about species loss that countless scientific reports, news stories, and documentary films elicit, he has chosen affective heterogeneity in the service of an open ethics of what Donna Haraway calls 'staying with the trouble'.[5]

In this way, Weaver takes his place at the forefront of an international group of theatre makers who have come to realize, as the Canadian playwright Chantal Bilodeau puts it, that 'we need to move beyond writing plays about climate change to writing plays that are climate change – plays that embody, in form, content, and process, the essence of the issues we are facing'.[6] With *The Unreliable Bestiary*, Weaver has set out to make a performance for every letter of the English alphabet, with each letter beginning the name of an endangered species or threatened habitat.[7]

---

[3] Deke Weaver, 'The Unreliable Bestiary', www.unreliablebestiary.org/, accessed 12 July 2019.

[4] Ibid.

[5] See Donna J. Haraway, *Staying with the Trouble: Making Kin in the Chthulucene*, Experimental Futures (Durham, 2016).

[6] Chantal Bilodeau, 'In Search of a New Aesthetic', *HowlRound*, 19 April 2015, https://howlround.com/search-new-aesthetic.

[7] www.unreliablebestiary.org/.

The *Bestiary* opened with *Monkey* in 2009, and Weaver has added four more works since: *Elephant* (2010), *Wolf* (2013), *Bear* (2016–17), and *Tiger* (2019).[8] With twenty-one letters left to go, and averaging one performance every two years, the fifty-something Weaver's plan betrays an aching irony: the project faces the same near-impossible timetable as global efforts to stave off catastrophic species loss. There is a very real chance that both performance and preservation will fail the species that the *Bestiary* contains.

Weaver himself has not – to our knowledge – broached the difficult question of whether or not he will ever complete the project he has set himself. He is, however, deeply invested in failure and what it reveals:

> I wonder what it will be like when these animals are gone. We're going to be left with these fragments, shards, whispers and cartoons of what the animal must have been like. As far as 'accurate' and 'truthful' representations, it's always always always going to fall short of the real thing. So I'm more interested in the failure of representation as a way to point out the absence of the real animal.[9]

Even if the species that audiences encounter in *The Unreliable Bestiary* go the way of the dinosaurs, something of them will be preserved in Weaver's performances; he has described the project as 'an ark of stories'.[10] Even more importantly, he will have provided us, letter by letter, with a new grammar of being in and with extinction. *The Unreliable Bestiary* cannot but fail to capture every aspect of each of the species it depicts, but that very failure provides us with a way of understanding what we (will) have lost. It is a sign of our topsy-turvy times that turning to two fixtures of the literary landscape – the unreliable narrator and the medieval bestiary – that blur the lines between myth and history, fact and fiction, has allowed Weaver to produce something that can be better relied upon than empirical data and factual description to help us navigate the erosion of all ecological, political, and cultural certainties. His simultaneous embrace and critique of science is a key element of the Anthropocenic species-thinking that lies at the heart of the new theatre of extinction. *The Unreliable Bestiary* suggests a 'more-than-scientific' relation to other animals – a relation that draws out new epistemological orientations, affective entanglements, and ethical commitments to

---

[8] For more information on the various versions of these pieces and their performance history, see www.unreliablebestiary.org/.

[9] Deke Weaver and Maria Lux, 'The Unreliable Bestiary', *Antennae: The Journal of Nature in Visual Culture* 22 (Autumn 2012): 34.

[10] www.unreliablebestiary.org/.

guide us across the increasingly devastated terrain of our shared planetary reality.

Squishy Science

When we arrive at the designated time and place to see *Wolf*, we're ushered onboard a bus by a uniformed Forest Ranger, a genial fellow who gives us an orientation to the unusual place we'll be visiting for this performance. (Of course, as is typical for Weaver's work, the performance has already begun.) Along with details about the area we're going to explore – an 'island' of forest among the monocultural Illinois farmlands – he mentions something called 'The Energy', and promises us an intense experience of it. His presentation includes video clips of wolf experts, wolf stories from world mythology, and drawings of wolf faces in various emotional states that he gets us to try out on each other. He also leads us in a singalong of 'Home on the Range'. When we arrive at our destination, he takes us through the moonlit forest, toward the mysterious sounds of 'The Energy' coming from deep within it. At one point we have to go around a red-hooded cape abandoned on the path. At another point there's a wolf lying by the side of the trail, and the Ranger whispers that he has been trapped and sedated in order to be studied. The wolf suddenly gets up on two feet and darts off. 'Wow!' says the Ranger. 'That's very unusual. Wow!' Giggling happily, we proceed to a glorious barn – a kind of grandmother's house for this radically reimagined 'Little Red Riding Hood' – for the rest of the show.

The Unreliable Bestiary abounds in characters like the Ranger in *Wolf* who seem to speak the language of scientific rationality and yet undercut it at every turn. They are adepts of what Weaver has called, in another context, 'squishy science'. If studies of various aspects of human and animal behaviour make up the 'soft sciences', then 'performance art and experimental theatre' comprise the 'reeeeally soft sciences .... the squishy sciences ... okay, the non-sciences' because there are at least as many variables as there are audience members, '[a]nd every night that equation shifts'.[11] Weaver's reluctance to accept that performance is entirely unscientific reveals something of his enthusiasm for science and at the same time his desire to integrate it into a broader epistemological project that takes up much that science excludes – like 'The Energy' or magic.[12]

---

[11] Deke Weaver, 'The Aura of Bad Maps', *Text and Performance Quarterly* 29, no. 4 (October 2009): 420.

[12] As he himself puts it: 'If I don't understand something and it blows my little mind, I use a suspicious word: magic.' Ibid., 418.

The intrusion of magic into the squishy science of Weaver's performance practice marks one of his many turns towards the bestiary. The art and philosophy of the Anthropocene logically seek inspiration from modernity's others – that is, spaces historically or geographically removed from the Euro-American cultural-industrial project out of which the conditions of climate chaos arose. It should come as no surprise, then, that an ecologically oriented postmodern artist like Weaver should reach back to a pre-modern genre, the bestiary, in order to mediate our currently terrifying relation to the more-than-human world.[13] As Susan Crane has argued, bestiaries put forward a remarkably holistic view of animal life, deploying complex taxonomies that entwine proto-scientific anatomical and behavioural observations of real and imagined creatures with dense allegorizations that fix the meaning of their characteristics within an expansive Christian cosmology and world view.[14] Michel Foucault has influentially claimed that the turn toward Linnaean taxonomy and natural history in seventeenth- and eighteenth-century Europe represented a profound loss of half of this inheritance: in the work of natural historians, '[t]he whole of animal semantics has disappeared, like a dead and useless limb. The words that had been interwoven in the very being of the beast have been unraveled and removed.'[15] *The Unreliable Bestiary* seeks to return animal semantics to the scene, clothing the 'beast' in the layers of meaning that revolutions in modern scientific thinking stripped away.

This tactic carries a great deal of political weight in the Anthropocene. The boldness with which modern biology and zoology reorganized our collective understanding of animals and the environment has now come under radical strain. While our increasing awareness of climate change derives from more sustained attention to – and respect for – scientific evidence, another, deeply paradoxical effect of the climate crisis is that it forces us to recognize how few and how limited the scientific and technological solutions to the crisis are. In this sense, the Anthropocene has plunged us into a post-scientific – or at least deeply science-sceptical – time. Life itself seems to be slipping beyond the reach of reliable knowledge systems, including those of the empirical sciences, which, over the past four centuries, have decisively remade the world. As climate change accelerates, it topples the very scientific models

---

[13] Like many others, we prefer this term to the more familiar 'nonhuman', which silently reinscribes the dualism between nature and culture, animal and human, matter and mind that contemporary, materially oriented ecocriticism fundamentally contests.

[14] Susan Crane, 'A Taxonomy of Creatures in the Second-Family Bestiary', *New Medieval Literatures* 10 (2008): 1–48.

[15] Michel Foucault, *The Order of Things: An Archaeology of the Human Sciences* (New York, 1994), 129.

and predictive systems through which we have been attempting to apprehend it, revealing the incommensurability of the atomistic protocols of modern science and the densely networked and interactive nature of the ecosphere. The ways of knowing that have long enjoyed the most respect and authority have been exposed as pillars of a dangerously limited world view, a 'great derangement'.[16] Why not turn, then, to a more capacious understanding of our creaturely existence? The medieval bestiary bespoke a marvellously legible natural world, its every beast and bloom inscribed with a message to aid in the moral conduct of human lives. A new bestiary might prove equally instructive.

Weaver's *Bestiary* attempts an epistemological rapprochement between science and magic by placing scientific literacy within a network of other explanatory systems: mythology, religion, cultural practice, sensory engagement, rumours, speculation, and outright lies. The *Bestiary*'s various performances abound in scientific information, which is often presented in ways that both reinforce and undermine its credibility. A character like the Forest Ranger in *Wolf* speaks with the institutional authority signalled by their uniform. At the same time, however, these same authority figures employ a folksy style of address and allow strange facts and odd analogies into their explanations of the science. For example, one Ranger in *Bear*, seeking to convey how enormous polar bears are, announces that '[t]he weight of this single bear is 50 pounds more than the combined weight of the starting 11 players for the men's 2014 US World Cup soccer team' (see Fig. 5.1). Not only is this a singularly unhelpful comparison, its absurdity is made manifest by the over-the-top way in which Weaver has chosen to theatricalize it: members of the audience are asked to stand behind a life-size image of the 2014 US World Cup men's soccer team, looking through holes cut out where the players' faces would be. Once they are all in place, and posing appropriately, the Ranger takes a photograph. This bit of country fair fun is one of many ways that Weaver's audiences are reminded that they are not only learning about the more-than-human world they have taken for granted, but also learning a new way to know it. They are practicing a new epistemology.

If audiences at *Unreliable Bestiary* performances learn by doing – posing for photos as a soccer team, traipsing over the river and through the woods looking for wolves – they also learn to content themselves with a base level of uncertainty about whether or not what they are hearing is objectively true. Weaver's facts about the size and weight of polar bears check out, but many

---

[16] See Amitav Ghosh, *The Great Derangement: Climate Change and the Unthinkable*, Berlin Family Lectures (Chicago, 2017).

Fig. 5.1 From Deke Weaver, *The Unreliable Bestiary: Bear* (2016): Ranger Joe with mask of polar bear expert Malcolm Ramsay. Photo by Nathan Keay; by courtesy of Deke Weaver.

others do not. *Elephant* opens with a kind of litany of the true, the false, and the unverifiable: 'Is it true that four elephants hold up the earth while standing on a giant turtle? Yes. It is true.'[17] In his commentary on *Monkey*, Cary Wolfe notes that many of the animals depicted in the piece are apes, not monkeys, and that Weaver seems to have cribbed some of his 'facts' straight from discredited Wikipedia pages.[18] This is not an oversight on Weaver's part. He has enormous respect for ethologists, animal experts, and wilderness thinkers. His research often includes taking courses or workshops on the species he is working on – including, for *Elephant*, a stint in a mahout-training course in Thailand. At the same time, he maintains a stubborn insistence on animal mystery and otherness. This is another way in which the unreliability of *The Unreliable Bestiary* makes itself plain: what we think we know about animals is as important as what is actually true. Moreover, Weaver – covert historian of science that he is – has noted that 'facts change'.[19] In other words, 'as science and technology improve, many things that artists and poets and old-wives-telling-tales have always known or

[17] Deke Weaver, 'Excerpts from *ELEPHANT*', in *Animal Acts*, 166.
[18] Cary Wolfe, 'Apes like Us', in *Animal Acts*, 156–62.
[19] Weaver and Lux, 'The Unreliable Bestiary', 36.

intuited are being "scientifically proven". And, suddenly, that piece of knowledge is removed from the "New Age Bullshit" category and enshrined in the "Validated by Science" category.'[20] Under other circumstances, the safest thing to do with knowledge that is still considered 'New Age Bullshit' is to keep it to oneself: 'you keep your mouth shut about visions and dreams and hunches and coincidences and trances'.[21] The squishy science of performance, however, allows Weaver a space to share all of this on an equal footing with knowledge 'Validated by Science' – precisely because all of it contributes to our patchwork understanding of animals, what they are, and what they mean.

The new epistemology that *The Unreliable Bestiary* proposes is also deeply embodied. Both *Wolf* and *Bear* are site-specific and mobile, with audience members traversing the territory of their beastly imaginations while walking through the fields and forests of central Illinois, where Weaver is based. *Elephant* was staged at the University of Illinois at Urbana-Champaign's Stock Pavilion – a space that could not help but activate and reconfigure audience members' kinaesthetic memories of attending circuses, rodeos, state fairs, and livestock auctions. Here, as elsewhere, the squishy science of performance and the historical legacy of the medieval bestiary converge. Foucault notes that European natural history changed 'the space in which it was possible to see ['exotic' plants and animals] and from which it was possible to describe them. To the Renaissance, the strangeness of animals was a spectacle: it was featured in fairs, in tournaments, in fictitious or real combats, in reconstructions of legends in which the bestiary displayed its ageless fables.'[22] The bestiary lends itself to performance, to 'the circular procession of the "show"',[23] to movement and spectacle. Weaver's performances reactivate this tradition in a postmodern mode, staging literal displacements of bodies in space – travelling, walking, wandering, searching – as well as mixing genres, moods, and media. Story-telling, dialogue, puppetry, and dance are accompanied by new video works of many kinds – animation, claymation, moving landscapes – as well as by archival film clips, documentary footage, photographs, drawings, maps, diagrams, and graphs. While of course carefully curated, the material included in *Bestiary* performances often feels profuse, cluttered, even random. This is epistemology in vivo, in the wild – a far cry from the highly constrained spaces in which science in the wake of the Enlightenment has encased and displayed its knowledge of the more-than-human world.

---

[20] Ibid., 33.   [21] Ibid.   [22] Foucault, *The Order of Things*, 131.   [23] Ibid.

Plain Old Wonder

This aesthetic can be affectively disorienting. Nigel Rothfels is not the only person to be 'perplexed' that 'Weaver repeatedly undermines the audience's desire that what they are seeing represents, in the style of old natural-history television, "authenticated facts".'[24] Notably, in his illuminating commentary on *Elephant*, Rothfels turns to the language of tragedy as a hedge against this uncertainty over what – and how – to feel. *Elephant* includes several different versions of the story of Hero, a circus elephant who was killed in South Dakota in 1916 after escaping his keepers' control. Rothfels argues that Weaver sees this as a tragedy:

> [I]t is clear enough that he finds plenty of room to blame the humans in these tragic events. For Weaver, the tragedy is obviously the events of May 15, 1916, but it is more than that; for him, the tragedy is the vexed encounter, seen in so many places, of humans with animals. But there is also hope in this piece: that by becoming more aware, by living differently, it is possible to have less destructive relationships with animals.[25]

Tragedy provides an affective framework within which we have become habituated to process loss. While he does not say so explicitly, Rothfels's argument requires him to move through a series of transpositions that is familiar to us from countless other examples. First, Hero's death was terribly sad, eliciting at least pity, one of the two emotions that define tragedy for Aristotle. Second, the audience understands that the sad thing that happened to this particular elephant is emblematic of a larger social and political problem – namely, 'the vexed encounter ... of humans with animals' in general. Third, this dawning awareness allows them a cathartic purgation of the emotional disturbance Hero's story has caused, which in turn leads them – fourth – to the hopeful conviction that 'by becoming more aware, by living differently', a new disposition towards other animals might be possible. This is Rothfels's road map for how to feel our way through *Elephant*'s panoramic array of truths, half-truths, and fantasies.

It is tempting to think of tragedy this way, but feeding our capacity to hope is not, in fact, its task. At most, one can claim that tragedy has a disciplinary function, impressing upon us the imperative to avoid the putatively amoral or antisocial behaviours that led to catastrophe. Killing poor Hero didn't go well for Hero or for the town of Elkton, South Dakota, so we must not do things like that in the future. This is a valuable lesson, especially if the goal of *Elephant* is, as Rothfels suggests, finding a new way of living

---

[24] Nigel Rothfels, 'A Hero's Death', in *Animal Acts*, 183.   [25] Ibid., 187.

with animals. Nevertheless, the principal affective dimension of tragedy is actually a kind of horrified resignation, as we watch characters struggle fruitlessly against their awful fate. The beauty of the tragic – and there is beauty in the mimetic representation of the most awful things, according to Aristotle, including 'the basest animals and corpses'[26] – inheres in the inevitability of suffering. In this way, the tragic dimension that so many discern in the deaths of particular animals like Hero and the extinction of entire species like elephants actually aligns much more closely with the most fatalistic responses to the challenges posed by the Anthropocene. As evidence of catastrophic climate change mounts, it is becoming more and more difficult for all kinds of environmentally oriented praxis to preserve a hopeful stance toward the future. Texts such as Paul Kingsnorth and Dougald Hine's *Manifesto* for the Dark Mountain Movement and Roy Scranton's *Learning to Die in the Anthropocene* chart a new path for ecological thought, urging a clear-eyed confrontation with modern civilization's pervasive alienation from ecospheric reality and an acceptance of that civilization's unfolding demise.[27] They trade comforting belief in a liveable future for acceptance of – or, at most, adaptation to – fate.

A hard-won hope is much more on offer in books like Donna Haraway's *Staying with the Trouble* and Anna Tsing's *The Mushroom at the End of the World*, which propose the cultivation of a new ecospheric consciousness and a renewed commitment to multispecies thriving through the use of experimental, interdisciplinary methodologies and life/art practices.[28] The undercurrent of hopefulness that Rothfels correctly identifies in *The Unreliable Bestiary* does not derive from any of the pseudo-tragic dimensions of the stories Weaver is telling but instead emanates from the conviction he shares with Haraway, Tsing, and others that radical openness to the more-than-human world may offer a way forward. In place of the linearity of tragedy, *Elephant* and the other performances in the *Bestiary* offer a loose, multimodal structure, an organic multiplicity of ideas. In place of the strong emotions associated with cathartic performance, Weaver favours a more 'everyday' affective repertoire, steering his audiences away from forceful positions and definitive conclusions towards a polymorphous feeling of

---

[26] Aristotle, *Poetics*, ed. and trans. Michelle Zerba and David Gorman, Norton Critical Edition (New York, 2018), 6.
[27] See Paul Kingsnorth and Dougald Hine, 'Manifesto' (2009), https://dark-mountain.net/about/manifesto/; Roy Scranton, *Learning to Die in the Anthropocene: Reflections on the End of a Civilization* (San Francisco, 2015).
[28] See Haraway, *Staying with the Trouble: Making Kin in the Chthulucene*; Anna Lowenhaupt Tsing, *The Mushroom at the End of the World: On the Possibility of Life in Capitalist Ruins* (Princeton, 2017).

exposure to the plenitude of animal life. The story of Hero's death is told over and over again in *Elephant* as the performance moves fluidly from talk-show banter to stop-motion animation to the reading of archival documents to singing. We never get the entire story, but we do slowly become more accepting of the feeling of not knowing, not understanding. Audience members at *Unreliable Bestiary* performances are – to return to Rothfels's characterization of his own feelings – 'perplexed', but pleasurably so. Because Weaver cannot be counted on to deliver the emotions we expect from other forms of performance – yet another way in which his *Bestiary* is unreliable – his work ends up cultivating curiosity and play.

Weaver has another word for this affect: wonder. He has noted that, as 'depressing' as living in the Anthropocene is, 'nobody wants to sit and be told how terrible and awful things are. People will walk out, turn the channel, click on another link.'[29] In order to hold our attention, he feels he must steer clear of the doom and gloom that have become de rigueur in many if not most accounts of the Anthropocene. Moreover, in order to help us adequately conceive of extinction, Weaver is aware that he must train us to think at the level of species, which is of course far beyond our ordinary, deeply individual experiences of life and death. He asks, 'How can you get people excited – or even to just pay attention to something incomprehensibly vast …? The *Unreliable Bestiary* is using humor, poetics and plain old wonder to inspire people to live differently.'[30] Note how Weaver's account-ing of the key features of his performances begins with tools at his disposal: humour and poetics. With 'plain old wonder', however, Weaver moves into the affective realm – that is, into the nebulous space of what he hopes his audiences will feel. He has not chosen to highlight his use of spectacle, which would seem best-suited to provoke wonder just as surely as humour occa-sions laughter, despite the fact that *The Unreliable Bestiary* contains many spectacular moments. (One reviewer notes, for instance, that, 'at a perform-ance of *ELEPHANT*, [his friend's] breath was literally taken away when, in a climactic moment, a huge elephant puppet, controlled from within by performers, appeared to the amazement of the assembled crowd.'[31]) Instead, Weaver counts wonder among the fundamental ingredients of the *Bestiary*, suggesting that it is the affective bedrock that defines even the quietest moments in his performances, such as the ceremonial naming and

---

[29] Weaver and Lux, 'The Unreliable Bestiary', 38.
[30] Deke Weaver, 'The Unreliable Bestiary Project' (March 26, 2011), TEDxUIUC, www.youtube.com/watch?v=RQwEABZq3vY.
[31] Matthew Green, 'Art in *WOLF*'s Clothing', *Smile Politely*, 11 September 2013, www.smilepolitely.com/arts/art_in_wolfs_clothing/.

erasure of threatened primate species at the beginning of *Monkey*. Once again, Weaver is reaching back to long-abandoned ways of thinking about other animals. In place of the anger, cynicism, and aversion that news coverage of climate change and mass extinction propagates, and in place of the benumbed enthrallment at the beauty of despair that tragedy instils, Weaver has given us 'plain old wonder': a quaint, even hokey, awe at the mystery and enormity of all that we are about to lose.

Extinction and the Ends of Performance

Plain old wonder is ethically agnostic. It is the product of one's encounter with an animal sublime, with all the indeterminacy that that term suggests. In and of itself, having one's breath taken away by an enormous elephant puppet is not especially virtuous – and there is no telling what, if anything, one will do with that feeling after the fact. On the surface, this seems to be yet another way in which Weaver's *Bestiary* is unreliable. Unlike its medieval predecessor, *The Unreliable Bestiary* cannot be counted upon to provide a framework for right living. It does not supply an allegorical key with which to understand the world and one's ethical orientation towards it.

At the same time, however, Weaver holds out hope that his project will 'inspire people to live differently'. Like Rothfels, who presumably got it from him, he never fully defines this phrase. Examples – including various forms of environmentalist protest – surface occasionally in his writing and public speaking, but often in somewhat subjunctive form. Notably, he has drawn on Rick Bass's *The Brown Dog of the Yaak*[32] to suggest that the political function of art is often deferred into an unknown future:

> Art can have tremendous long-term effects if it burrows into somebody's imagination, like a seed growing into an oak tree. But, if the chain saws are whining and the bulldozers are moving – a poem might not save the last acre of old-growth forest … but a human-chain might.… I'm never going to be bold or committed enough to live in the branches of a redwood tree for months on end. But maybe some of my work will sink into one or more people who might carry the idea somewhere else.[33]

Inspiration, like wonder, is unpredictable: it might or might not 'sink into one or more people'. But what will these people do as they 'carry the idea somewhere else'? Weaver has his own preferences, of course, as his call to

[32] Rick Bass, *Brown Dog of the Yaak: Essays on Art and Activism*, the Credo Series (Minneapolis, 1999).
[33] Weaver and Lux, 'The Unreliable Bestiary', 36–7.

'live differently' by 'sav[ing] the last acre of old-growth forest' makes clear. But what if there are too many crises to attend to, too many species and habitats to save, each of them rapidly approaching a tipping point that will render even drastic action moot? Is there an ethical function for performance if there is no guarantee that there is a future in which its 'tremendous long-term effects' can play out? Why make art if we are running out of time?

This is another way of asking an old-fashioned question: What are the ends of performance? Aristotle conceived of the form, function, and purpose of performance in much the same way as he conceived of the form, function, and species-specific essence of the animals he observed in his study of the natural world. Michelle Zerba and David Gorman note that the *History of Animals*, which came out of sustained research that Aristotle conducted on Lesbos, 'established the framework for ... [his] approach in the *Poetics*. He organizes his subject matter within a system of classification that treats individual works as if they were living organisms in an ecosystem.'[34] This isomorphism extends still further: for Aristotle, art, like nature, has a kind of 'organic form', meaning that it 'endows matter with a form that has a function and an end', like a 'biological entity with a coherent design that connects all the parts in a necessary fashion'.[35] We have already established that Weaver does not subscribe to the dogmatic strain of Aristotelianism that continues to dominate Western theatre making. That said, his approach to the fertile intersection between the animal sciences and theatrical perform-ance is deeply, if unexpectedly, Aristotelian. Like Aristotle, he conceives of individual performances as 'living organisms in an ecosystem' – *The Unreli-able Bestiary*, but also the broader space of what Foucault calls animal semantics more generally. Weaver also speaks and writes of the genesis of the *Bestiary* in strikingly organic terms: 'the performances and stories have different seeds and different ways of growing'.[36] And of course, in uniting Aristotle's twin interests in animals and performance, he takes the dictum 'art imitates nature' much more literally than most. In so doing, he reframes the old-fashioned question about the ends of performance for the Anthropocene: What are the ends of performances about species that are themselves ending?

Just as the bearness of a bear is contained, for Aristotle, within bears, and therefore inductively discoverable through close observation of their physi-ology and behaviour, so too the ethical core of *Bear* – and that of the other pieces in *The Unreliable Bestiary* – resides within it. In other words, leaving

---

[34] Michelle Zerba and David Gorman, 'Introduction', in *Poetics*, by Aristotle, ed. and trans. Zerba and Gorman, x.
[35] Ibid., xviii.   [36] Weaver and Lux, 'The Unreliable Bestiary', 36.

to one side Weaver's entirely understandable hope that his work will eventually inspire us to reorganize our lives around ecologically sustainable principles, these pieces actually advance their own ethical project in the here and now of live performance. We 'live differently' as we watch and walk and wonder our way through Weaver's work. As Aristotle might have intuited, the 'organic form' that governs the *Bestiary* – Weaver's use of squishy science and its epistemologies to wed the most fantastic flights of the animalized imagination with the most astonishing facts discovered by animal science, his cultivation of unsettled affect in the face of the spectacular enormity and mystery of animal life – leads us inexorably to its end. As we take in these performances, we reconceive of monkeys, elephants, wolves, bears, and tigers not only as moving memorials to a lost relation or as hopeful harbingers of a more genuinely reciprocal future, but also as real beings who remain to be encountered, even belatedly, even now. In the 'field guide' – a combination program and explanatory booklet, complete with diagrams of bear claws – that accompanies the various actions and performances that comprise *Bear*, Weaver writes: 'To put the genie back in the bottle, we need to bring back the bears. . ... With your help, we will bring back the bears by telling and re-telling a story, by walking a path for hours and hours.' While Weaver supports conservation efforts aimed at restoring bear populations and 'bring[ing] them back' from the brink of extinction, that is not quite what he has in mind here. Instead, he is advancing the radical proposition that by – forgive us – bearing witness, by participating in the performance, 'by telling and re-telling a story, by walking a path', audiences are in fact actively helping to 'bring back the bears'. Even if we have run out of time, even if – returning for a moment to Tsing – *The Unreliable Bestiary* is a play at the end of the world, this is the ethical commitment it makes. For now, at least, here, these animals are among us still. We've brought them back together.

Suggested Reading

Bass, Rick. *Brown Dog of the Yaak: Essays on Art and Activism*. The Credo Series. Minneapolis, 1999.

Bilodeau, Chantal. 'In Search of a New Aesthetic'. *HowlRound*, 19 April 2015. https://howlround.com/search-new-aesthetic.

Chaudhuri, Una, and Holly Hughes, eds. *Animal Acts: Performing Species Today*. Ann Arbor, 2014.

Crane, Susan. 'A Taxonomy of Creatures in the Second-Family Bestiary'. *New Medieval Literatures* 10 (2008): 1–48.

Foucault, Michel. *The Order of Things: An Archaeology of the Human Sciences*. New York, 1994.

Ghosh, Amitav. *The Great Derangement: Climate Change and the Unthinkable*. Berlin Family Lectures. Chicago, 2017.

Green, Matthew. 'Art in WOLF's Clothing.' Smile Politely, 11 September 2013. www.smilepolitely.com/arts/art_in_wolfs_clothing/.

Haraway, Donna J. *Staying with the Trouble: Making Kin in the Chthulucene*. Experimental Futures. Durham, 2016.

Kingsnorth, Paul, and Dougald Hine. *Manifesto*. Oxford, 2009. https://dark-mountain.net/about/manifesto/.

Kolbert, Elizabeth. *The Sixth Extinction: An Unnatural History*. New York, 2014.

Scranton, Roy. *Learning to Die in the Anthropocene: Reflections on the End of a Civilization*. San Francisco, 2015.

Tsing, Anna Lowenhaupt. *The Mushroom at the End of the World: On the Possibility of Life in Capitalist Ruins*. Princeton, 2017.

Weaver, Deke. 'The Aura of Bad Maps'. *Text and Performance Quarterly* 29, no. 4 (October 2009): 418–37.

'Excerpts from ELEPHANT'. In *Animal Acts: Performing Species Today*, ed. Una Chaudhuri and Holly Hughes. Ann Arbor, 2014, 163–81.

Weaver, Deke, and Maria Lux. 'The Unreliable Bestiary'. *Antennae: The Journal of Nature in Visual Culture* 22 (Autumn 2012): 31–40.

6

STANTON B. GARNER, JR.

Bodies of Knowledge

Theatre and Medical Science

Since its emergence in the ancient world, Western theatre has enjoyed an intimate relationship with Western medicine and the scientific theories on which it rests. Galen's medical theory of the humours influenced dramatic characterization in classical and early modern theatre, and Aristotle employed the medical term *catharsis* in his *Poetics* as a metaphor for tragedy's effect on its spectators. The appearance of modern theatre buildings in the late sixteenth century coincided in Italy and then elsewhere in Europe with the construction of anatomical theatres, where spectators watched the dissection of animal and human bodies (the latter were often executed convicts). In the early nineteenth century, this spectatorial practice was extended to live operations, which took place in surgical, or operating, theatres. Witnessed by medical practitioners, students, and other interested bystanders, operations in these venues were often crowded affairs, with surgeon-performers, sometimes hundreds of spectators, and patients who – until the introduction of anaesthetics in the latter nineteenth century – remained conscious throughout the procedure. Although such performances declined in the early twentieth century, the continuing use of *operating theatre* to designate the room where surgery is conducted is a reminder that medicine, like theatre, is a visual discipline grounded in embodiment, observation, and performance.

The influence of medical understandings of the body on theatre intensified in the nineteenth century, a period that saw unprecedented innovations in medical technology, advances in medical theory, and medical specialization. Instruments such as the stethoscope, microscope, thermometer, and X-ray made the body's interior newly accessible, and the discipline of physiology was transformed by the Frenchman Claude Bernard into a science for studying this internal environment. The development of germ theory and microbiology by Louis Pasteur, Robert Koch, and others transformed the understanding of infectious disease and led to the discovery of vaccines for typhoid fever, cholera, diphtheria, smallpox, and other medical scourges.

The birth of modern theatre paralleled and was influenced by these changing medical conceptions of the body and its biological environment. Émile Zola, for example, used Bernard's writings on physiology as a reference point for the naturalist theatre he championed. In place of the conventional representations that dominated the nineteenth-century stage, Zola called for the 'gradual substitution of physiological man for metaphysical man' and the 'thorough analysis of an organism'.[1] Germ theory and bacteriology also had an impact on modern theatre by activating and reframing the association of theatre with contagion, a centuries-old trope in antitheatricalist discourse.[2] Although Antonin Artaud's Theatre of Cruelty rejected the positivism of science, for example, his call for a 'plague theatre' played off the preoccupations of the microbiological revolution. Other medical and medicine-related sciences that had an influence on theatre during the nineteenth century include tropical medicine, modern anaesthesiology, hereditary science and eugenics, experimental psychology, and theories of hysteria.[3]

Along with these developments – and, in part, because of them – the period saw a vast increase in the professional status and cultural authority of medicine as a discipline, which was linked to the rapid growth and escalating prestige of scientific medicine during the century. As medicine claimed its place as an experimental science, it increasingly became a discipline of the laboratory as well as the clinic. With the advent of the modern research hospital – the London Hospital became the London Hospital Medical College in 1785 – these activities were combined. Medical discoveries and innovations were disseminated in the popular and scientific press for a readership with a high level of medico-scientific literacy, and figures

---

[1] Émile Zola, 'From *Naturalism in the Theatre*', trans. Albert Bermel, in *The Theory of the Modern Stage: An Introduction to Modern Theatre and Drama*, ed. Eric Bentley (Middlesex, 1968), 367, 363.

[2] In 1633, the English Puritan William Prynne characterized playgoers as 'many in number, contagious in quality, more apt to poison, to infect all those who dare approach them, than one who is full of running Plague-sores' (*Histrio-Mastix: The Player's Scourge or Actor's Tragedy* [1633; reprint, New York, 1972], 1.152).

[3] Fuller discussion of the intersections between medical science and modern theatre can be found in Stanton B. Garner, Jr., 'Physiologies of the Modern: Zola, Experimental Medicine, and the Naturalist Stage', *Modern Drama* 43 (2000): 529–42, and 'Is There a Doctor in the House?: Medicine and the Making of Modern Drama', *Modern Drama* 51, no. 3 (September 2008): 311–28; Kirsten Shepherd-Barr, *Science on Stage: From Doctor Faustus to Copenhagen* (Princeton, 2006); and *Performance and the Medical Body*, ed. Alex Mermikides and Gianna Bouchard (London, 2016), which includes Shepherd-Barr's essay 'The Diagnostic Gaze: Nineteenth-Century Contexts for Medicine and Performance' (37–49). The relationship of theatre and medicine has also been explored in special issues of *Modern Drama* (2008), *Performance Research* 19 (2014), and *Critical Stages/Scènes critiques* (2018).

such as Pasteur and the American military physician Walter Reed, who confirmed the theory that yellow fever was caused by mosquitoes on a research expedition to Cuba in 1900–1, became household names.

The influence of science on medicine did not begin in the nineteenth century, of course. Ancient Mesopotamians, Egyptians, and Greeks applied proto-scientific procedures to the study and treatment of disease, and early modern medicine drew upon the research of anatomists and physician-scientists such as William Harvey, who studied and mapped the circulatory system. Before the emergence of modern experimental medicine, though, scientific procedures and discoveries competed with, and were frequently eclipsed by, nonempirical explanations of human physiology and disease. The doctrine of *vitalism*, for one, which originated in the ancient world, held that the functions and processes of living organisms are determined by immaterial forces and that these operations cannot be explained by purely physical or chemical processes. Claude Bernard challenged this doctrine in his influential 1865 treatise *An Introduction to the Study of Experimental Medicine*. If medicine was to extend its understanding and therapeutic power over the human body, he claimed, it had to re-establish itself on the foundation of experimental science. It 'should delve into the interior of organisms and find ways of altering and, to a certain extent, regulating the hidden springs of living machines'.[4] Central to Bernard's experimentalist view was scientific determinism, the principle that natural phenomena are associated with specific conditions or determining causes. Against the proponents of vitalism, Bernard maintained that bodily operations are subject to physico-chemical laws and that the operations of these laws and the relations among bodily phenomena are determinable through controlled experimentation. In the absence of rigorous scientific method, he insisted, medicine cannot extricate itself from received authority, untested observation, and superstition.

As scientific medicine gained ascendancy in nineteenth-century Europe and North America – and as its methods and perspective were taken up by hospitals and medical schools – the human body became increasingly objectified in medical and scientific terms. Bernard's 'living machine' is a body that can be studied, experimented on, and measured. Reduced to physiological and pathological processes and subject to what Michel Foucault referred to in *The Birth of the Clinic* as the 'medical gaze', it is an objectified body rather than an experiential body-subject conscious of itself and its environment. In Hsuan L. Hsu and Martha Lincoln's useful

---

[4] Claude Bernard, *An Introduction to the Study of Experimental Medicine*, trans. Henry Copley Greene (New York, 1957), 197.

explanation, 'facilitated by the medical technologies that frame and focus the physician's optical grasp of the patient, the medical gaze abstracts the suffering person from her sociological context and reframes her as a "case" or a "condition"'.[5] The body as an object of medical knowledge is also a technologized body, and from the early nineteenth century on its organicity was complicated by the discourse and interventions of machines. Illness, from this perspective, is a scientific problem, not an experiential and emotional phenomenon. The ethical implications of this objectification are significant for a profession that was once considered a humanistic discipline and has always included care as one of its mandates.

Theatre, which assumed its status as a modern art form during this period of medical advancement, became an important site for the examination of scientific medicine's aspirations, achievements, limitations, and dangers. Reinforcing the heroic narrative of scientific discovery, a number of early twentieth-century plays celebrated the pioneers of modern disease research and their accomplishments. Sacha Guitry's 1919 play *Pasteur*, which enjoyed success in Paris, London, and New York before being made into a film, commemorated the career of the French scientist, while Sidney Howard and Paul De Kruif's 1934 play *Yellow Jack* presented the story of Reed's pioneering yellow fever research. Arthur Sundgaard's Living Newspaper *Spirochete* (see Fig. 6.1), which was produced in 1938 by the Federal Theatre Project, chronicled the spread of syphilis in early modern Europe as a result of New World expeditions and the scientific efforts to find a cure, which led to the development of an effective treatment in 1910.[6]

In each of these plays, medical research embodies the promise of a scientific modernity presided over by the researcher's objective, and objectifying, gaze. Anna Ziegler's 2015 play *Photograph 51* reinforces this narrative of scientific breakthrough by dramatizing the story of English chemist and X-ray crystallographer Rosalind Franklin, whose important but unacknowledged research contributed to the discovery of the DNA molecule's double-helix structure. Although James Watson and Francis Crick relied on Franklin's work, she was not recognized when they and Maurice Wilkins were awarded the Nobel Prize for Physiology or Medicine in 1962.

In the later twentieth and early twenty-first centuries, however, tributes to medical progress such as these were overshadowed by a growing critique of

---

[5] Hsuan L. Hsu and Martha Lincoln, 'Biopower, "Bodies . . . the Expedition", and the Spectacle of Public Health', *Discourse* 29, no. 1 (Winter 2007): 23.

[6] Living Newspapers are a twentieth-century theatre genre that dramatizes current events and social problems in order to advocate for progressive political and social change. The form was popularized in the US from 1935 to 1939 as part of the government-subsidized Federal Theatre Project.

Fig. 6.1 Poster for the Federal Theatre's production of *Spirochete* in Chicago (1938).

scientific medicine and its conception of the body as an object of medical knowledge. Theatre is a natural medium for this critique because the spectatorial dynamics it employs evoke yet also resist the objectifying perception of medical science. Like the anatomical and operating stages of earlier centuries, the lunatic asylums of early modern England that admitted members of the public so that they could observe the inmates, or the ethnological exhibits that displayed 'exotic' human beings as anthropological specimens, theatre offers actors' bodies as objects of spectatorial interest. In this sense, theatre aligns itself with medicine's objectifying gaze. But while theatre may aspire to scientific ways of seeing in the modern period – Zola, we have seen, modelled his theory of naturalism on experimental physiology, and Bertolt

Brecht invoked science as a paradigm of theatrical spectatorship – theatre also measures their limits, especially when the analytical eye seeks to penetrate the body and explore its inner regions.[7] As an interactive medium, theatre confronts the medical gaze with multiple points of view, each with its claim to autonomy. The body as object of theatrical spectatorship, in other words, is also the body as a locus of subjective experience. Theatre empowers this embodied subject, allowing it to express itself in an intersubjective field with other individuals on stage and off.

While theatre sometimes aspires to objectivity, then, it also provides a space where objectifying modes of spectatorship are themselves examined and subject to critique. Scientific medicine and its excesses have provided contemporary drama with an important field for this critique. If early twentieth-century theatre commemorated the life-saving discoveries of medical researchers, later playwrights and theatre artists confronted the legacy of officially sanctioned biomedical abuses. German and Japanese doctors conducted medical experiments on prisoners during World War II, and Soviet and American researchers used human subjects in radiation, chemical, and other forms of research. One of the most infamous experiments conducted in the interests of medical knowledge was the Tuskegee syphilis study conducted between 1932 and 1972 by the US Public Health Service and the Tuskegee Institute, in which 399 African American sharecroppers in Alabama who tested positive for syphilis were told that they were being treated for 'bad blood' when in fact they were denied available treatment for their actual disease. The study came to light in 1972 when the Associated Press reported that all but a handful of its participants had gone untreated for forty years.

David Feldshuh's 1989 play *Miss Evers' Boys* explores the human and ethical stakes of this biomedical scandal. The title character, Eunice Evers, is based on the African American nurse who recruited and cared for the subjects of the Tuskegee experiment. As a trusted health-care professional who worked for years with Alabama's rural poor before joining the study, Feldshuh's Evers attempts to mediate between the medical research establishment and the infected sharecroppers to whom she grows close. The ethical contradictions of her position become increasingly clear as the play progresses. Evers advocates on behalf of the men to the doctors conducting the

---

[7] For Brecht's discussion of his Epic Theatre's scientific spectator, see *Brecht on Theatre*, ed. Marc Silberman, Steve Giles, and Tom Kuhn (London, 2015), 65–67 and 275–301.
Dramatist August Strindberg, who was also influenced by science, compared his work as a writer to vivisection, the experimental use of surgery on living organisms. See Amy Strahler Holzapfel, 'Strindberg as Vivisector: Physiology, Pathology, and Anti-Mimesis in *The Father* and *Miss Julie*', *Modern Drama* 51, no. 3 (Fall 2008): 329–52.

study – pleading with them to treat their subjects with penicillin, for instance, which had recently been proven to cure syphilis – but when her superiors rebuff her intercessions, she continues to withhold information from the men who would benefit from it. As Evers establishes in the play's opening lines, her life has been guided by the nursing profession's pledge, which includes the promise 'to devote myself to the welfare of those patients entrusted to my care'.[8] When human welfare conflicts with science, however, this duty risks being compromised by experimental exigencies and the valorizing of medical knowledge. Dr. Eugene Brodus, whose character is based on the African American hospital director who helped administer the Tuskegee study, comments on this ethically troubling double role from a doctor's point of view: 'Physician and scientist ... That can be an uneasy combination.'[9]

At the centre of this ethical dilemma are the patients who become unwitting objects of scientific observation. The four tenant farmers in Feldshuh's play are richly individualized, and their fears, aspirations, and shared affection are amplified through their growing relationships with Evers and their participation in a makeshift band that competes in rural dance contests. After they agree to join the study that Evers proposes in return for free government medical care, however, their bodies are co-opted by the demands of medical research. The objectifying nature of this activity is rendered explicit at the end of Act 1. While the men perform their music-and-dance routine at an increasingly frenzied pace, the stage lighting 'surrounds the men in a confining, microscopic circle, burning bright', and the circular seal of the United States Public Health Service appears.[10] When the play resumes in Act 2, the stage is divided into three separate playing areas. In one, the members of the band watch Willie Johnson, their dancer and front man, practice his steps. In another, Brodus and Dr John Douglas (the head of the Tuskegee study) study microscope slides and plot points on a blackboard graph. In the third, Evers testifies in 1972 before a US Senate committee investigating the abuses that occurred when medical research trumped the claims of humanity. *Miss Evers' Boys* ends with this testimony and with the image of Willie's lost, graceful dance.

The Tuskegee Study of Untreated Syphilis in the Negro Male was not the only example of unethical medical research conducted as part of the fight against syphilis. Between 1946 and 1948, US researchers infected Guatemalan soldiers, sex workers, mental patients, and prisoners with syphilis and other sexually transmitted disease in order to test the effectiveness of

---

[8] David Feldshuh, *Miss Evers' Boys* (New York, 1995), 14.   [9] Ibid., 42.   [10] Ibid., 62.

penicillin as a treatment. The choice of subjects in these experiments reflects medical science's historical use of socially marginal and disadvantaged populations as research subjects. Charly Evon Simpson's 2019 play *Behind the Sheet* examines a particularly egregious example of this practice: the use of enslaved African American women for surgical experiments by J. Marion Sims, the 'father of modern gynecology', during the 1840s. In his trial-and-error search for a technique for closing vaginal fistulas, Sims operated on slave women without anaesthesia in the belief that African Americans do not feel pain to the same extent that Caucasians do. Simpson's play explores the human cost of this medical exploitation. Philomena, who serves as assistant and mistress to the slave-owning doctor, George, develops a fistula during labour and ends up undergoing thirty surgical procedures. The operations that are enacted on stage are excruciating to witness: Philomena cries out in pain, and it takes several other assistants to hold her down on the operating table. When George discovers a procedure that works after years of trial and error, the triumph is all his. Philomena is exhibited to white audiences as evidence of his success, and the other slave women in the play who suffered from the same condition must wait to be healed until white women who need it are given the procedure – with ether to numb their pain.

The medical objectification of marginalized bodies is also evident in the historical study of those with anomalous, or extra-ordinary, bodies. The fact that many of these individuals were exhibited in freak shows, ethnographic exhibitions, and other forms of public demonstration indicates the close association between medicine, science, and popular performance during the nineteenth and early twentieth centuries. Conjoined twins, individuals with disabilities, and racial 'exotics' were the objects of medical study as well as popular display. As Fiona Pettit explains, these fields often traded on each other. Freak show exhibitors employed medical language when promoting their attractions, and the published accounts and preserved remains of these human curiosities 'became important sites of reference in the development of medical knowledge'.[11] The skeletons and organs of those who were displayed were often exhibited after their deaths in medical research collections, ethnographic collections, and museums of human oddities such as the Mütter Museum in Philadelphia, which was founded in 1858. The skeleton of Joseph Merrick – the severely disfigured 'Elephant Man' of nineteenth-century renown and the protagonist of Bernard Pomerance's 1977 play of

---

[11] Fiona Pettit, 'The Afterlife of Freak Shows', in *Popular Exhibitions, Science and Showmanship, 1840–1910*, ed. Joe Kember, John Plunkett, and Jill A. Sullivan (London, 2012), 62. Also see Shepherd-Barr, *Science on Stage*, 38–40.

that title – remains on private display 130 years after his death in the Queen Mary University medical school.

Suzan-Lori Parks stages this intersection of medico-scientific and popular exhibition in *Venus*, her 1996 play about Saartjie Baartman, the Khoikhoi woman who was brought to Europe from southern Africa in 1810 and exhibited to audiences in London and Paris under the name 'Hottentot Venus'. During her time in Paris, Baartman was studied by French scientists, and after her death in 1816 her preserved skeleton, brain, and sexual organs were placed on display at the Paris Musée de l'Homme (Museum of Mankind), where they were housed until their repatriation and burial in 2002. Parks's *Venus* forcefully dramatizes this medical preoccupation with Baartman's body, particularly the buttocks and genitals, that made her an example for those attempting to prove the evolutionary inferiority of Africans to Europeans. From the moment she is brought to England to her time in Paris as a mistress/object of the Baron Docteur, the Venus (as she is referred to in Parks's text) is an object of medical and voyeuristic interest. The Mother-Showman who advertises her in London as the lowest rung of the evolutionary ladder invites spectators to gawk at her and the other freaks in her employ: 'Waiting for yr gaze here inside / theyre all freaks and all alive.'[12] Parks's Baartman is also the object of anatomical study, an activity that begins with her first appearance and continues after her death. In the play's overture, a member of the Chorus addresses her living and postmortem status as medico-scientific specimen: 'I look at you, Venus, and see: / Science. You / in uh pickle / on my library shelf.'[13] The anatomical perspective is underscored by the Negro-Resurrectionist, who recites historical extracts from medical texts and Baartman's autopsy report, and the Baron Docteur, who gives a lengthy anatomical lecture on the Venus in two scenes subtitled 'The Dis(re)memberment of the Venus Hottentot'. This text, which is drawn from Georges Cuvier's autopsy of the historical Baartman, is accompanied by a glossary of medical terms at the end of the published play.

While Parks's Venus lives under the gaze of others who seek to objectify her as anatomical and ethnographic spectacle, however, she maintains her individuality and agency. She has a say in her own career as an object of display and speaks on her own behalf in her interactions with those who seek to manipulate her. Moreover, when she exhibits herself onstage, the look that she directs back at her spectators challenges her objectification and fetishization. As Harry J. Elam, Jr., and Alice Rayner observe in their analysis of Parks's play, 'the pose is an act that paradoxically accepts and

---

[12] Suzan-Lori Parks, *Venus* (New York, 1997), 31.   [13] Ibid., 8.

refracts the gaze of the spectator and turns the play into a test *of* the audience, not *for* the audience. It arrests the line of sight and transfixes the one who is looking.'[14] In a play that resurrects Saartjie Baartman from the relics and traces of history – the term 'resurrectionist' was used to refer to those in the eighteenth and nineteenth century who exhumed corpses to sell to anatomists – it is Venus who speaks the closing words ('*Kiss me Kiss me Kiss me Kiss*').[15]

Looking back – and speaking back – are also central to Margaret Edson's 1995 play *Wit*, which explores the conflict between scientism and subjectivity in the context of the modern research hospital. Its protagonist, Vivian Bearing, is a professor of seventeenth-century English poetry and an authority on the metaphysical poet John Donne who is diagnosed with advanced (stage 4) metastatic ovarian cancer. Edson's play shows the course of her treatment with an aggressive experimental regimen of chemotherapy: her consent to receive the maximum dose of these powerful drugs, the steady increase of debilitating side effects, and her eventual death under sedation. With the exception of a series of flashback scenes in her oncologist Dr Harvey Kelekian's office when she receives her diagnosis, her father's study during her childhood, her scholarly mentor E. M. Ashford's office, and the university classroom where she lectures, the play takes place in her hospital room and other rooms where she is undergoes a battery of X-rays and diagnostic tests. In her position as protagonist and narrator of her life story, Bearing opens the play by addressing the audience, and from that point until she is sedated with morphine near the play's end she discusses her life and career, her deteriorating condition, and her interactions with those who treat her.

By setting her play in a cancer ward, Edson depicts the interpenetration of medical science, clinical practice, and end-of-life care in the modern hospital's totalizing environment. When Bearing enters, she wears two hospital gowns, one tied in front and one in the back, and a baseball cap to cover her bald head. She has a central venous access catheter over her left breast that is attached to a wheeled IV pole with bottles that change over the course of the play (see Fig. 6.2). When she is not in bed, she wheels the IV pole around or sits in a wheelchair while others move her and her intravenous apparatus.

Bearing's subjection to a phalanx of medical technologies indicates her new-found place in the institutionalized world of medical science. From the perspective of the researchers, clinicians, and most of the hospital staff who

---

[14] Harry J. Elam and Alice Rayner, 'Between Body Parts: Story and Spectacle in *Venus* by Suzan-Lori Parks', in *Staging Resistance: Essays on Political Theater*, ed. Jeanne Colleran and Jenny S. Spencer (Ann Arbor, 1998), 278.

[15] Parks, *Venus*, 162.

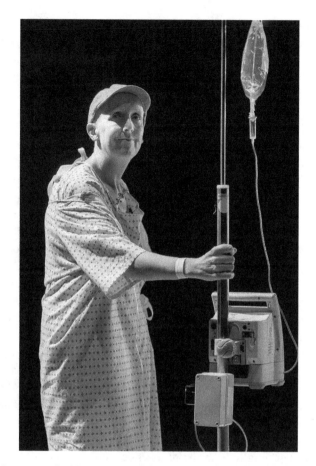

Fig. 6.2 Julie Hesmondhalgh as Vivian Bearing in Margaret Edson's *Wit* (Manchester Royal Exchange Theatre, 2016). By permission of Jonathan Keenan.

interact with her, she is a medical case, not an individual – a collection of internal processes, symptoms, and measurements, not a conscious agent in relation to herself and her world. Her situation recalls Foucault's description of the medical gaze: 'Paradoxically, in relation to that which he is suffering from, the patient is only an external fact; the medical reading must take him into account only to place him in parentheses. Of course, the doctor must know "the internal structure of our bodies"; but only in order to subtract it, and to free to the doctor's gaze "the nature and combination of symptoms, crises and other circumstances that accompany diseases".'[16]

---

[16] Michel Foucault, *The Birth of the Clinic: An Archaeology of Medical Perception*, trans. A. M. Sheridan Smith (New York, 1994), 8.

The objectifying nature of this attitude is evident throughout Edson's play. Kelekian, for example, explains Bearing's diagnosis to her in highly specialized language, making no attempt to translate these terms to her or gauge their emotional impact on a woman who is suddenly being faced with the possibility of premature death. When he urges her to consent to the experimental drug treatment he is developing, he describes the likely side effects in detached, clinical terms and assures her that 'as research', her treatment 'will make a significant contribution to our knowledge'.[17] Edson, who drew on her earlier experience of working in the AIDS and Oncology unit of a research hospital to write the play, is clear about the stakes involved in this medico-scientific enterprise. Bearing's best chance at surviving advanced ovarian cancer requires that her body be scanned, measured, and treated as a biochemical entity – that it be hooked up to machines and serve as an object of medical analysis. She is a *patient* in the etymological sense of someone who is acted upon, and this passivity is an inevitable consequence of the fact that others have the training and technology to treat her, whereas she does not. Cancer, in this sense, is a problem to be solved. That Bearing is a patient in a research hospital intensifies the medical profession's interest in her pathology, since the success (or nonsuccess) of the chemotherapeutic treatment she agrees to will enable more effective treatment options for future patients. Bearing, herself an expert, can appreciate this accomplishment. It is also the case, however, that cancer is a trauma to be lived, a transformative physical and psycho-emotional event in the life of an individual. In her book *The Meaning of Illness*, S. Kay Toombs writes, 'One does not "see" one's own illness primarily as a disease process. Rather, one experiences it essentially in terms of its effects upon everyday life.'[18] Illness has a landscape of its own, and its radical subjectivity resists the objectifying perception of scientific medicine.

The tension between objectification and first-person experience that *Wit* foregrounds finds a natural home in Edson's theatre of direct address. As *Miss Evers' Boys*, *Behind the Sheet*, and *Venus* have demonstrated, theatre empowers the embodied subject, allowing it to express itself in an intersubjective field with other individuals on stage and off. *Wit* stages these competing points of view. In this overt way, theatre undermines scientific medicine's tendency to reduce illness to a physico-chemical problem and the patient to a scientific case study. During the play's grand rounds sequence, when Kelekian leads a group of fellows through a review of Bearing's medical

[17] Margaret Edson, *Wit* (New York, 1999), 11.
[18] S. Kay Toombs, *The Meaning of Illness: A Phenomenological Account of the Different Perspectives of Physician and Patient* (Dordrecht, 1992), 11.

condition and symptoms, Bearing offers a running commentary on the examination while her body is being analyzed as a medical object. '[I]n Grand Rounds, *they* read *me* like a book,' she wryly observes. 'Once I did the teaching, now I am taught.'[19]

Bearing's scholarly training bears on her present efforts to understand and come to terms with her present predicament. A specialist in words, she attempts to master the discourse through which her body is objectified: 'I want to know what the doctors mean when they ... anatomize me. And I will grant that in this particular field of endeavor they possess a more potent arsenal of terminology than I. My only defense is the acquisition of vocabulary.'[20] Schooled in New Criticism, a twentieth-century critical school that advocated disciplined, highly refined close reading of a literary work's textual elements, she breaks down specialized medical language into its Latin roots as a way of mastering the unthinkable through intellect and analysis. Linguistic training, though, cannot protect Bearing from the fact that she is now the object of scientific analysis, the complex problem against which intellect tests itself. Reduced under medical scrutiny to her pathological symptoms, she is the one being read, parsed, and explicated. In her own words, 'What we have come to think of as *me* is, in fact, just the specimen jar, just the dust jacket, just the white piece of paper that bears the little black marks.'[21] In its progression from specimen jar to printed page, Bearing's self-description mirrors her body's subordination to the hospital's regimen of diagnosis and treatment and its eventual reduction to words and numbers in the journal article that she imagines Kelekian and Jason will eventually write about her. Edson underscores this textualization in an earlier flashback scene. While delivering a lecture to her students on one of Donne's sonnets, Bearing walks in front of the projector when lecturing to her students and Donne's words are momentarily projected on her double-gowned, terminally ill body.

As her condition worsens, Bearing addresses the challenge of empathy and relationship in her medico-scientific environment.[22] One of the most telling interactions she has is with Jason Posner, a clinical fellow under Kelekian's supervision who monitors her treatment throughout the play. During grand rounds, Jason distinguishes himself from the others in his medical and scientific understanding. He is also a former student of Bearing's, having taken her course on seventeenth-century poetry as a biochemistry major

---

[19] Edson, *Wit*, 37.   [20] Ibid., 43–4.   [21] Ibid., 53.

[22] Kate Rossiter discussed the ethics of relationality in Edson's play in 'Bearing Response-ability: Theatre, Ethics, and Medical Education', *Journal of Medical Humanities* 33 (2012): 1–14.

because it was one of the hardest on campus. Jason relishes intellectual challenges and shares, with Bearing, a fascination with the metaphysical poet John Donne. Donne, he says, wrote sonnets so difficult that 'your whole brain had to be in knots before you could get it'.[23] Confronting topics like the dilemma of salvation, Donne created convoluted puzzles for his readers. The game of trying to solve these puzzles is the same, Jason suggests, as scientific research: 'The puzzle takes over. You're not even trying to solve it anymore. Fascinating, really. Great training for lab research. Looking at things in increasing levels of complexity.'[24] One of the things that Jason appreciates about seventeenth-century poetry, he acknowledges, is its rejection of sentimentality. Jason's impatience with feeling and what he calls 'that meaning-of-life garbage' is consistent with his antipathy toward clinical work and the human element of relationship. He speaks eloquently about how 'awesome' cancer is, how audacious its proliferating cells are in defying normal intercellular regulatory mechanisms.[25] His interest in cancer, however, does not extend to what Bearing wryly calls 'the part with the human beings'.[26] As someone who has to prompt himself with the word 'clinical' to attend to his patient, he is impatient with the interpersonal demands of his hospital fellowship.

When Bearing finally loses consciousness under sedation, the tension between impersonal protocols and compassionate treatment comes to a head in a confrontation between Jason and Susie, the nurse looking after Vivian. Throughout the play, Susie's care for Bearing stands in sharp contrast to Jason's commitment to research and established hospital protocols. Susie urges Jason to lower the level of chemotherapy to alleviate Bearing's suffering, and when this request fails, she urges Kelekian to provide a patient-controlled analgesic that Bearing can use to control her pain treatment instead of the morphine that he ends up ordering. In the scene immediately before this, Susie sits with Bearing and comforts her when she admits to being afraid. The two share a popsicle, and Susie encourages her to think about her resuscitation options in the event that her heart stops beating. As she explains, doctors want to save lives at all cost even when the body is dependent on machines. Bearing decides on a 'do not resuscitate' order, and this is added to her chart. When her heart finally does stop under sedation, however, Jason calls for a 'code blue' without looking at the chart. While Susie physically tries to restrain him, the code team rushes in and violently manipulates Bearing's body for defibrillation and artificial respiration in 'a whirlwind of sterile packaging and barked commands'.[27] During this brutal,

[23] Ibid., 75.   [24] Ibid., 76.   [25] Ibid., 56–7.   [26] Ibid., 57.   [27] Ibid., 83.

98

undignified sequence Bearing's treatment presents a harrowing image of depersonalizing medical treatment. It ends only when Jason realizes his mistake and cancels the code in dismay at what he has done.

While the code team express their resentment at Jason's error, Bearing rises from her hospital bed, sheds her hospital attire, and reaches – 'naked, and beautiful' – for a light that shines on the stage.[28] In keeping with John Donne's spiritual meditations, the moment suggests an afterlife – momentary or enduring – in which Bearing is freed from her suffering body. Mike Nichols's 2001 television film of *Wit*, which he adapted with actress Emma Thompson, mutes this suggestion of transcendence. In the film's closing moments, the camera rests on Bearing's lifeless but peaceful face as her voice is heard reciting Donne's Holy Sonnet 'Death be not proud'. This image eventually gives way to a photograph of Bearing that was taken before the onset of cancer. Looking directly at the camera, her eyes assert the subjectivity that scientific medicine failed to eclipse. This subjectivity, we have seen, is even more pressing in theatre, the medium – as Herbert Blau memorably insisted – 'most dependent upon, fascinated with, drawn, quartered by, and fixated upon the body, its vulnerabilities, pain, and disappearance'.[29] This body – living and dying, available and inaccessible – is where medicine, science, and theatre have historically converged. Medical science may formulate this body as an object of knowledge, but theatre's bodies look back in the midst of their display. Scientific looking, as *Wit* and the other examples of contemporary medical drama make clear, is a two-way street.

Suggested Reading

Bernard, Claude. *An Introduction to the Study of Experimental Medicine*, trans. Henry Copley Greene. New York, 1957.

Edson, Margaret. *Wit*. New York, 1999.

Feldshuh, David. *Miss Evers' Boys*. New York, 1995.

Foucault, Michel. *The Birth of the Clinic: An Archaeology of Medical Perception*, trans. A. M. Sheridan Smith. New York, 1994.

Garner, Stanton B., Jr. 'Physiologies of the Modern: Zola, Experimental Medicine, and the Naturalist Stage'. *Modern Drama* 43 (2000): 529–42.

'Is There a Doctor in the House?: Medicine and the Making of Modern Drama'. *Modern Drama* 51, no. 3 (September 2008): 311–28.

Parks, Suzan-Lori. *Venus*. New York, 1997.

Pettit, Fiona. 'The Afterlife of Freak Shows'. In *Popular Exhibitions, Science and Showmanship, 1840–1910*, ed. Joe Kember, John Plunkett, and Jill A. Sullivan. London, 2012, 61–78.

---

[28] Ibid., 85.

[29] Herbert Blau, *To All Appearances: Ideology and Performance* (New York, 1992), 1.

Rossiter, Kate. 'Bearing Response-ability: Theatre, Ethics, and Medical Education'. *Journal of Medical Humanities* 33 (2012): 1–14.

Shepherd-Barr, Kirsten. 'The Diagnostic Gaze: Nineteenth-Century Contexts for Medicine and Performance'. In *Performance and the Medical Body*, ed. Alex Mermikides and Gianna Bouchard. London, 2016, 37–49.

Sundgaard, Arnold. *Spirochete: A History. Federal Theatre Plays*, ed. Pierre De Rohan. New York, 1973, 1–90.

Zola, Émile. '*Naturalism in the Theatre*', trans. Albert Bermel. In *The Theory of the Modern Stage: An Introduction to Modern Theatre and Drama*, ed. Eric Bentley. Middlesex, 1968, 351–72.

7

FINTAN WALSH

Pathogenic Performativity

Urban Contagion and Fascist Affect

In Arinzé Kene's *Misty* (Bush Theatre, 2018) and Neil Bartlett's *The Plague* (Arcola Theatre, 2017), cities are under siege.[1] Contagions spread among residents, destroying lives and tearing the fabric of the urban environment. In both productions we find the city caught up in a drama of violence invisible to the audience's eye, in which described or recounted contamination effects biological death and cultural cleansing. This chapter examines how ideas of contagion are mobilized in these works to capture a sense of intangible danger spreading throughout the city, especially London, and how this formulation finds inspiration in contemporary political discourse that heralds the risk of economic, cultural, and political contagion as part of divisive rhetoric. I track the often contrasting relationship between what is narratively described and aesthetically evoked on stage in each production, and how this relates to the broader cultural climate in which group feeling is systematically roused and harnessed for political effect. These interrelated dynamics are viewed in light of contemporary theatre studies' widespread assumption of the general beneficence of shared affect, towards considering its more sinister implications. The chapter analyzes how we might understand these entangled forms of representation and discourse in light of the broader prevalence of what I describe as 'pathogenic performativity', in which the language and phantasmagoria of contagion are deployed as tactics of abjection and governance, while assessing theatre's role in their perpetuation or disruption. Thinking through these plays and productions reveals some of the ways in which theatre and contagion have long been implicated, and their more specific intersections in contemporary theatre.

---

[1] *Misty* was written by Kene and directed by Omar Elerian, and it opened at the Bush Theatre in March before transferring to Trafalgar Studios in September 2018. *The Plague* was directed and written by Bartlett, and so far has had two runs at the Arcola Theatre in 2017 and 2018.

Urban Spread

Misty tracks movement between central London and the borough of Hackney, where the play's author and central performer grew up, having emigrated from Nigeria as a child. Accompanied by live music, Kene performs most of the monologues and songs that comprise the production, shifting between ostensibly telling his own story and that of his friend Lucas – with whom his identity tends to blur. In his opening address, Kene speaks directly to the audience as 'Virus', describing the city as a living entity, while comparing its boroughs and streets to organs and veins: 'Our city's organs function like any living creature / Our city is a living creature ... You might liken the borough that I live in to the bowel.'[2] If the city is a creature, Kene initially likens himself and his black family and community to viruses, who pass through London's transport networks and streets, to contaminate neighbouring 'blood cells', or white population.

This cellular drama is visualized scenographically by orange balloons – at one point Kene steps inside one, and at another they take over his onstage studio. Narratively, the balloons represent the last thing Lucas claims to see before he dies due to police brutality, but theatrically they perform the immunizing function of spherical shapes in culture, which Peter Sloterdijk describes as 'immune-systemically effective space creations for ecstatic beings that are operated upon by the outside'.[3] As the play unfolds, and the performer engages in conversations with family and friends on stage, his viral formulation flips to frame the city's gentrifying forces as maligning residents' lives, in particular by pushing black people out of their neighbourhoods and homes: 'Call it virus invasion / Call it gentrification, / Call whatever you want, / It's nothing but modern-day colonisation.'[4] Kene also cautions that 'too much compromising' will lead to 'black smoke rising', an apparent allusion to the London riots of 2011,[5] which are also referenced in his other play *Good*

---

[2] Arinzé Kene, *Misty* (London, 2018), 14.
[3] Peter Sloterdijk, *Bubbles, Spheres I*, trans. Wieland Hoban (Los Angeles, 2011), 28. Thanks to Lynne McCarthy for this reference.
[4] Kene, *Misty*, 54.
[5] The riots took place 6–11 August 2011. They started in Tottenham, London, following the fatal shooting of young black man Mark Duggan, and spread across London and the UK. A report by the London School of Economics and *Guardian* concluded that the most significant contributing factors included opportunism, social injustice and deprivation, and frustration with police/policing. See *Reading the Riots* (2012), http://eprints.lse.ac.uk/46297/1/Reading%20the%20riots%28published%29.pdf, accessed 1 May 2019.

Dog (2017), prompting *Spectator* critic Lloyd Evans to claim that 'his songs encourage riots in London'.[6]

Kene's play explores how black people are imagined as corrupting presences within the city – not least black men and the kinds of masculinity they are presumed to represent or embody. Ultimately, however, it exposes the more culpable destructiveness of governing economic imperatives, especially gentrification processes. Critiquing gentrification is not easy for the writer and performer, whose friends and family accuse him of misrepresenting their lives and even colluding with gentrification in his artistic ambitions – arguably compounded by the move of his play from the small Bush Theatre in West London to Trafalgar Studios in the West End (where I saw it) later the same year.[7] Indeed, the emergence of theatres in city neighbourhoods is often central to regeneration initiatives, potentially conspiring with and benefitting from the structures that oppress local communities.

Aesthetically, *Misty* mainly operates on two levels. Musically and visually, it takes the form of a grime gig, with rap, music, moments of spoken word, and movement. Grime is a form of electronic dance music that developed in London in the 2000s, the term indicating the genre's focus on the 'dirty' dimensions of London, in particular deprived urban experience. Narratively, the plot focuses on Kene's grappling with London and its pressures and biases, largely described via lyrics and occasional dialogue. Operating within this dual register, *Misty* practices a form of aesthetic contamination that speaks to different ethnic, age, and class constituencies, troubling any attempt to locate the production as being about or for a specific demographic.

According to Kene's onstage sister, called Girl, violence against black people is now more psychological than physical: 'disseminated to you through news, education, radio, television, film – deployed in all sectors right from government to ... the theatre. It engenders in our people feelings of self-doubt, self-hatred, and when that's what you're telling, you could totally make up stories like, well, the one you seem to be writing right now.'[8] The real danger threatening the city, Kene's final song suggests, is not black people or communities of colour, but the tearing-up of the environment through corporate initiatives and gentrification processes. As Ben Campkin

---

[6] Lloyd Evans, 'Blacktivist Rhetoric and Impenetrable Symbols: *Misty* Reviewed', *The Spectator*, 22 September 2018, www.spectator.co.uk/2018/09/blacktivist-rhetoric-and-impenetrable-symbols-misty-reviewed/, accessed 1 May 2019.

[7] Lynette Goddard explores the significance of black British theatre becoming more mainstream and commercial in her book *Contemporary Black British Playwrights: Margins to Mainstream* (Basingstoke, 2015).

[8] Kene, *Misty*, 32–3.

has argued, throughout the twentieth century these transformations have often been defended using 'socio-biological metaphors' of regeneration.[9]

Bartlett's play is an adaptation of Albert Camus's 1947 novel of the same title, which imagines a plague spreading through the Algerian city of Oran, a former French colony with a large Arab population. Set in an unnamed city, with mixed gender and ethnic casting (contrary to Camus's novel, which lacks central Arab and female characters), Bartlett's version is framed as an inquiry, the stage set with a couple of tables, chairs, and mics against the theatre's exposed brick walls. Combining narration and dialogue, the play recounts the rapid spread of plague throughout the city over a number of days, decimating its population. First, dead rats appear on the street, and people start to wonder where the plague has come from, before turning to the city's Arab community. But no straightforward cause can be found, and Doctor Rieux ultimately suggests that this plague was lying dormant all along within the city's infrastructure: 'It was as though the source of infection had been here all the time and was now coming up from under our houses and erupting like a sewer.'[10]

Camus suffered from tuberculosis, and his experience of illness no doubt influenced themes in *The Plague*. But after its initial publication, the novel was received foremost as an allegory of fascism, in particular the occupation of France by the Nazis. In this, the text continued Camus's broader exploration of French colonialism and its noxious effects, though his perceived ethnocentrism has been met with criticism.[11] In his preface to the play, Bartlett claims his adaptation should represent every city of its production, 'every city, that is, where Arabs live in the poorer parts of town, where near-strangers collide on the stairs of apartment blocks, where doctors are overworked, where the newspapers are irresponsible and the authorities use the words "infection" and "crisis"'.[12] Bartlett describes his version as an attempt to 'get us through the impossible and the hateful'[13] and mentions 'the dangerous, unstable spring of 2017',[14] a reference to the effects of Donald Trump's election as US president, the rising populism across Europe, and the political turmoil in the UK following the Brexit referendum of 2016. But given Bartlett's long commitment to queer politics and activism, the play

---

[9] Ben Campkin, *Remaking London: Decline and Regeneration in Urban Culture* (New York, 2013), 4.

[10] Neil Bartlett, *The Plague*, after *La Peste* by Albert Camus (London, 2017), 18.

[11] Some critics have challenged the ethnocentrism of Camus, in particular Conor Cruise O'Brien, who queried the French focus of Camus's concerns in *The Plague*. See Conor Cruise O'Brien, *Camus* (1970) (London, 2015), 33–51. Thanks to Caoimhe Mader McGuinness for drawing my attention to this literature.

[12] Bartlett, *The Plague*, 6.   [13] Ibid., 3.   [14] Ibid.

also nods to the pathologization of the LGBTQ community, not least given that 2017 marked the fiftieth anniversary of the Sexual Offences Act 1967, which partially decriminalized sexual acts between men.

In its two Arcola runs to date, *The Plague* struck a particular resonance with the neighbourhood of its production. The Dalston of the Arcola's setting (and the Hackney borough in which it sits and which provides the background for *Misty*) is not just a historically mixed neighbourhood that has experienced high migration and population growth, but one that witnessed extraordinary changes in the past ten years due to so-called regeneration initiatives. While rooted in programmes originated in the 1980s, in East London these were accelerated by the 2012 Olympics.[15] It is difficult not to read the destruction that the play enacts as alluding to the violence of this gentrification process and to the 2011 riots referred to in Kene's play, which were arguably fuelled by this disruption. Writing about the 2017 production in the *Independent*, Andy Martin describes leaving the theatre only to discover someone stabbed to death at the adjacent Dalston Junction, finding in the play a comment on gang violence in light of rising knife and gun crime.[16] In the range of meanings that cluster around contagion in Camus's novel and Bartlett's stage adaptation, multiple socioeconomic ills emerge as potentially responsible for the community's ruin.

Ideas of blood contamination have a particular resonance in the UK's history of imagining race relations, providing the central and abiding image of Enoch Powell's racist anti-immigration 'Rivers of Blood' speech of 1968 in which, referencing the *Aeneid*, he said: 'As I look ahead, I am filled with foreboding; like the Roman, I seem to see "the River Tiber foaming with much blood".'[17] While in both plays the blame for disease is initially directed towards annexed communities of colour – black communities in *Misty* and Arab communities in *The Plague* – the two productions share the sense of neighbourhoods crushed by a densely populated and gentrifying

---

[15] London 2012 included plans for large-scale redevelopment and regeneration across the boroughs of Hackney, Tower of Hamlets, and Newham. Jen Harvie argues that the 2012 Games were less advantageous for East Londoners than promised and that this was foreshadowed by their comparative occlusion from the visual representation of the Games. See Jen Harvie, 'Brand London 2012 and "The Heart of East London": Competing Urban Agendas at the 2012 Games', *Contemporary Theatre Review* 23, no. 4 (2013): 486–501 (488).

[16] Andy Martin, 'The Parallels between Albert Camus's 'The Plague' and London's Growing Problem with Knife Crime', *Independent*, 5 May 2017, www.independent.co.uk/news/long_reads/albert-camus-the-plague-london-violent-knife-crime-police-a7717851.html, accessed 1 May 2018.

[17] The speech is widely available online, including at BBC Archive on 4 at www.bbc.co.uk/sounds/play/b09z08w3, accessed 22 July 2019.

city, particularly the changing face of Hackney. As Loretta Lees observes, gentrification is often pitched with the promise of social mixing, 'as an attempt to reduce socio-spatial segregation and strengthen the "social tissue" of deprived neighbourhoods',[18] though in reality this has resulted in the decimation of established communities through hiked prices, over-crowding, and displaced populations. While in each play contagion initially figures as the projected racialized others' impact on the city, requiring social rather than medical cleansing, we are left with a sense that violent structural reorganization is itself pathological and productive of social pathology.

Contagion and the Political

The issues these plays raise find form in the broader contemporary climate in which ideas of contagion are frequently activated to describe the unpredict-able workings of politics, culture, and economics. The term 'contagion' suggests that we are living through times when imperceptible dangers abound, ready to sprout and spread before we have a chance to grasp what is really going on, let alone to intervene. Economists describe the financial crash of 2008 as the most recent pivotal moment of economic contagion, which led to the manufacture of austerity policies to protect against the negative diffusions that we are still processing.[19] More recently still, with the Brexit vote and the election of Trump in 2016 supplying some of the most obvious political coordinates, the rise of populism and fascism and the ongoing migration crisis are frequently characterized with the language of contagion to suggest that swathes of populations are always at risk of sudden penetration and corruption. Prior to the Brexit vote, for instance, then-UK Prime Minister David Cameron set the standard of hyperbole by warning of 'a swarm of people coming across the Mediterranean', while Trump's justification for a US–Mexico border is that Mexicans carry 'tre-mendous infectious disease' in addition to moral and criminal corruption.[20]

---

[18] Loretta Lees, 'Gentrification and Social Mixing: Towards an Inclusive Urban Renaissance?', *Urban Studies* 45, no. 12 (November 2008): 2449–70 (2452).

[19] Gavin Hewitt, 'The Contagion of Austerity', [BBC News blog], 25 May 2010, www.bbc .co.uk/blogs/thereporters/gavinhewitt/2010/05/the_contagion_of_austerity.html, accessed 3 May 2019. It is worth noting, too, that economic contagion is sometimes caused by bio-medical contagion, which negatively impacts theatre business in particular ways. We have witnessed this in the shutting down of theatres in the sixteenth and seventieth centuries due to bubonic plague, and in the early twentieth century owing the Spanish flu; and in the impact of AIDS on the livelihoods of gay men in particular in the latter part of twentieth century.

[20] Cameron's comments to ITV aired on 30 July 2015, while Trump tweeted on 19 June 2018: 'Democrats … want illegal immigrants, no matter how bad they may be, to pour

These images compound the migrant's alignment with disease and pestilence, invoking Nazi-era propaganda that associated Jews with vermin, which was repeated in relation to migrants and refugees in a cartoon by Stanley 'Mac' McMurtry for the *Daily Mail* in November 2015. In light of these analogies, what Emma Cox has described as the 'processional aesthetics' of migrant representation might also be viewed as the aesthetics of streaming or overflow.[21] Instances of email hacking, viral attacks, and misinformation campaigns in recent UK and US elections have enhanced the sense that we now live always at risk of techno-psychological infiltration.[22]

Writing in the *Guardian* in 2017, Jonathan Freedland invoked the language of contagion to describe the mobilization of fascism in global politics, from Trump's America to Brexit Britain. It was precisely to guard against the spread of fascism, Freedland suggests, that the EU was set up: 'Trump and the fascist contagion is reminding us why the EU exists: to ensure that the neighbourhood we live in is never again consumed by the flames of tyranny and hatred.'[23] While populism and fascism may be understood to have a contagious dimension, its proponents typically imagine the source of infection to lie among migrants, asylum seekers, and people of colour, so that taking back control of UK borders, or erecting a wall between Mexico and the US, are offered as defence mechanisms to maintain the healthy sovereign state in the face of external threat.

Sara Ahmed, responding to a British National Front poster that used the language of 'swarm' to claim that '[e]very day of every year, swarms of illegal immigrants and bogus asylum seekers invade Britain', has suggested that narratives of soft touch are used to justify racist and fascist policies. That Britain will not be a 'soft touch', Ahmed writes, 'suggests that the nation's borders and defences are like skin; they are soft, weak, porous

---

into and infest our Country, like MS-13.' For more on contagion's history and relationship to politics, see Fintan Walsh, 'Contagious Performance: Between Illness and Ambience', in *Theatres of Contagion: Transmitting Early Modern to Contemporary Performance*, ed. Fintan Walsh (London, 2019), 3–20, especially 8–9.

[21] Emma Cox, 'Processional Aesthetics and Irregular Transit: Envisioning Refugees in Europe', *Theatre Journal* 69, no. 4 (December 2017): 477–96.

[22] For example, we can think of reports of email hacking and Russian social media interference in the 2017 US election, and the reported role of Cambridge Analytica in harvesting data and circulating misinformation for the same election and the Brexit referendum.

[23] Jonathan Freedland, 'Trump's Fascist Contagion Gives the Anti-Brexit Cause What It Lacked: An Emotional Heart', *Guardian*, 8 September 2017, www.theguardian.com/commentisfree/2017/sep/08/trump-brexit-fascist-european-union-eu, accessed 1 May 2019.

and easily shaped or even bruised by the proximity of others'.[24] To protect itself, and the typically white sovereign subject, Ahmed maintains, the political demand is for a nation to be less porous, harder, to be a nation that is 'less emotional, less open, less easily moved, one that is "hard", or "tough"'.[25] Within this same imaginary, 'nonwhite' people are often perceived to be perpetual migrants – always arriving, never quite belonging – regardless of citizenship, ethnicity, or family history, and therefore vulnerable to the same kind of defensive assault.

It is a short leap from the language of swarms, deployed by Cameron and the National Front, to the language of contagion, which was used to characterize the UK riots in 2011. These were read by many as a symptomatic flare of austerity's effects and frequently described in terms of violence spreading uncontrollably from borough to borough, place to place. Writing in the *Guardian* at the time, epidemiologist Gary Slutkin claimed:

> That violence is an epidemic is not a metaphor; it is a scientific fact. To review the events of the past week in London through this lens, we see a grievance (citizens upset that a civilian has been shot by law enforcement officials) that occurs within in the context of frustration and general dissatisfaction (poverty, unemployment) serving as the precipitating cause for an outbreak of violence. These conditions set the stage for an outbreak in the same way that poor sanitation, overcrowding, and contaminated water set the stage for cholera. Once the event is triggered, it moves from person to person, block to block, town to town. This pattern is not unique to London: it is evident in past riots throughout the US, from Cincinnati to Crown Heights in New York to the Los Angeles riots ignited by the Rodney King beating.[26]

While there may be some truth to Slutkin's diagnosis, there are dangers of understanding phenomena such as riots solely through a contagious lexicon. First, it feeds the idea that the working class and communities of colour are somehow particularly dangerous agents, while concealing the psychic and material conditions that lead to the rise and spread of violence. Second, it risks absorbing other forms of organized dissent, such as protest, into riotous form. Third, it may further sensationalize both protest and violence, contributing to what some critics refer to as riot porn – the fetishistic representation of violence as erupting and spreading. Attempting to resist these dangers, the Canadian artist Stan Douglas's large-scale photographs of the riots cast a rather cool, clear eye over its proceedings, depicting scenes of

[24] Sara Ahmed, *The Cultural Politics of Emotion* (New York, 2004), 2.   [25] Ibid.
[26] Gary Slutkin, 'Gary Slutkin: Rioting Is a Disease Spread from Person to Person – The Key Is to Stop the Infection', *Guardian*, 14 August 2011, www.theguardian.com/uk/2011/aug/14/rioting-disease-spread-from-person-to-person, accessed 1 May 2019.

anticipation and inertia across intricate streetscapes rather than outbursts of violence and its uncontrollable spread.[27]

Both *Misty* and *The Plague* are clearly attuned to the dangers of playing out their dramas of contagion in the context of specific communities, but avoid them by attending to some of psychic and material conditions that give rise to the destruction enacted. Contagion is disentangled from originating in particular social groups and presented as an affective performative that actually produces the very categorizations and conditions it names.

Pathogenic Performativity

While I have suggested that the term 'contagion' has been harnessed to account for a range of social, economic, and political processes, I'm less interested in the descriptive accuracy of these claims than their capacity to actually produce the feelings of invasion and ruin they index. Indeed, it may be more helpful to think of contagion in the politicized context I've sketched out – which takes us from the 2008 global financial crash to the present (though of course it has other historical manifestations and roots too) – less as a process or event and more in light of pathogenic performativity. In medicine, pathogenicity describes the capacity of an agent to cause disease, and in the plays in question, we see this largely attributed to urban communities of colour. But as a discursive tactic, the attribution of pathogenicity strives to create division and pit groups against one another by effecting the sensation it evokes, while occluding the conditions that give rise to certain circumstances, subjectivities, and dispositions, thus also obscuring or redirecting causal responsibility.

The pathogenic performative operates via language, images, and gestures; however, it is primarily an affective technique that works by suggestion to imply that the world is perpetually porous to disease and collapse – politically, culturally, economically – while often placing blame on people of colour and migrant communities, and of course other minorities throughout history too, for it is fundamentally a mobile category. This is not to say that contagion is baseless as a descriptive biological, cultural, or economic phenomenon, but rather that its primary political deployment is psychologically suggestive and divisive, producing fear to qualify defence. Moreover, in provoking anxiety around perceived unhygienic difference, contagious

---

[27] In 2017, Douglas's photographs were included in Tate Modern's *Soul of A Nation: Art in the Age of Black Power* exhibition and at Victoria Miro, London, www.victoria-miro .com/exhibitions/515/, accessed 1 May 2019.

discourse wills the production of cultural homogeneity and impermeability, the foundational impulses of fascist thought.

Pathogenic performativity is evidenced in *Misty* and *The Plague* in each play's preoccupation with the city succumbing to disease. The changing urban environment in the shadow of austerity policies supplies the most particularized conditions for biomedical and cultural annihilation in each play, and of course *The Plague* is more firmly rooted in early twentieth-century fascist critique. Certainly, the plays are troubled with specific and localized instances of racialized labelling and targeting, but they are also concerned on a narrative and referential level with a more nebulous and pervasive sort of contamination that spreads beyond those on whom disease is projected. Crucially, this is not something that happens *to* society (though it may be manipulated top-down), but in a more complicated, sinister way, emerges *from* it, is part of it.

Contagion has long associations with fascism, taking us back to the pioneering work of nineteenth-century social psychologist Gabriel Tarde. Tarde considered imitation central to interpersonal and group dynamics and to the means by which traits and behaviours spread. His ideas were influential to the group analyses of Sigmund Freud, as well as to Gilles Deleuze and Félix Guattari's rhizomatic conceptualizations and Bruno Latour's actor-network theory.[28] More recently, Tarde's ideas have been drawn upon by Tony D. Sampson to describe how feelings, affects, and emotions can spread in digital networks.[29] For Tarde, the group can be manipulated insofar as people are imitative at a psychological and organic level: 'the social being, in the degree that he is social, is essentially imitative, and that imitation plays a role in societies analogous to that of heredity in organic life or that of vibration among inorganic bodies'.[30] According to Tarde's contemporary Gustav Le Bon, the imitative nature of crowds is matched by their suggestibility: 'When defining crowds, we said that one of their general characteristics was an excessive suggestibility, and we have shown to what an extent suggestions are contagious in every human agglomeration; a fact which explains the rapid turning of the sentiments of a crowd in a definite direction.'[31] Freud makes a distinction between the crowd, as disorganized, and

[28] See, for example, Latour's *Reassembling the Social: An Introduction to Actor-Network-Theory* (Oxford, 2005) and Deleuze and Guattari's *A Thousand Plateaus*.

[29] See Tony D. Sampson, *Virality: Contagion Theory in the Age of Networks* (London, 2012).

[30] Gabriel Tarde, *The Laws of Imitation* (1903) (Worcestershire, 2013), 19.

[31] Gustav Le Bon, *The Crowd: A Study of the Popular Mind* (1895) (Scotts Valley, CA, 2010), 18.

the group, as regulated by an authority: 'A group is an obedient herd, which could never live without a master. It has such a thirst for obedience that it submits instinctively to anyone who appoints himself its master.'[32] Tarde's focus on how crowds could be controlled and manipulated made his work of interest to twentieth-century fascist thought; Le Bon's writings were read by Hitler and Mussolini.[33]

The seeds of fascism as group-mind infiltration and synchronization can be found in some of these late nineteenth- and early twentieth-century writings, whose natural conclusion is a form of biocultural cleansing in which people conspire in the destruction not only of individuals but whole communities, cities, even nations via a drive to homogenization. Guattari draws a distinction between fascism on a macro and molecular level. The former emerges from the structures and institutions of the state, he suggests, which saw their most elaborate manifestation in concentration camps, but the latter belong to the chemistry of the individual and society; 'a slow burning fascism in familialism, in school, in racism, in every kind of ghetto, which advantageously makes up for the crematory ovens'.[34] In his introduction to Deleuze and Guattari's *Anti-Oedipus*, which also addresses fascism, Foucault stresses its double nature: 'the fascism of Hitler and Mussolini – which was able to mobilize and use the desire of the masses so effectively – but also the fascism in us all, in our heads and in our everyday behavior, the fascism that causes us to love power, to desire the very thing that dominates and exploits us'.[35]

Misty and *The Plague* are also interested in these macro and micro politics, though they blend and blur. To desire the very thing that dominates and exploits, as Foucault puts it – whether gentrification or cultural domination – is to desire not only another's death but our own too. This alignment brings fascism and capitalism into intimate contact, insofar as capitalism colonizes desire to benefit the profit economy at all cost. As Cameron Crain argues, 'Fascism would seem to be, importantly, a response to capitalism: it

---

[32] Sigmund Freud, 'Group Psychology and the Analysis of the Ego' (1921), in *The Standard Edition of the Complete Psychological Works of Sigmund Freud, vol. 18 (1920–2): Beyond the Pleasure Principle, Group Psychology and Other Works* (London, 2001), 65–144.

[33] For a discussion of Le Bon's work and legacy, see Stephen Reicher, '"The Crowd" Century: Reconciling Practical Success with Theoretical Failure', *British Journal of Social Psychology* 35, no. 4 (June 2011): 535–53.

[34] Félix Guattari, 'Everybody Wants to Be a Fascist', in *Chaosophy: Texts and Interviews, 1972–1977*, ed. Sylvère Lotringer, trans. David L. Sweet, Jarred Becker, and Taylor Adkins (Los Angeles, 2007), 154–75 (171).

[35] Michel Foucault, 'Preface', in *Anti-Oedipus: Capitalism and Schizophrenia* (Minneapolis, 1987), xi–xiv (xiii).

involves an attempt to impose order on the chaos of desire.'[36] This colonization of desire is also what makes fascism dangerous to capitalism, for it is fundamentally a suicidal impulse that would annihilate worlds for an idea of profit. 'Fascism's drive toward homogeneity is ultimately suicidal', Crain continues, 'We are all (only) the same in death.'[37] Like desire, fascism is productive and contagious. 'It passes through the tightest mesh', Guattari tells us, 'it seems to come from the outside, but it finds its energy right at the heart of everyone's desire.'[38] For Guattari, fascism is a 'cancerous body'[39]; for Wilhem Reich, a 'vampire leeched to the body'.[40] In *Misty* and *The Plague*, we too see how disease spreads well beyond those on whom it is projected, ultimately becoming a force of mass destruction – we are all the same only in death.

Audience Affects

Crowds, we have seen, have been considered ripe for contagious behaviour in the form of imitative or suggestible action. But what sort of a gathering is a theatre audience, and how might it conspire with or resist such processes? For Tarde, the theatre audience was indeed a crowd, whose behaviours spread throughout the group: 'Individuals in a crowd have achieved both the highest degree of mutual moral attraction and mutual physical repulsion.... They elbow each other aside, but at the same time they visibly wish to express only those sentiments which are in agreement with those of their neighbours.'[41]

Of course, all audiences vary, not least since Tarde's time, and are often arranged in different ways, sometimes to deliberately heighten awareness or provoke questioning. But many contemporary immersive modes at least strive to engineer blanket group feeling and coercive behaviour, with which theatre studies' investment in affect has sometimes uncritically corroborated. Affective literacy is important – that is, studied attentiveness to the production of both feeling and its discourses – but broad-based interpretations and

---

[36] Cæmeron Crain, 'Microfascism', *The Mantle*, 5 June 2013, www.mantlethought.org/philosophy/microfascism, accessed 1 May 2019.

[37] Ibid.   [38] Guattari, 'Everybody Wants to Be a Fascist', 171.

[39] Gilles Deleuze and Félix Guattari, *A Thousand Plateaus: Capitalism and Schizophrenia* (1980), trans. Brian Massumi (Minneapolis, 1987), 215.

[40] Wilhelm Reich, *The Mass Psychology of Fascism* (1933), trans. Vincent R. Carfagno (New York, 1970), xvii.

[41] Gabriel Tarde, 'The Public and the Crowd' (1901), in *Gabriel Tarde on Communication and Social Influence: Selected Papers*, ed. with intro. by Terry N. Clark (London, 1969), 277–96 (291).

deployments of affect as assumed valuable shared sensation, many of which draw on Antonin Artaud's plague-inspired writings (which also inspired Deleuze and Guattari),[42] run the risk of obscuring detail, desire, and power relations. Of course, Bertolt Brecht originally alerted us to some of these dangers by developing a dramaturgical form that might counter theatre's naturalizing tendencies in the early twentieth century, against the backdrop of Weimar fascism. As we find ourselves again in a time when right-wing political establishments draw deeply on affect's fascist potential to shape feelings and moods, *Misty* and *The Plague* invite us to think more critically about the machinery of political and theatrical affect, and theatre's capacity to intervene its own tools.

While both productions allude to the projection of pathogenicity on communities of colour, they resist this themselves (except perhaps, according to *Misty*, through theatre's own inevitable collusion with gentrification and classism). This largely happens narratively, via the ways in which we see how suggestive language and imagery work to engineer this pathogenic affect. This power is compounded by the fact that neither production actually shows any of the biomedical crises mentioned; rather, they are conjured into being mainly through direct address or recounting. Each production exposes the power and fraudulence of other forms of public discourse that assign pathogenicity to specific groups through the performative production of contagious affect. In their narrative-driven, direct-address modes, both productions seem to offer theatre as a form of witnessing, of testimony, that asserts the need to cut through the miasma of dominant discourse to hear the stories of specific communities and histories in their own aesthetic terms and dramaturgical forms. In this regard they correspond with the distinction Teresa Brennan makes between negative and positive affect, with the latter conforming to a form of living attention, which she associates with love and joy, that 'directs positive feelings towards the other by attending to the specificity of the other (rather than seeing him or her through idealizing or demonizing projections'.[43]

According to Cottard in *The Plague*, what's needed to intercept the virulence of the contagion is an earthquake to kill everybody.[44] A more

---

[42] Artaud famously aligned the theatre with plague, for its visceral capacity to work on and through the body (rather than language), awakening repressed impulses and sensations. While Artaud's interest in plague is chiefly metaphorical, the essay 'The Theater and the Plague' opens with a dream of an actual plague in Marseille in 1720, before tracking other occurrences in the fourteenth, sixteenth, and nineteenth centuries. See Antonin Artaud, *The Theater and Its Double* (1938), trans. Mary Caroline Richards (New York, 1958).

[43] Teresa Brennan, *The Transmission of Affect* (New York, 2004), 32.

[44] Bartlett, *The Plague*, 21.

modest proposal comes from Tarrou, who maintains the need for wilful forgetting: 'You think about bathing in the sea – thick as velvet, supple and smooth as a wild animal. You think about swimming naked and at night, with the stars and a friend.'[45] His vision extends to imagine a world in which freedom is experienced as the pleasurable rather than pathologized synchronization of rhythm – sensation shared rather than blocked: 'Swim till you're far from the world, and breathing together the same rhythm, and free of absolutely everything.'[46] His words are obliquely echoed in Kene's closing gambit in *Misty*, a powerful freestyle refrain in which the now topless performer champions his so-called 'jungle shit', which raises most of the audience to its feet. It's these rhythms led by Kene and his band that eventually take over the production and become its closing gift. The final impression both productions offer is that while the attribution of pathogenicity to certain individuals and groups is often a pernicious form of policing and containment, cultures are irrepressibly transmissible in all sorts of enriching ways.

Conclusion

Theatre has long been considered a site for the transmission of feelings, behaviours, illnesses, and ideas. In contemporary theatre about London, contagion captures the city fraught with uncontainable sociopolitical ills. While chiefly played out as a biocultural phenomenon affecting the whole city, the blame for destruction is largely directed at people of colour and migrant communities. In this regard, the two plays discussed here resonate with contemporary political rhetoric that mobilizes contagion as a category to produce fears of everything from migration and cultural takeover to crime spread and economic meltdown. However, whereas some strands of political discourse would have us accept contagion as a descriptive, even diagnostic category, these productions help us see it more accurately as an affective performative that produces the sensation named in the service of politically legitimated social othering and cultural cleansing. Our current political circumstances demand of us finely honed skills in affective literacy and criticality, as well as an appreciation of and openness to those forms of transmission and exchange that are not predicated upon the paranoid production of pathology.

[45] Ibid., 55.   [46] Ibid., 55.

Suggested Reading

Artaud, Antonin. *The Theater and Its Double* (1938), trans. Mary Caroline Richards. New York, 1958.

Brennan, Teresa. *The Transmission of Affect.* New York, 2004.

Campkin, Ben. *Remaking London: Decline and Regeneration in Urban Culture.* New York, 2013.

Deleuze, Gilles, and Félix Guattari. *A Thousand Plateaus: Capitalism and Schizophrenia* (1980), trans. Brian Massumi. Minneapolis, 1987.

Goddard, Lynette. *Contemporary Black British Playwrights: Margins to Mainstream.* Basingstoke, 2015.

Guattari, Félix. *Chaosophy: Texts and Interviews, 1972–1977,* ed. Sylvère Lotringer, trans. David L. Sweet, Jarred Becker, and Taylor Adkins. Los Angeles, 2007.

Harvie, Jen. 'Brand London 2012 and "The Heart of East London": Competing Urban Agendas at the 2012 Games'. *Contemporary Theatre Review* 23, no. 4 (2013): 486–501.

Le Bon, Gustav. *The Crowd: A Study of the Popular Mind* (1895). Scotts Valley, CA, 2010.

Reich, Wilhelm. *The Mass Psychology of Fascism* (1933), trans. Vincent R. Carfagno. New York, 1970.

Sampson, Tony D. *Virality: Contagion Theory in the Age of Networks.* London, 2012.

Tarde, Gabriel. *The Laws of Imitation* (1903). Worcestershire, 2013.

Walsh, Fintan, ed. *Theatres of Contagion: Transmitting Early Modern to Contemporary Performance.* London: Bloomsbury, 2019.

8

JON VENN

Theatres of Mental Health

The strands and complications of contemporary mental health – coupled with the immense variety of theatrical engagement – pose a challenge to anyone attempting to detail the relationship between theatre and mental health. The issue of mental health is labyrinthine, not confined to any single problem, splaying out in multiple directions. Part of this difficulty is the fundamental heterogeneity of mental disorders themselves. Each manifested or identified 'disorder' – such as major depression, post-traumatic stress, schizophrenia – brings a different genealogy, societal stigma, legal consequence, relationship to care, and etiology (the explanation of the cause of the disorder).

The expansion of categories of mental disorder has been a core component in the development of mental health and its claims as a medical science. Across the post-war period, the *Diagnostic and Statistical Manual of Mental Disorders* (DSM) and *International Classification of Disease* (ICD) have seen an exponential increase in size. Nikolas Rose suggests these developments are bound up with two central shifts: the emergence of neuroscience as an explanatory model and of psychopharmacology as a mode of treatment. For Rose, this represents a shift in diagnosis as a process: 'The broad categories of the start of the twentieth century – depression, schizophrenia, neurosis – are no longer adequate.... The psychiatric gaze is no longer molar but molecular.'[1] Under this view, psychiatric diagnosis has shifted from judging the concentration and intensity of broad categories of mental disorder to identifying the precise classification from an ever-expanding taxonomy.

The significance of psychiatric diagnosis, or what it constitutes, has been contested. For Michel Foucault, references to nosology, to particular identifiable illnesses or disorders, are immaterial: 'I think all this is only a superficial and secondary activity in relation to the real question posed in every diagnosis of madness, which is not whether it is this or that form of madness,

---

[1] Nikolas Rose, *The Politics of Life Itself: Biomedicine, Power, and Subjectivity in the Twenty-First Century* (Princeton, 2007), 199.

but whether it is or is not madness.'[2] Diagnosis, in the context of psychiatric power, is simply the power to judge who is or is not 'mad'; the specificity of the classification is irrelevant compared with the broader context of madness. However, Foucault's perspective seems simplistic; the legitimization of psychiatry as a medical science has been predicated upon its analogy with other forms of medicine. The creation of a nosology of psychiatric disorder, the mapping-out of madness into a multitude of mental disorders, and the ability to attribute specific disorders from identifiable symptoms have played a core role in psychiatry's claim to legitimacy.

This chapter examines the potential of theatre as a means to examine the process of psychiatric diagnosis. The staging of diagnosis has often been critiqued as a potentially regressive act that simply replicates the power structures of the diagnostic gaze. In *Unmaking Mimesis*, Elin Diamond observes how the dramaturgical implications of diagnosis can reproduce expectations of gendered performance; she suggests that 'Ibsenite realism guarantees its legitimacy by endowing the fallen woman of popular melodrama with the symptoms and etiology of the hysteric.'[3] For Diamond, Ibsen's plays draw upon the process of psychiatric diagnosis, replicating its power structures and its investigative dramaturgy to facilitate the shift from melodrama to realism.

While Diamond provides a powerful example of how the staging of diagnosis simply results in the replication of psychiatric power, I am interested in how theatre can, potentially, move beyond such a replication. I explore examples of contemporary British theatre in which the staging of diagnosis does not lead to such a reification, but rather offers a site through which to think 'upon' rather than 'with' diagnosis. Anna Furse's *Augustine (Big Hysteria)* (1993), Joe Penhall's *Blue/Orange* (2000), and Lucy Prebble's *The Effect* (2012) stage the process of diagnosis in order to offer a critique of it. This chapter suggests that these plays facilitate a step back from the diagnostic process and initiate a fundamentally diagnostic question – one that quickly dissolves within the social, historical, and bureaucratic context of the diagnosis. The plays become a dramaturgic interrogation of diagnosis itself.

Concepts of Diagnosis

For some, a radical shift in terms of mental health can be achieved only by moving away from the diagnostic; Anna Harpin advocates 'a shift from the

---

[2] Michel Foucault, *Psychiatric Power: Lectures at the College de France*, trans. G. Burchell (Basingstoke, 2003), 266.
[3] Elin Diamond, *Unmaking Mimesis: Essays on Feminism and Theatre* (London, 1997), 4.

fixity of identity to a fluidity experience as a model of thinking ... from "I *am* schizophrenic" to "I hear voices"; from "I *am* bipolar" to "I sometimes experience joyful cosmic connections that other people do not"'.[4] Under this understanding, diagnosis is a process that isolates and transmogrifies a span of experience to a static topology of pathology. While I have sympathies with such a position, this chapter is not concerned with what psychiatric diagnosis should be. Rather, it is interested in an investigation of what diagnosis constitutes, as a social technology that remains a core component in the legitimization of psychiatry as a science, and how theatre can cast a light on its processes.

Diagnosis is often framed as a denotative process: a straightforward act of naming, of providing the correct definition based upon the underlying symptoms. The doctor is a detective who studies the behaviour of the patient for clues, finds the solution, and ascribes the correct name. In contrast, I am interested in presumptions underlying diagnosis as an *act*: while diagnosis is an act of naming, it is a naming that occurs within a sociohistorical environment. Diagnosis is a performance. Specifically, diagnosis is a speech act, as defined by J. L. Austin, in which the language of diagnosis does not merely 'describe' the world, but fundamentally alters it. Austin himself termed diagnosis as 'verdictive', as passing a verdict.[5] As a result, the performance of diagnosis reshapes the social worlds of both doctor and patient. To diagnose a psychiatric patient is not merely to attempt to describe their mental health disorder; it is to imbue the body with a label, authenticated through expertise, with potential legal and medical repercussions. To be diagnosed with a mental health disorder can give you access to certain rights, in terms of both state benefit and antidiscrimination law. However, it can also expose the individual to the potential of stigma and discrimination, particularly for disorders such as schizophrenia and borderline personality disorder. A diagnosis can potentially give access to new forms of care and medication; however, it can also be used as a pretext for institutionalization and sectioning. Diagnosis, as a speech act, at once draws upon the social world (leaning upon institutional authority, possible modes of treatment, existing categorizations) and reshapes it.

The diagnosis does not simply 'name' the patient's ailment; it can actively shift the lives and experiences of the diagnosed. For the writer and schizophrenic Esmé Weijun Wang, her diagnosis provides comfort 'because it provides a framework – a community, a lineage – and, if luck is afoot,

---

[4] Anna Harpin, *Madness, Art, and Society: Beyond Illness* (London, 2019), 11, emphasis in original.
[5] J. L. Austin, *How to Do Things with Words* (Oxford, 1962), 152.

a treatment or cure'.[6] Diagnosis can give an explanatory framework for those confused by their experiences of extreme distress and can give access to provisional communities. However, studies have also suggested negative responses to diagnosis, finding it confining or leading to social stigma, with one participant stating: 'It's horrible having a label, having a label done to you.'[7] Alongside the experience of being diagnosed are the manners in which diagnosis becomes 'performed' by those who are diagnosed; as Chris Millard puts it, 'how diagnosis intervenes upon a person's sense of self, and how that self might change'.[8] Ian Hacking has written extensively about how psychiatric diagnosis results in a performance of psychiatric disorder, establishing the two 'technologies' of 'Making Up People' and 'Looping' through which diagnosis is inculcated by the patient.[9] Diagnosis is not merely felt: it structures the patient.

To unfold psychiatric diagnosis is therefore to examine two interlinked components: the social and conceptual lines upon which the diagnostician draws, and the manners in which diagnosis is then written upon the body and experience of the diagnosed. The plays discussed in this chapter slip from a purely denotative mode of explaining diagnosis into one that explores the concerns of diagnosis as a speech act. I suggest that theatre can reveal the historical, bureaucratic, and economic motivations and assumptions upon which diagnosis is made and experienced. In this regard, this chapter suggests that theatre can have an active role in unfolding diagnosis as a performance, for both the doctor and patient, and resisting the understanding of diagnosis as simply a denotation or revelation.

Augustine (Big Hysteria): A Genealogy of Diagnosis

Hysteria stands as a core example of a diagnosis that was formed around intersecting social expectations of gender, behaviour, and madness. The diagnosis of hysteria was popularized during Jean-Martin's Charcot's reign at the Parisian teaching hospital, the Salpêtrière. Charcot's period at the

---

[6] Esme Weijun Wang, *The Collected Schizophrenias* (London, 2019), 5.

[7] Amorette Perkins, Joseph Ridler, Daniel Browes, Guy Peryer, Caitlin Notley, and Corinna Hackmann, 'Experiencing Mental Health Diagnosis: A Systematic Review of Service User, Clinician, and Carer Perspectives across Clinical Settings', *Lancet Psychiatry* 5, no. 9 (April 2018): 747–64 (757).

[8] Chris Millard, 'Concepts, Diagnosis and the History of Medicine: Historicising Ian Hacking and Munchausen's Syndrome', *Social History of Medicine* 30, no. 3 (2016): 567–89 (568).

[9] Ian Hacking, *Rewriting the Soul: Multiple Personality and the Sciences of Memory* (Princeton, 1995).

Salpêtrière was marked by his proclamations and theories concerning hysteria, as he forged a detailed account of hysteria as an illness, with stages of epileptic fits, contortions, and hallucinations before a slow regaining of consciousness. His public seminars, in which he would demonstrate symptoms and perform hypnosis of patients, became famous; attendees included figures such as William James and the actor Sarah Bernhardt. Anna Furse's *Augustine (Big Hysteria)* details the experiences of Augustine, Charcot's most famous patient, during her period at the Salpêtrière. Augustine survived sexual abuse and rape as a young woman at age thirteen, before her mother took her to the Salpêtrière. While there, she became the star of Charcot's Grand Hysteria, the main attraction of the public seminars, and 'was the perfect archetype of hysteria, achieving leading lady status in Charcot's medical freakshow'.[10] Eventually, she would escape the hospital, dressed as a man.

Furse's play exists within a wider lineage of 'plays of hysteria', from Hélène Cixous's *Dora: A Portrait of Hysteria* (1976) to Kim Morrisey's *Dora: A Case of Hysteria* (1993), works that sought to reimagine and investigate the legacy of 'hysteria' as a diagnosis. The gendered aspect of 'hysteria' is well documented, including its etymology in the Greek wandering womb, and the sexual abuse inflicted on patients. The legacy of hysteria has been noted as central in the dynamics of gender in psychiatry, leading Elaine Showalter to term madness 'the female malady'.[11] Charcot, in a notorious lithograph, would propagate the patriarchal dynamics visually: the knowing male doctor gesticulating over the unknowing female patient. The diagnosis of hysteria is, thereby, legitimized through a concoction of gender and theatricality.

Furse's representation of the historical circumstances of hysteria does not, inherently, offer a radical perspective on contemporary diagnoses. To stage the past as a place of abjection can be to partition it, to closet it away from having a lineage to the present: that was then, but this is now and things are different. In her examination of depictions of the asylum in contemporary horror, Harpin suggests that 'the historical othering that takes place in representations of asylums evidences an implicit desire to consign psychiatric failure and cruelty to the (falsely) distant past'.[12] If history can be a useful tool through which to expose the sociohistorical contingencies of the

[10] Anna Furse, 'Augustine (Big Hysteria): Writing the Body', *Theatre Review* 2, no. 1 (1994): 25–34 (28).
[11] Elaine Showalter, *The Female Malady: Women, Madness, and English Culture, 1830–1980* (London, 1987).
[12] Anna Harpin, 'Revisiting the Puzzle Factory: Cultural Representations of Psychiatric Asylums', *Interdisciplinary Science Reviews* 38, no. 4 (2013): 335–50 (341).

diagnostic process, it can also hold a danger of sectioning off past abuses from the present. The sexist tropes of hysteria can become a cushion for the present, rather than implicating a genealogy of gendered violence in psychiatry.

Furse evades such a static historical depiction through adding fictional components to Augustine's life; her role is not to chronicle the past but to remember through reimagination. She invents an encounter between Sigmund Freud and Augustine (their presence at the Salpêtrière was separated by a decade). In part, this allows for a juxtaposition of their approaches to Charcot and Freud, their debates concerning hysteria, of Charcot's concern with the spectacle in contrast to Freud's obsession with listening. But it also allows the piece to interpret hysteria not as a moment in psychiatric history but as part of a wider genealogy. The piece interrogates psychiatric violence on women, the silencing of their abuse, common to both Charcot and Freud. Charcot shows no concern with the testimony of the women he diagnoses, only the showmanship of his weekly seminars. Freud, in contrast, listens attentively, but his formulation of the psychoanalytic denies the reality of sexual abuse. Furse demonstrates the legacy of sexism in psychiatric diagnosis as persistent across generations. She proactively attempts to implicate the audience within this diagnostic gaze and its inherent violence, noting that 'the audience is deliberately placed in the role of voyeur'.[13] They are situated as the attentive attendees to Charcot's lectures, encouraged to unpack the question of Augustine's hysteria, its cause and its performance. While acknowledging the dangers of simply replicating patriarchal power, Furse suggests that 'when all parties concerned are made aware of their function, this kind of role-play becomes most fruitful for challenging perception'.[14]

Furse uses theatre as a mode to imagine the circumstances, memories, and lives bound behind the archival remnants. She not only uses Charcot's famous photographs of Augustine; she stages their creation. Far from recorded instances of truth, the stillness of nineteenth-century photography is revealed whereby the slow exposure requires a single stance to be maintained for extended periods of time. At one point in the play, Augustine expresses a desire to see the photos, and is shocked at how she appears. Freud attests to the veracity of the photograph, that 'the camera doesn't lie', to which Augustine responds, 'People do. Their eyes do.'[15] Augustine disturbs the archival and historical claims on her hysteria.

---

[13] Furse, '*Augustine (Big Hysteria)*: Writing the Body', 31.   [14] Ibid.
[15] Anna Furse, *Augustine (Big Hysteria)* (London, 1997), 62.

Beyond a disturbance of this archival recreation, Furse is using this photographic restaging to demonstrate how the diagnosis of hysteria is performed. Across the play, Augustine is shown to consciously identify the prompts of Charcot and respond to them. However, in the staging of the photographs, Furse plays upon the inherent component of duration in performance. Staging these photographs, introducing a temporal component to their creation, allows us to more keenly anticipate Augustine's hysteria as a performance, one requiring exceptional endurance and skill. Far from the reproduction of the past, it forms an active engagement, becoming an act of memory as radical political engagement. Charcot would use these photos to uphold an objective portrayal of symptoms; photos would be labelled as representing the different 'stages' of hysteria. But, through the performance of the photography, these catalogued and static symptoms are reframed as a performance by the patient. For Furse, Augustine's photo-performance reflects how she maps out the diagnosis thrust upon her: 'this is Augustine's particularly interesting message – she takes on the qualities by which she herself is described by others'.[16]

Furse's understanding of Augustine's performance of her diagnosis is not of capitulation to the social structures of the doctors. For Furse, Augustine ingested the feature of the diagnosis, before creating a performance of her own: 'This I believe was her art – self-parody.'[17] Far from the structures of governmentality or 'looping' suggested by Foucault and Hacking, Furse sees the performance of the diagnosed as agentic. In Christina Wald's terms, as Augustine frees herself from the doctor's control, it is not 'a renewed integrity beyond performativity but rather a new performance'.[18] The finale of the play – Augustine dressed as a man in clothes stolen from Freud and Charcot – suggests she has taken her diagnosis and played upon it. Her exit from the stage is an exit from the gaze of others, both of her doctors and of the audience.

In *Augustine (Big Hysteria)*, Furse exposes the historical legacy of hysteria, the genealogy of patriarchal violence, and how psychiatric diagnosis has been forged through the denial (or overlooking) of the sexual abuse of women. The play dramatizes the diagnosis of hysteria by both Charcot and Freud, representing violent forms of spectacle and listening and situating the audience within these diagnostic processes. However, the performance of the diagnosis gives way to an interrogation of the historical processes behind diagnosis. The performance of the photographs becomes a microcosm of this

---

[16] Furse, 'Augustine (Big Hysteria): Writing the Body', 27.   [17] Ibid.
[18] Christina Wald, *Hysteria, Trauma and Melancholia: Performative Maladies in Contemporary Anglophone Drama* (London, 2007), 60.

process, where the duration of nineteenth-century photo-performance subverts archival imaginations of the veracity of hysteria. Augustine wears her diagnosis almost as a parody.

Blue/Orange: Interrogating Bureaucracies of Care

If *Augustine (Big Hysteria)* demonstrates how performance can reveal a genealogical approach to diagnosis, what does it mean to interrogate diagnosis in contemporaneous structures? Joe Penhall, playwright of *Some Voices* (1994) and *Blue/Orange*, has specialized in dramatizing the bureaucratic structures of 1990s psychiatry. Previously, Penhall had worked as a writer for the *Hammersmith Guardian*; during this time, he encountered the disastrous consequences of the National Health Service and Community Care Act 1990, a policy that called for psychiatric patients to be treated in the familiar structures of their family and friends, rather than contained in psychiatric units. Penhall, however, encountered a series of bereft and vulnerable individuals who had been abandoned by the government, cared (or not cared) for by a community that was incapable of the task given.

In *Some Voices*, Penhall excavates the 'community' in which the patient is meant to be receiving care: it is a community broken by underinvestment, familial tension, and violence. The political and dramaturgic role of the play is one of exposure, to reveal the vacuity of the abstract, ideal communities the Conservative government posited while pursuing fiscal gains. *Blue/Orange* analyzes how this practice shapes and alters the diagnostic process. The play is set entirely in a room on a psychiatric ward, while a patient, Christopher, waits to be released from his involuntary admission. We never see the outside 'community' that Christopher wishes to rejoin. Rather, the dramatic question of the piece is the argument between the doctors Robert and Bruce concerning Christopher's diagnosis: Does he have borderline personality disorder or is he schizophrenic?

As with *Augustine (Big Hysteria)*, the audience are encouraged to participate in this diagnostic process. A range of 'symptoms' are variously revealed, withheld, or reinterpreted. Christopher claims he is the son of Idi Amin – only to reveal later he suspects his father to be Muhammad Ali. The original production was staged like a boxing ring, with rising seating set in the round, with the audience voyeurs to the diagnosis-as-combat between Bruce and Robert. Watson sees this scenography as reflecting the architecture of older medical buildings, noting that 'the audience looked down on the claustrophobic space of the examining room from vertiginously raked seating that surrounded the stage on all sides like an old-fashioned operating or anatomical theatre'.[19] The audience are encouraged to compare and evaluate Robert's and Bruce's varying diagnoses, to partake in the diagnosis itself.

The play, however, quickly shifts from the accuracy of diagnosis to the desirability of care. For Robert, Christopher's diagnosis of borderline personality disorder facilitates a return to his community. If this is partly motivated by his political leanings to the theories of R. D. Laing, it is consolidated by economic benefits, and the availability of one more bed. For Bruce, the diagnosis of schizophrenia is more accurate, as he relies upon his faith in the various labels of modern psychiatry. However, as the play develops, we see Bruce as also believing in an imperative of confinement. His diagnosis, and his pursuit of the diagnosis, emerges from a wish to keep Christopher under direct observation and care, so he can be regularly monitored.

Care is a central purpose to diagnosis and is, as Caroline Whitbeck states, 'aimed at creating the best outcome for the patient'.[20] For Annemarie Jutel, 'diagnosis guides medical care. It organises the clinical picture, determines intervention, and provides a framework for medical education.'[21] The epistemological operations of psychiatric diagnosis (of ascribing a psychiatric classification to a patient) are thereby primarily valuable in instrumental terms; the diagnosis is only as useful as our ability to treat the condition. Robert's and Bruce's argumentation concerning Christopher's diagnosis reveals how, under current structures of psychiatric diagnosis, the veracity of diagnosis becomes subservient to the political underpinnings of care. In Blue/Orange, both Robert and Bruce focus on models of care, with diagnosis a means to this end. Robert claims his process is more traditional – 'That's the ICD 10 for you. Observation and interview.'[22] However, when asked to justify the diagnosis, he quickly shifts to desired care, saying that 'we believe this patient will receive the treatment he needs in the community'.[23] Penhall thereby demonstrates how any psychiatric diagnosis is necessarily embedded within, and emerges from, bureaucratic systems of care. The questions of the 'accuracy' of Christopher's diagnosis are quickly subsumed by the question of treatment.

Penhall is alert to the manners in which the act of diagnosis shapes and alters the patient. At the beginning of the play, Christopher is articulate, providing witty challenges to Bruce. However, across the piece, caught

[19] Ariel Watson, 'Cries of Fire: Psychotherapy in Contemporary British and Irish Drama', Modern Drama 51, no. 2 (Summer 2008): 188–210 (201).

[20] Caroline Whitbeck, 'What Is Diagnosis? Some Critical Reflections', Metamedicine 2, no. 3 (1981): 319–29 (326).

[21] Annemarie Jutel, 'Sociology of Diagnosis: A Preliminary Review', Sociology of Health and Illness 31, no. 2 (2009): 278–99 (279).

[22] Joe Penhall, Blue/Orange (London, 2000), 94.   [23] Ibid.

between the two doctors and their competing diagnoses, Christopher is gradually silenced by their debate. The play is pessimistic about Christopher's ability to navigate the power structures of contemporary psychiatry. Christopher is a young black man with acute mental health difficulties: there is no realistic prospect of him adopting tactics to circumvent or resist the diagnosis and treatment that are determined for him. Far from an active contender in a competition, Christopher is the ball kicked between Bruce and Robert. In the final scene, Christopher's sense of self has been fundamentally ruptured by the diagnostic debate, as he exclaims, 'the thoughts I have are not my thoughts'.[24] Diagnosis, as warped by the bureaucratic wrangling of the two doctors, has actively harmed a vulnerable patient.

The politics of race adds further dimensions to the silencing of Christopher. The legacy of the relationship of race and madness is long and complicated, including the legacy of psychiatry as a colonial tool (for instance, the use of craniology in framing 'race' as natural and 'white' as inherently superior), and *Blue/Orange* stages a contemporary unveiling of this history in relation to Britain's black diaspora. Race inflects every concern of *Blue/Orange*, from diagnostic criteria to the containment of Christopher. Both doctors express racist sentiments, whether through the ethnocentric stereotypes of Robert or Bruce's crass description of Robert's research as 'R. D. Laing in a gorilla suit'.[25] Crucial, however, is that racism itself is deployed as yet another tactic between Bruce and Robert; in the political machinations of psychiatric diagnosis, Christopher's race is simply another facet to be exploited. Diagnosis, and the silencing of Christopher, is enacted through white supremacy.

If Penhall reveals some of the philosophical quandaries of psychiatric diagnosis, his plays are less interested in an investigation of their epistemological underpinnings than in how these debates are mobilized for fundamentally political aims. In *Blue/Orange*, the relationship between diagnosis and care is warped by the bureaucratic system within which the doctors operate. Diagnosis results in the deterioration of Christopher's identity, representing how the multivalent levels of diagnosis as a speech act, as crossing medical, legal, and bureaucratic contexts, can potentially result in the silencing of the patient.

The Effect: Causation and Diagnosis

The Effect follows the experience of two test subjects, Connie and Tristan, as they voluntarily participate in a clinical drug trial for a new antidepressant.

[24] Ibid., 104. [25] Ibid., 92.

As the play develops, the two subjects fall in love. However, is their mutual attraction natural or has it been instigated by the drug? Unlike *Blue/Orange* and *Augustine (Big Hysteria)*, the two test subjects in *The Effect* are not identified with any form of psychiatric disorder. The character with the closest proximity to depression is, ironically, Doctor James, who monitors and measures the test subjects. Rather, the play interrogates the diagnosed 'madness' of Connie and Tristan's love. In part, this reflects a social readjustment with mental health. As mental health awareness has improved, 'madness' has ceased to be solely defined by extremities of mental distress requiring sectioning or direct care. Regardless of whether we understand the rise in mental health problems as a genuine increase due to contemporary social pressures, increased reported numbers due to a reduction in social stigma, or a reconfiguration of previously deemed 'ordinary' mental distress as pathological, our relationship to mental health has broadened away from the remote and confined space of the asylum.

However, the play also facilitates a theatrical investigation of a core component of diagnosis: the aetiology of mental disorder. Unlike the previous two plays, the diagnostic gaze of the play is not concerned with the identification of a particular malady (hysteria, borderline personality disorder, schizophrenia) within an established nosology. Rather, diagnosis concerns the origins of behaviour: Is their love a 'natural' response to mutual attraction or a 'madness' brought on by the antidepressants? As its title suggests, this is a play that is centrally concerned with causation and consequence, and the way in which the search for causation is variously exploited and affecting.

Offering a causational account is one of the key purposes of psychiatric diagnosis; as Hane Htut Maung notes, the explanatory component of psychiatric diagnosis is most commonly causational, as in 'the diagnosis explains the patient's data by indicating its cause'.[26] However, it also offers one of the chief epistemological challenges to psychiatry: How do we distinguish the first cause of a psychiatric disorder? At the beginning of *The Effect*, Connie and Dr James discuss sadness and depression, and the question of when one fades into the other. Connie expresses the common view that depression is distinguished from sadness on a neurological basis, as 'an abnormal amount of chemical – in the brain or anything'.[27] This common

---

[26] Hane Htut Maung, 'The Functions of Diagnoses in Medicine and Psychiatry,' in *The Bloomsbury Companion to Philosophy of Psychiatry*, ed. Serife Tekin (London, 2019), 507–26 (509).

[27] Lucy Prebble, *The Effect* (London, 2012), 5.

belief is then challenged across the play: Is such chemical imbalance the cause of depression or is depression the cause of such imbalance?

This debate over causation becomes the central quandary of the play: locating the cause of Connie and Tristan's affection. This fundamentally diagnostic question is posed directly to the audience. Information is provided or withdrawn; the audience is informed that one of the volunteers is on a placebo, but the stage directions clearly state that 'which scan belongs to which volunteer is unknown'.[28] The audience is informed that Tristan is on the placebo, only to be informed later he was not. Through this narrative twist, the audience is led to one understanding of the characters' actions, only to be informed that it was wrong. The play encourages the audience to read, interpret, and guess the cause of the characters' behaviour, mimicking the approach of the clinical psychologists on stage as well as in real life.

However, concern for causation in *The Effect* is tethered to capitalist exploitation. Between the two perspectives of the doctors is a clear expression of how profit motivation distorts our perspective. Beyond a purely epistemological interrogation of the aetiology of mental health (namely, to what extent we can establish causation from a neurological perspective), the play demonstrates how such an interrogation is distorted by market forces. The debates between Dr James and Toby are revealed to have personal or economic motivation. Dr James, attempting to evade medication and the experience of her depression, seeks to deny the efficacy of the drug whose trials she is supposed to be impartially leading. Toby, pharmaceutical businessman and the sponsor of the trial, argues for the discovery of a 'love potion', seeing potential financial benefit. The 'effects' are manipulated and rebranded, as Dr James remarks of undesirable responses to the drug: 'They're not side effects, Toby, they're just effects *you* can't sell.'[29] In this, Prebble echoes developments in contemporary psychiatry, where causation and medication are enmeshed, and contemporary attitudes 'weld psychiatric etiology to psychopharmacology'.[30]

If the aetiology of their condition is sparked through capitalist motivation, the anxieties of capitalism are passed on to the lives and experiences of Connie and Tristan. Vicky Angelaki notes that 'Prebble locates love and depression within a purely individualized and neoliberalist framework'.[31] The anxieties of Connie and Tristan are an extension of capitalist structures; the confusion of 'real' feelings with manufactured ones is possible only within the pharmaceutical testing chamber, a microcosm of the

---

[28] Ibid., 42.   [29] Ibid., 78.   [30] Rose, *The Politics of Life Itself*, 200.
[31] Vicky Angelaki, *Social and Political Theatre in 21st-Century Britain: Staging Crisis* (London, 2019), 240.

collaboration between psychiatry and capitalist forces. Prebble situates diagnosis within a capitalistic setting that proliferates anxiety. As with *Augustine (Big Hysteria)* and *Blue/Orange*, this anxiety is experienced and performed through the bodies of the diagnosed. *The Effect* repeatedly returns to the measurement and assessment of Connie and Tristan's bodies, demonstrating the relentless measurement and control of the diagnosed body in extremis. Scans are incessantly performed on Connie and Tristan, who are displayed as automatons to the audience, their arms shifting to stock positions of *The Vitruvian Man*. Under this, their bodies are schematized and static, observed rather than active. This observational function then becomes internalized, in an echo of Bentham's and Foucault's panopticon; the incessant search for causation (as a psychiatric and capitalist desire) causes a crisis for their relationship. *The Effect* represents the diagnostic gaze as a process of governmentality, of the external gaze internalized. Yet, unlike previous plays, this is then starkly contrasted by spaces in which the pair are free to move and shift, outside the watchful eye of the testing centre. Ironically, in one scene, they escape and find freedom in a dilapidated and abandoned Victorian asylum: they enjoy and explore the space, running around the edges, doing handstands. Under the watchful eye of the testing chamber, their bodies are observed; in the asylum, they are observing, viewing their bodies as things that can enact and do. When they eventually have sex, it is possible only by taking off their heart monitors and evading the gaze of the experiment.

The Effect, as with the two previous plays, encourages a diagnostic gaze, only for it to be dissolved in the play's wider conceptual and political dramaturgy. The question of the cause of Connie and Tristan's attraction is framed as the crux of the play, the two doctors incessantly scrutinizing their bodies and their behaviour, the audience encouraged to 'solve' this quandary. But the play steps back from this enquiry, demonstrating instead how the search for the aetiology of behaviour is co-opted by capitalist and market forces. In this regard, the play facilitates a more self-reflexive examination of diagnosis and looks back upon its own looking.

Conclusion

Diagnosis, across all these plays, is never settled. At points, these plays deliberately tease a simplistic dramatic question out of standardized diagnostics: Is Augustine a genuine hysteric? Is Christopher schizophrenic? Are Connie and Tristan mad? The plays are often staged in a manner that encourages such diagnosis from the audience, using dramatic irony to provide clues to a guessing game about the bodies of the diagnosed. The plays can initially appear to offer simply a staging of the diagnostic gaze, a reproduction of the power structures that underlie psychiatric diagnosis.

However, these questions are dissolved into a wider enquiry of diagnosis itself, a gaze that looks back on itself. The psychiatric diagnosis shifts and warps according to political and social contexts. It possesses a genealogy, a fraught relationship to care, and a troubled aetiology. Far from simply identifying the 'correct' diagnosis, these plays test the presumptions that enable the diagnosis in the first place. The diagnoses at the heart of the plays vary from antiquated hysteria, the more 'legitimate' schizophrenia, and the curious love-madness of the drug trial. But, across these plays, psychiatric diagnosis necessarily emerges from surrounding historical, bureaucratic, and economic structures.

These social forces are felt upon the bodies of the diagnosed. What it means for diagnosis to inscribe itself upon the body varies across these plays. In *Augustine (Big Hysteria)*, it is an active, purposeful performance, almost a parody; as Augustine responds to the prompts of Charcot and Freud, she takes on the control of a virtuoso. No such control is allowed Christopher in *Blue/Orange*, who is silenced between the arguments of the two doctors and each aspect of his voice and identity stripped away in the political power play of modern psychiatry. The two test subjects of *The Effect* veer between passivity and joy, their bodies and actions mechanized for measurement, their love possible only outside the testing chamber's gaze. Despite this variety, all these plays stage diagnosis as something proactive, not merely descriptive, and shifting the sense of self.

The critique of psychiatric diagnosis as a speech act should not be mistaken for its renunciation. However, by staging the diagnostic process only to sublimate the question, these plays facilitate a richer understanding of psychiatric diagnosis. Rather than simply identifying psychiatric disorder, these plays explore the implications of diagnosis as a speech act, emerging from a social environment, shifting the social world, and acting upon the lives and experiences of the diagnosed. As they reveal the potentially damaging effects, sifting through the sociopolitical influences and the epistemological dilemmas, these plays puncture the hegemony of standard psychiatric diagnosis, its self-conception as a concrete process and a nosology based upon natural kinds. The conceptual unfolding of diagnosis is, in this regard, not a rejection, but an enrichment.

Suggested Reading

Angelaki, Vicky. *Social and Political Theatre in 21st-Century Britain: Staging Crisis*. London, 2019.
Austin, J. L. *How to Do Things with Words*. Oxford, 1962.

Diamond, Elin. *Unmaking Mimesis: Essays on Feminism and Theatre*. London, 1997.

Foucault, Michel. *Psychiatric Power: Lectures at the College de France*, trans. G. Burchell. Basingstoke, 2003.

Furse, Anna. '*Augustine (Big Hysteria)*: Writing the Body', *Theatre Review* 2, no. 1 (1994): 25–34.

Augustine (Big Hysteria). London, 1997.

Hacking, Ian. *Rewriting the Soul: Multiple Personality and the Sciences of Memory*. Princeton, 1995.

Harpin, Anna. 'Revisiting the Puzzle Factory: Cultural Representations of Psychiatric Asylums'. *Interdisciplinary Science Reviews* 38, no. 4 (2013): 335–50.

Madness, Art, and Society: Beyond Illness. London, 2019.

Millard, Chris. 'Concepts, Diagnosis and the History of Medicine: Historicising Ian Hacking and Munchausen's Syndrome'. *Social History of Medicine* 30, no. 3 (2016): 567–89.

Penhall, Joe. *Blue/Orange*. London, 2000.

Prebble, Lucy. *The Effect*. London, 2012.

Rose, Nikolas. *The Politics of Life Itself: Biomedicine, Power, and Subjectivity in the Twenty-First Century*. Princeton, 2007.

Wald, Christina. *Hysteria, Trauma and Melancholia: Performative Maladies in Contemporary Anglophone Drama*. London, 2007.

Watson, Ariel. 'Cries of Fire: Psychotherapy in Contemporary British and Irish Drama'. *Modern Drama* 51, no. 2 (Summer 2008): 188–210.

Whitbeck, Caroline. 'What Is Diagnosis? Some Critical Reflections'. *Metamedicine* 2, no. 3 (1981): 319–29.

9

MIKE VANDEN HEUVEL

Devised Theatre and the Performance of Science

Two questions bring devising to the fore with respect to relations between science and theatre. First, is there something about collective or ensemble creation that lends itself particularly to the treatment of scientific concepts and themes? After all, if devised theatre simply mimics the way science is represented in single-authored plays, there is little need for a separate chapter in this volume. Second, what lies behind the recent claim by Andy Jordan that 'there are far more devised and cross-disciplinary productions dealing with science than there are conventional (text-based) plays being presented'?[1] There may be material reasons for this – for instance, that much devised work falls under applied theatre (discussed by Michael Carklin in this volume), and so examples multiply in educational and science outreach contexts – but it seems an accurate observation nonetheless based on my findings. Indeed, research for this chapter created a Borgesian garden of forking paths leading to thickets of science-based work by ensembles and featuring every variety of devised performance: verbatim, live art, postmodern, new circus, postdramatic, visual theatre, physical performance, and more. The few examples I provide below in no way represent the breadth of work and the curiosity in science that devising ensembles evince.

Several deeply intertwined factors help explain why ensemble creation becomes well suited for engaging with science. There has been a shift away from the conception of science as an autonomous form of knowledge production whose stature derives from its strict disciplinary procedures, such as controlled experiments, falsifiable and value-free theories, and the carapace of objectivity constructed around the methods and objects of inquiry.[2] This conception of science certainly remains active, and is deeply embedded in conventional narratives within the history of science. These typically

---

[1] Andy Jordan, 'Science-in-Theatre: A Significant New Genre?', in *Consciousness, Theatre, Literature and the Arts 2013*, ed. Daniel Meyer-Dinkgräfe (Cambridge, 2014), 1–32 (9).

[2] Bruno Latour, *Laboratory Life: The Construction of Scientific Facts* (Princeton, 1986).

position scientific practice and knowledge in a separate domain mostly anterior to, isolated from, and superior to social influences and popular culture. The discourse produced by science in this model could circulate authoritatively simply, as James Secord writes, 'because it was true'.[3] This orthodox image of science continues to provide artists seeking to dramatize it through conventional dramatic texts with a robust line-up of people, situations, and ideas from which to extract characters, plots, and action, all 'mediated' (to use Kirsten Shepherd-Barr's term) through biographies and historical events that assure a linear and historically grounded narrative.[4] These may question, overturn, or complicate the internal histories of science – in fact, this is the strategy underlying the majority of science dramas from *Galileo* to *Arcadia* to *Photograph 51* – but they continue to represent them, in part because those familiar, and familiarly positivist, histories are so ingrained in cultural memory that they easily establish common ground with audiences.

But science is growing increasingly interdisciplinary, especially in just those fields of research that most directly evoke contemporary anxieties and aspirations, such as cognitive science, neurobiology, genetics, and climate research. In part owing to the nature of the research across several disciplines, the histories of such scientific fields appear less settled because their evidential structure, by which the scientific theories are falsified, leaves them open to multiple interpretations. Such entangled fields of inquiry also reveal a kind of epistemological porousness that often manifests for the nonscientific public as some form of complexity, as something too convoluted to grasp; a 'great immensity' (to cite the title of a devised science play discussed below). In the parlance of inter- and transdisciplinarity, these are known as 'wicked problems', knotty and recursive complications that are 'highly complex (typically a mixture of social and natural factors) and difficult to define; their nature may not become apparent until after they have been solved'.[5] Wicked problems often arise in ecology, but haunt other scientific fields as well and seem to call forth what Sleigh and Craske define as transdisciplinary approaches that feature a 'multi-pronged, democratic and critical method as the only kind of approach likely to produce any kind of solution' (320). For example, 'cognitive science' actually describes less a coherent discipline than the means by which research into the relatively

[3] James A. Secord, 'Knowledge in Transit', *Isis* 95, no. 4 (December 2004): 655.
[4] Kirsten Shepherd-Barr, '"Unmediated" Science Plays: Seeing What Sticks', in *Staging Science: Scientific Performance on Street, Stage and Screen*, ed. Martin Willis (London, 2016), 108.
[5] Charlotte Sleigh and Sarah Craske, 'Art and Science in the UK: A Brief History and Critical Reflection', *Interdisciplinary Science Reviews* 42, no. 4 (2017): 320.

discrete fields of linguistics, artificial intelligence, anthropology, neuroscience, psychology, and philosophy of mind come into contact and establish robust but contingent and centreless interdisciplinary networks. Owing to the breadth of its research portfolio and the myriad wicked problems this generates, cognitive science would be nearly impossible to portray effectively in a literary drama based on discrete characters and a conventional plot encompassing its multiple and entangled histories (as Stoppard's difficulties in *The Hard Problem* demonstrate).

Yet 'wicked problems' often comprise the very genesis of devised theatre, which is driven less by explication than by exploration. Devised creation responds to the challenge of interdisciplinarity by resisting the drive toward literary coherence and wholeness. It accomplishes this in two ways: first, by avoiding a single point of view in favour of group creation, which generates dialogue and multiple strands of research that are animated by the social and artistic exchanges at the heart of devising, and, second, by blending multiple storytelling modes (dance, multimedia, physical theatre, installation, live art, and so on) that resist transformation into well-crafted works of literature. The various performance modes, like the manifold stories brought into the devising process by multiple authoring agents, operate nonhierarchically, creating layered verbal, visual, kinetic, and acoustic scores that do not prioritize dialogue, coherent character, and plot. Such seemingly unwieldy assemblages generate their own kinds of wicked problems that elude closure and, ideally, call the audience's attention to the quality of process, of how these elements might come together to create possibilities of contingent meaning and understanding. Nicola Shaughnessy argues that 'the space between disciplines and dualisms is where meaning is made as new epistemologies predicated on *process* create bridges between different discourses'.[6] The practices of devised theatre engaged with science bear this out. Jean-François Peyret's Feuilleton company, for instance, discusses its practice of publishing multiple versions of its performance texts (as 'partitions') on its website, emphasizing that 'it avoids the single viewpoint of any one person; it is theatre as the result of dialogue and debate'.[7] As I suggest below, this reflects the discourse of science in the contemporary world, not governed by its own positivist history but open to an exchange in which scientific ideas are not discrete and stable forms of knowledge to be passed along to the spectator but are, themselves, in process.

---

[6] Nicola Shaughnessy, 'Introduction', in *Affective Performance and Cognitive Science: Body, Brain, and Being* (London, 2014), 4.

[7] Shepherd-Barr, '"Unmediated" Science Plays', 110.

Regarding the recent upsurge of ensemble-devised science plays, we should attend not only to recent developments in theatre-making practices but also to evolving cultural notions of science itself.[8] I argue that devised theatre comprises a set of methods that align with the altered social dynamics of contemporary science and thereby make devised science performance a viable platform for addressing themes, ideas, and concepts from science that are difficult for single-authored plays to encompass. Perhaps emboldened by the success of plays like *Copenhagen* and *Arcadia*, devising companies eagerly sought out scientific content and concepts beginning in the 1990s, and quickly discovered strong correlations between the more complex and interdisciplinary sciences and their own methods of creating theatre. As Stephen Di Benedetto has shown, such multisensory and nonlinear forms of storytelling elicit unique phenomenological and cognitive reactions, creating complex embodied responses from audiences.[9] Indeed, as Alan Hancock has suggested, devising processes can usefully be understood by metaphorical references to sciences like chaos and complexity theory, and devised creation mimics in surprising ways the cognitive operations of distributed systems.[10] As well, devised work often eschews the fourth wall of representational theatre and thus offers opportunities to engage directly with audiences so that performances may enact forms of communicative action. This is not to say that devised performance supplant more conventional dramatic treatments of science; both have shown to be successful. But owing to a particular set of historical circumstances only recently coming into perspective, devised work engages with science in ways that audiences have thus far responded to enthusiastically.

One historical cause stems from the influence – mostly indirect – that science and technology studies (STS) has exerted on the public understanding of science, reshaping the public's relationship to scientific knowledge. The emergence and explosive growth of this field, and its consequences for the public understanding of science, comprise a vast history too complex for anything but a brief summary here.[11] Perhaps most significantly, STS,

---

[8] See Shaughnessy, 'Introduction', and Shepherd-Barr, '"Unmediated" Science Plays'.

[9] Stephen di Benedetto, *The Provocation of the Senses in Contemporary Theatre* (New York, 2011).

[10] Alan Hancock, 'Chaos in Drama: The Metaphors of Chaos Theory as a Way of Understanding Drama Process' [online], *N.A.D.I.E. Journal* 19, no. 1 (1995): 15–26; and Rick Kemp, 'Devising – Embodied Creativity in Distributed Systems', in *The Routledge Companion to Theatre, Performance, and Cognitive Science*, ed. Rick Kemp and Bruce McConachie (New York, 2019), 48–57.

[11] See Georgina Born and Andrew Barry, 'Art-Science', *Journal of Cultural Economy* 3, no. 1 (2010): 103–19; and Sleigh and Craske, 'Art and Science in the UK'.

alongside other social influences, shifted the understanding of the history of science outward, away from a sequestered internalist narrative shut off from the processes of everyday social and political life and toward a broader, externalist conception of science as a sociopolitical activity bound by many of the same dynamics that govern the civic sphere. These and similar factors have pulled science ever more deeply into the public view with consequential results, making it necessary for science not simply to report its discoveries but to perform them for public debate and engagement. As Nicola Triscott frames it, 'a new generation of historians and philosophers have pointed out that science doesn't just think about the world, it makes the world and then remakes it'.[12]

Thus, we see a roughly parallel movement: first, with regard to science, knowledge conceived (in James Secord's formulation) 'in transit' rather than as stabilized within past contexts, and, second, with regard to theatre, a movement away from the fixed literary work to the performed event.[13] By virtue of the historical conditions that have externalized science and its manner of constructing knowledge, Secord argues that such knowledge, in its popularized form, has acquired new forms of mobility and circulation, new networks that combine to shape scientific knowledge in ways that disperse its origin stories and 'great discovery' narratives (which emphasize the linear progress of knowledge production) into more complex forms of discourse that highlight the means and processes of communicating knowledge by the stories about it that we share, revise, and adapt. Science becomes 'performative' in the sense of being an exchange of embodied, social, and material practices. With scientific knowledge always already in transit, the emphasis falls instead on how that knowledge is communicated through social networks and how it transforms over time under the influence of new relations. Similarly, the typically presentational style of devised theatre, which constructs the experience as an event in real time rather drawing the spectator into an already established fictive world, allows meanings to multiply and circulate, and to emerge only with the active participation of the spectator.

Not, I think, by coincidence, these various trajectories in the public understanding of science culminated at just about the time devised theatre practice was becoming institutionalized. By the 1990s, devising was being taught widely in schools and conservatories – just about the time STS was

---

[12] Nicola Triscott, 'Performative Science in an Age of Specialisation: The Case of Critical Art Ensemble', in *Interfaces of Performance*, ed. Maria Chatzichristodoulou, Janis Jefferies, and Rachel Zerihan (London, 2009), 153–68 (156).

[13] Secord, 'Knowledge in Transit', 664.

being recognized. These trajectories between new conceptions of science and new ways of assembling performance run on parallel tracks, and so the interactions that begin in the late 1990s between an 'alternative' understanding of science and what was originally an alternative method for creating performance seem, if not predetermined, then at least unsurprising. The new alignment appears in scholarly treatments of theatre and science at about the same time. Shepherd-Barr devoted the concluding chapter in her 2006 *Science on Stage* to what she titled 'Alternating Currents: New Trends in Science and Theater', which focused mainly on the director-led companies of Peyret and Luca Ronconi, as well as Britain's pre-eminent devising company, Complicité.[14] Building upon an essay by David Barnett that proposed dramaturgical interventions in Frayn's *Copenhagen* to realize its potential as 'postdramatic' theatre, Shepherd-Barr also deployed the postdramatic as a genre of the science play.[15] While not exclusively devised, most postdramatic work utilizes many of the same formal aesthetic strategies as devised theatre, such as an open, non-Aristotelian form, the mitigation of a self-contained 'fictive cosmos', a dehierarchization of theatrical elements (which deprivileges dialogue and narrative as the central components of a performance to feature visual, sonic, and physical elements), and more varied and direct relations with the audience.[16] A later article by Shepherd-Barr and Liliane Campos extends these investigations, again using Peyret and Ronconi as case studies, and Campos uses a similar lens in an essay on Complicité's *Mnemonic* and *A Disappearing Number*.[17] Thus the confluence of STS, devised theatre, and a critical apparatus informed by theories of postdramatic theatre, all arriving in the 1990s, created a vector for new work to approach science as a question open to debate and direct engagement rather than a source of closed narratives.

Turning now to examples of such devised work addressing science, the first observation is that while a general 'devised aesthetic' is discernible, there is tremendous variety in terms of goals and outcomes. While most

---

[14] Kirsten Shepherd-Barr, *Science on Stage: From Doctor Faustus to Copenhagen* (Princeton, 2006); and Shepherd-Barr, '"Unmediated" Science Plays'.

[15] David Barnett, 'Reading and Performing Uncertainty: Michael Frayn's *Copenhagen* and the Postdramatic Theatre', *Theatre Research International* 30, no. 2 (July 2005): 139–49; and Hans-Thies Lehmann, *Postdramatic Theatre*, trans. Karen Jürs-Munby (New York, 2006).

[16] Lehmann, *Postdramatic Theatre*.

[17] Liliane Campos and Kirsten Shepherd-Barr, 'Science and Theatre in Open Dialogue: *Biblioetica*, *Le Cas de Sophie K.* and the Postdramatic Science Play', *Interdisciplinary Science Reviews* 31, no. 3 (September 2006): 245–53; and Liliane Campos, 'Searching for Resonance: Scientific Patterns in Complicité's *Mnemonic* and *A Disappearing Number*', *Interdisciplinary Science Reviews* 32, no. 4 (December 2007): 326–34.

ensembles, for example, establish devising methods that work to avoid the conventional predicates of dramatic writing – the focus on character as fully separate from, and 'played' by, the actor; linear narrative structure that aspires to bring the audience to its moments of tension and release collectively and simultaneously; a fictive cosmos into which the spectator is fully absorbed; a setting that simply contains or serves as a backdrop to the action and language; and so on – they produce widely different responses to their scientific themes. But all the companies I discuss fully utilize the particular opportunities that devising affords to grapple with scientific knowledge that is 'in transit' and unmoored from traditionally entrenched disciplinary structures. They recognize that it is not sufficient simply to present science or its history as givens through traditional representation; instead, they devise work in order to activate different forms of public engagement with it.

To begin, we can consider the work of Complicité to see how creative responses to science find exemplary expression in devised theatre. The company's reputation for science-based work rests on two productions, *Mnemonic* (1999, toured through 2003) and *A Disappearing Number* (2007–10). Interestingly, both are thematically grounded in actual transit, and both evince Complicité's famed fluidity and pace of action to convey viscerally a sense of breathless and constant transformation: the set, choreography, and special effects elements become a substantial 'character' that assumes a kind of agency in performance. *Mnemonic* presents Alice's quest to find her father (whom she thought dead) as well as the attempts by scientists to retrodict the past travels of the Iceman, the 5,300-year-old corpse discovered in the Alps between Italy and Austria in 1991. *A Disappearing Number* conveys the unsettling migration of the mathematician Srinivasa Ramanujan from India to Cambridge, and presents his collaborations with G. H. Hardy in the traditional quest/discovery motif represented in many science plays, but given pointedly different treatment here. In the present-day action, Ruth grapples with the mathematical paradoxes of infinite series, and her desire to connect with Ramanujan's origins ends unsuccessfully when she is struck down by a fatal aneurysm (while in transit). Her husband, Alex, criss-crosses the world as a hedge fund manager preoccupied with risk, and his search for understanding following her death leads him to India. Yet, consonant with the contemporary understanding of scientific knowledge as open-ended and caught in complex social feedback loops, these acts of transit share the quality of nonlinearity. Travel and memory are wayward, falling off traditional maps and revealing not fixed routes but rather fractal patterns that assume shape as characters move and wander, like motes dancing in Brownian motion. This kind of kinesis in *Mnemonic* finds its scientific analogue in neural activity and memory (neural sprouting, brain plasticity, synaptic connections), which lack origin, *telos*, and centre. Alice's quest proceeds haphazardly and eventually frustrates the play's apparent search-for-origins story when she declines to interact with her father just when she appears to have found him. The archaeologists similarly fail to come to agreement on the history (and provenance) of the Iceman. In *A Disappearing Number*, the quest to acclimatize Ramanujan to England and complete his collaboration with Hardy is deflected by food, weather, and loneliness, and reflected, as Campos argues, by the work he does with Hardy on the mathematical problem of partitions, which both divide and draw sets together.[18] In both plays, the purpose of the science is not to present the knowledge it represents as fixed but to convey how the concepts themselves make stable knowledge improbable, inviting the spectator to join the company in, using Campos's apt phrase, 'searching for resonance'. Thus, the pieces not only combine form and content but present an analogy between the means by which the productions come into being – the improvisational give-and-take of devising – and the performativity of science.

The British company Third Angel, founded in 1995 and consisting of co-artistic directors Rachael Walton and Alexander Kelly and a revolving cohort of regular collaborators, often engages with science in both deep and rhizomatic ways. According to their website, Third Angel 'regularly collaborate with experts from other fields, such as geography, cartography, psychology and astrophysics', and in a recent article Kelly is quoted saying, 'When we began it was a bit insular, it was given the term "sciart", whereas now it's diffused into the culture and it's not unusual to see scientists working with performers.'[19] Their work, along with companies like Curious Directive, Menagerie Theatre Company, Kings of England (all in the UK), Phantom Limb (New York), and Rimini Protokoll (Germany and the UK) that are also invested in science, exemplifies the widest range of devising's potential. It cuts across and often doubles back to scientific themes and research to produce not just stand-alone plays but also 'performance lectures' (*Hurrysickness* [2004]), durational performances (*600 People* [2015]), installations, relational and site-specific events, film, video, and design projects.[20] The performance lectures, such as *600 People*, tend to present the

---

[18] Campos, 'Searching for Resonance', 331.

[19] Tim Bano and James Doeser, 'Stage of Reason: How Theatre Is Being Used to Engage People in Science', *The Stage* (7 November 2018), www.thestage.co.uk/features/2018/stage-reason-theatre-used-engage-people-science/.

[20] For Curious Directive's work, see Laura Barnett, 'Curious Directive, the Theatre Company Experimenting with Science', *Guardian* (3 August 2014), www.theguardian.com/science/2014/aug/03/curious-directive-theatre-company-experiments-scientific-

scientific content more straightforwardly, intending to evoke wonder and awe from the spectator. But Third Angel is also likely to send that knowledge 'in transit' by rendering it performative and on the move. Philip Stanier's essay on the evolution of 9 *Billion Miles from Home* (based on Kelly's fascination with the *Voyager 2* spacecraft and its ever-increasing distance from earth) vividly describes the long genesis and multiple platforms that this leads to: 'a lecture-demonstration, autobiographical monologue, environmental collage, the hosting of a fake research/balloon launch and a performance ritual'.[21] Highlighting the intuition that scientific knowledge, like *Voyager 2*, is on the move, Third Angel is not preoccupied with notions of 'science-in-theatre' for which nailing the scientific concepts is paramount and failure to do so cause to dismiss the work.[22] They explore forms of storytelling that do not conclude with the sort of science explanation, delivered by the appropriate character in order to advance the plot, that we have become used to in text-based science dramas. Kelly is forthright that Third Angel works in the grey area between truth and fiction by devising work that 'incorporates documentary detail and fiction but doesn't bother to point out which is which'.[23] Behind that seeming nonchalance lies, in fact, a deep commitment to the time, research, and creative energy required to stay engaged with science, not in the sense of accumulating facts and data but of allowing the audience to discover different access points to the ongoing story.

Unlimited Theatre, another Yorkshire-based ensemble, similarly consults regularly with scientists as part of their play development. The company runs its own space agency as part of their ongoing youth program that includes a spaceship that tours museums and science fairs. Like Third Angel, the company's work sometimes takes the scientific content developed via their consultancies and renders it as straightforward science education, as in *The Ethics of Progress* (2008), Jon Spooner's tour de force lecture on quantum science and teleportation based on his conversations with physicist Vlatko Vedral. Several company-performed works, however, including *The Noise* (2013, and available as an immersive online text) and the recent *Future Bodies* (2018, produced in collaboration with the physical theatre

subjects. Kings of England produced *Elegy for Paul Dirac* (2011) as part of their 'In Eldersfield' cycle.

[21] Philip Stanier, 'The Distance Covered: Third Angel's 9 *Billion Miles from Home*', in *Devising in Process*, ed. Alex Mermikides and Jackie Smart (Houndmill, 2010), 110–27 (125).

[22] See, for instance, Carl Djerassi, 'Contemporary "Science-in-Theatre": A Rare Genre', *Interdisciplinary Science Reviews* 27, no. 3 (2002): 193–201.

[23] Quoted in Stanier, 'The Distance Covered', 111.

company Rashdash), decentre the propositional knowledge of science by dramatizing it as caught in the social and ethical nets surrounding environmental catastrophe and transhumanism.[24] *Future Bodies* questions the benefits of human 'upgrading' through the use of smart drugs, bionic implants, prosthetics, and even total brain emulation or 'uploading'. But the performance is not based in discursive dialogue and continuous narrative but structured instead as a series of vignettes (some movement- rather than text-based) connected by the songs of a posthuman Moritat singer – described as a 'blue skinned, gender switching angel winged demi god' – and featuring subtitles projected directly onto the set and actors' bodies. The sensuality of the environment, music, choreography, and even language situates scientific and technological knowledge (all of which, with reference to transhumanism, is directed at transcending the body) on a plane of immanence that stubbornly locates flesh and world in the physical present. The feverish intensity of the production's pace and its rhizomatic structure prevents the spectator from assuming a single point of view, a strategy that disperses the knowing subject and thereby invites the audience to create patterns of associations in the moment. The full benefits of devising the piece among a number of different creative staff bringing their own viewpoints produced a fertile friction. Spooner was initially enraptured by the technological potential of enhancements before encountering other points of view, which faceted the perspectives presented in the show and kept the piece from becoming another science lecture. 'I started making this show excited by the possibility of becoming an internet connected, blue-skinned, 300-year-old, winged demi-god', he reported. 'As a result of the depth of conversation with my collaborators, particularly Abbi [Greenland] and Helen [Goalen] from RashDash, I've become surprisingly reinvested in exploring the full potential of the body I was born in. I'd still like wings though.'[25]

Perhaps the most robust conversations that touch upon science today take place in reference to climate change. Performance practices that address environmental crisis often take forms of applied theatre, such as the Climate Change Theatre Action playwriting initiative and the participatory devised work of youth-based devising companies such as Inside the Greenhouse, as well as activist site-specific work (like the audio-based ambulatory performances on the order of Platform's *And While London Burns*, and the

---

[24] http://uneditions.com/the-noise/.
[25] Carmel Thomason, 'John Spooner Talks Future Bodies and Biological Enhancement', *Quay's Life* (3 October 2018), https://quayslife.com/people/future-bodies/.

relational performances of the Critical Art Ensemble).[26] Conventional plays and devised work that overtly confront issues of climate change denial, government vacillation, and public nonchalance, however, are until quite recently surprisingly rare.[27]

Given the interdisciplinarity of climate science and the many difficult social, ethical, and conceptual challenges it generates, there is great pressure on the quality of research and the verifiability of the data presented. This would seem to make forms of investigative and verbatim theatre particularly well suited to dramatizing climate change. However, as was evident in the production of *The Great Immensity* by the New York–based Civilians, the sheer volume of information brought to the table (as well as the volatile politics surrounding the issue) can prove problematic. Indeed, based on the company's previous productions, they were awarded a substantial grant from the National Science Foundation to produce *The Great Immensity* at the Kansas City Repertory Theatre and New York's Public Theatre in 2014 (the grant became a flashpoint in 2017 for the Trump administration and right-wing groups opposed to climate change research).[28] The play is based in deep research and curated discussion, not only among the company's devisers but with scientists and citizens across several years of development. The company's trademark use of song, movement, and spectacle (in this case, mostly digital projections) created distancing effects that attested to the company's mission to avoid a form of documentary performance that artistic director Steve Cosson calls a 'theatre of assurance'.[29] Although the work implicitly celebrates the pleasures and utility of deep scientific research (in part by mimicking its research methods), it also satirizes the scientific community's narrow disciplinary enclaves that often inhibit effective communication of the science to the public.

However, the piece was critiqued for its somewhat conventional presentation and narrative structure.[30] A more adventurous application of research

---

[26] See Joanne Tompkins, 'Site-Specific Theatre and Political Engagement across Space and Time: The Psychogeographic Mapping of British Petroleum in Platform's *And While London Burns*', *Theatre Journal* 63, no. 2 (2011): 225–43.

[27] See Julie Hudson, '"If You Want to Be Green Hold Your Breath": Climate Change in British Theatre', *New Theatre Quarterly* 28, no. 3 (August 2012): 260–71; and Una Chaudhuri, *Research Theatre, Climate Change, and the Ecocide Project* (New York, 2016).

[28] Diep Tran, 'How a "Climate Change Musical" Became a Right-Wing Punching Bag', *American Theatre* (5 June 2017), www.americantheatre.org/2017/06/05/how-a-climate-change-musical-became-a-right-wing-punching-bag/.

[29] 'Discovering What We Don't Know: An Interview with Steve Cosson of the Civilians', *TDR/The Drama Review* 54, no. 4 (December 2010): 188–205 (197).

[30] Nicole Seymour, Review of The Great Immensity, in *Resilience: A Journal of the Environmental Humanities* 2 (2014): 1 (n.p.).

informs the work of Glass Half Full Theatre, located in Austin, Texas. Self-described as a 'theatre of objects and ideas', the company uses object puppetry and low-tech dioramic environments to create interactive shows based in research into climate science and environmental justice issues. Artistic director Caroline Reck studied history and learned the value of research before moving into theatre because '[her] drive is creating live visual performances that allow people to experience ideas in an empathetic, simultaneous way'.[31] Their signature piece, *Once There Were Six Seasons* (2013–14), manipulated its tiny, featureless puppets across landscapes being transformed or destroyed by catastrophic weather events, creating strong visual images that conveyed the ultimately human control over climate change. The visible puppeteers both create empathy for the silent victims by their manipulation of their motions and reactions but also physically cause the violent cataclysms that destroy the landscape. 'I wanted to puppeteer the effects of climate change as well as puppet characters to whom this is happening, to illustrate that humans are the cause as well as the solution to this problem'.[32] Following the success of the show, Glass Half Full co-created (with Indigo Rael) *Polly Mermaid: Apocalypse Wow* (2018), a queer take on oceanic pollution, while plans are underway to mount a virtual reality experience entitled *Trash Trial/Trash Trail*.

Una Chaudhuri's Ecocide Project at New York University develops from the position that the climate crisis should elicit new forms of inquiry and response in order both to represent the Anthropocene and to know how to 'think and feel about it'.[33] Continuing her decades-long work in ecocriticism, the work evolves out of what she and her collaborators, Fritz Ertl and Shonni Enelow, call 'Research Theatre'. Using both conventional scientific research and theoretical models that seek to complicate conventional scientific practice – some of it based, for instance, in Artaud's thought ('Eco-Cruelty') – Research Theatre develops a specific aesthetic form (Ecotheatre) that is highly attuned to our period of environmental transformation. Although limited in scale (several pieces have been devised and staged in and around New York), the work, by virtue of its conceptual rigor and unique devising practices, may provide a route toward performance forms that emphasize communicative action over the simple communication of 'science' by traditional means.

---

[31] Michael McFadden, 'A Theater of Objects, Ideas and Ideals: Glass Half Full Theater in Austin', http://artsandculturetx.com/a-theater-of-objects-ideas-and-ideals-glass-half-full-theatre-in-austin/.

[32] Ibid.   [33] Chaudhuri, *Research Theatre*, viii.

Finally, there are works that stand at the postdramatic end of the devised science theatre continuum and that fully explore the particular attributes that ensemble-created theatre may bring to scientific themes. The Phantom Limb Company of New York City is just preparing to tour the final section of its trilogy, *Falling Out*, exploring the human relationship to nature under the threat of climate change. Speaking 'for' the elements under hazard rather than featuring scientists explaining what is happening, the three pieces address, in order, ice, wood, and water. The company's signature combination of puppetry and Butoh dance feels especially pertinent in the third section, given that its focus is the devastated Fukushima nuclear plant and irradiation of Japanese water supplies following the 2011 Tōhoku earthquake and subsequent tsunami. Rimini Protokoll, the celebrated German company made up of Helgard Haug, Stefan Kegi, and Daniel Wetzel, experiment with new forms of documentary theatre that shift authority and positions of knowledge away from the science expert characters who usually deliver the scientific content in literary drama. In works addressing environmental issues such as *Welt-Klimankonferenz* (*World Climate Change Conference*), the spectator is situated as an 'expert of the everyday' partaking in actual research related to climate change with fellow audience members, guided by members of the company. Produced in 2014 just prior to the Conference of Parties 21 (out of which emerged the Paris Accords), the performance modelled the global participation of the actual conference by designating spectators as delegates from individual countries and including breakout sessions and a final plenary panel. As Vicky Angelaki points out, this 'did not take a symbolic approach to the universality of the issue but rather a corporeal and literal one, with bodies at work on the ground: from discussions about to simulations of climate change conditions, this was a densely lived rather than merely live event'.[34] Such participatory forms of documentary theatre profoundly change the way scientific knowledge is positioned within performance, and offer perhaps the most effective means to shift authority from the dramatic text to the moment-by-moment exchanges between artists and participants that devised theatre pursues.

And yet devised theatre can still create surprises when it addresses scientific themes from within the proscenium. Mole Wetherell, artistic director of Reckless Sleepers, formed the ensemble in 1988 on a principle of 'smallness'; thus, it's little wonder that the company's signature science play, *Schrödinger's Box* (created 1997; redevised and retitled *Schrödinger* in 2011), is based on the quantum-particle thought experiment intended to serve as a

---

[34] Vicky Angelaki, *Theatre & Environment* (London, 2019), 42.

reductio ad absurdum to the Copenhagen Interpretation but which has instead become its signature mnemonic.[35] Noting that early audiences sometimes struggled with the content – 'perhaps expecting a stage version of "Quantum Theory for Beginners"' – Wetherell is adamant that 'it was never intended to popularize or explain science'.[36] Instead, Schrödinger's uncanny box becomes literalized on stage as a closed system in which uncertain and complementary realities prevail, forcing the performers to negotiate – through intense experimentation and frantic, often repeated, actions – how meaning must, in the fluctuating reality of the quantum universe, be made and unmade. Metonymically, the box is a built proscenium set inside a (usually) proscenium space, but instead of doubling theatrical space it challenges and deconstructs it, creating a dramatic contradiction between conventional theatrical space and the spaces devised theatre may open up. Rather than encapsulating a fictive world and containing and stabilizing its energy and signification, as the traditional proscenium does, the box remains somehow both impenetrable and porous: while the performers cannot stay out of it for any length of time, they rapidly enter and exit through a maze of traps and doors. Instead of allowing the spectator to peer into the (proscenium) box in order to render the fictive world coherent, to align narrative, character, and plot and thus open the box to know what's inside (in quantum terms, to 'collapse the wave function' and either kill or free the cat), Schrödinger's box is a purely liminal space, both claustrophobically confining but also free of orderly/ordering structures like narrative. Meaning is sought by various means – writing, enumeration, interrogation, recall through repetition – but, like zed particles, these all decay or are washed away by rainwater almost as soon as they come into existence. Knowledge is fluid and in transit, conveyed as only devised performance can render it.

Suggested Reading

Angelaki, Vicky. *Theatre & Environment*. London, 2019.
Brown, Andrew, and Mole Wetherell. *Trial: A Study of the Devising Process in Reckless Sleepers' 'Schrödinger's Box'*. Plymouth, UK, 2007.
Campos, Liliane, and Kirsten Shepherd-Barr. 'Science and Theatre in Open Dialogue: *Biblioetica, Le Cas de Sophie K.* and the Postdramatic Science Play'. *Interdisciplinary Science Reviews* 31, no. 3 (2006): 245–53.

---

[35] Scientific concepts are active in other productions, such as *Breaking Symmetry* (1999), *The Turing Test* (2001), and *Negative Space* (2016).
[36] Andrew Brown and Moe Wetherell, *Trial: A Study of the Devising Process in Reckless Sleepers' "Schrödinger's Box"* (Plymouth, 2007), 15.

'Searching for Resonance: Scientific Patterns in Complicité's *Mnemonic* and *A Disappearing Number*'. *Interdisciplinary Science Reviews* 32, no. 4 (2007): 326–34.

Chaudhuri, Una. *Research Theatre, Climate Change, and the Ecocide Project*. New York, 2016.

Hancock, Alan. 'Chaos in Drama: The Metaphors of Chaos Theory as a Way of Understanding Drama Process'. *N.A.D.I.E. Journal* 19, no. 1 (1995): 15–26.

Heddon, Deirdre, and Jane Milling. *Devising Performance: A Critical History*. Houndsmills, UK, 2006.

Jordan, Andy. 'Science-in Theatre: A New Genre?' In *Consciousness, Theatre, Literature and the Arts 2013*, ed. Daniel Meyer-Dinkgräfe. Cambridge, 2014, 1–32.

Kemp, Rick. 'Devising – Embodied Creativity in Distributed Systems'. In *The Routledge Companion to Theatre, Performance, and Cognitive Science*, ed. Rick Kemp and Bruce McConachie. New York, 2019, 48–57.

Lehmann, Hans-Thies. *Postdramatic Theatre*. New York, 2006.

Secord, James A. 'Knowledge in Transit'. *Isis* 95, no. 4 (December 2004): 654–72.

Shaughnessy, Nicola. *Affective Performance and Cognitive Science: Body, Brain, and Being*. London, 2013.

Shepherd-Barr, Kirsten. *Science on Stage: From "Doctor Faustus" to "Copenhagen"*. Princeton, 2006.

Sleigh, Charlotte, and Sarah Craske. 'Art and Science in the UK: A Brief History and Critical Reflection'. *Interdisciplinary Science Reviews* 42, no. 4 (October 2017): 313–30.

Stanier, Philip. 'The Distance Covered: Third Angel's *9 Billion Miles from Home*'. In *Devising in Process*, ed. Alex Mermikides and Jackie Smart. Houndsmills, UK, 2010, 110–27.

Vanden Heuvel, Mike. '"The Acceptable Face of the Unintelligible": Intermediality and the Science Play'. *Interdisciplinary Science Review* 38, no. 4 (2013): 365–79.

10

MICHAEL CARKLIN

Theatre and Science as Social Intervention

In January 2018, I directed Lauren Gunderson's play *Silent Sky* as part of a season of theatre and science at the University of South Wales in Cardiff. The play is about Henrietta Leavitt, who worked as a 'computer' at Harvard College Observatory in the early 1900s. She is credited with discovering the relationship between period and luminosity in Cepheid stars, leading to a system for working out the distances of stars and galaxies from the earth. The theatre-science season, entitled 'Theatre through the Telescope', also included productions of *Mnemonic* by Complicité and *Incognito* by Nick Payne. The preparation for this season included workshops with students exploring science and theatre more generally, investigating the contribution of women to science, and enhancing audience access by working with Taking Flight Theatre Company to incorporate integrated British Sign Language interpretation into the performances. Alongside the performances we also hosted a pre-show public panel discussion on theatre and science. In many senses, this season of plays can be understood from an 'interventionist' perspective – there was a deliberate decision to introduce our theatre students to scientific ideas and history as part of their education; there was an attempt to subvert the traditional separation of arts and sciences in higher education (at my own university, arts and sciences are not only in different faculties but in different towns); and the panel discussion served as a springboard for public discussion and debate, not just about theatre and science, but about science in society today. Taken as a whole, the programme was an opportunity to provoke an engagement with science through theatre, for both students and the general public.

In September 2018, a few months after directing *Silent* Sky, I was invited to chair a post-show panel discussion after a performance of *2023*, a new play by Lisa Parry, produced by Illumine Theatre at the Chapter Arts Centre in Cardiff. The play, set in the near future, focuses on the impact of the change in the law allowing for the release of sperm donors' personal information. Parry says that she was partly motivated to write the play because the change of the law had such significant implications and yet there was hardly any media coverage of it. In the panel discussion she stated:

> What gets complicated when you bring in people into that [legal] situation, *characters* into that situation, is that the law looks very clearly at: there's the donor, there's the child; but the donor is going to have a different life in eighteen years' time, and is going to have responsibility for people who aren't involved in this situation at all, and children that they're not even aware of. I found that really really fascinating, that a decision you could make eighteen years ago, and the implications that has when technologies change, when your family situation has changed, can impact on a completely different set of people.[1]

For her, writing the play was about raising a social issue with profound implications that is not being addressed in the mainstream press or social media. The panel discussion offered further opportunity for a public forum to explore these implications through its inclusion of Jacky Boivin, professor of health psychology specializing in reproductive health, and consultant embryologist Dr Lyndon Miles, in addition to Parry. Members of the audience were keen to ask questions, offer points of view, and share personal experiences, including people who had themselves conceived and raised children through sperm donation. The word 'complex' came up numerous times in discussion, and in a real sense the play opened the door to considering the complexity of the relationship between science and society at this particular moment in time. What was striking about the discussion was that when I occasionally tried to steer the conversation towards the play itself and theatre as a medium, the audience was particularly keen to talk about the science, or at least the social implications of it. In this sense, then, the play was, amongst other things, a catalyst, an intervention aimed at raising public discussion and debate.

The focus of this chapter is on how drama, theatre, and performance might be used, or be seen, to deliberately *intervene*. Of course, it might be argued that *all* theatre offers some form of intervention, or at least has the potential to do so. Every theatre experience has the potential to be transformative for an audience member, to shift their thinking, feeling, or perspective in even small ways. Here, however, I am concerned with the ways that drama, theatre, and performance may be understood or applied with the specific intention of intervening, of impacting on the audience or participants' engagement with science. This suggests a broad spectrum of practice that includes plays about science, theatre education projects, work in

---

[1] A video recording of the panel discussion can be viewed at www.illuminetheatre.org/2023-1.

schools, public engagement activities by scientists, performances at science centres, lecture demonstrations, and post-show discussions.

With the development of drama in education, the growth in community theatre and applied drama, the impact of social media technologies in the twenty-first century, and the increasing popularity of 'citizen science', it seems inevitable that explorations of science through theatre and participatory arts methodologies become a fertile ground for social intervention. Whether teaching science in the school classroom through drama or provoking audiences with the ethics of biotechnology in the theatre, at root is a desire to stimulate people in critically engaging with science in society, including:

- encouraging public understanding of science
- exploring the complexity, ethics, implications, and ambiguity of scientific experimentation
- engaging communities in considering the implications of science for themselves
- addressing a lack of information or countering misinformation
- offering historical contexts and perspectives
- challenging prevailing moralities, ethical frameworks, political agendas, or social norms.

Writing of intervention in relation to applied theatre, Tim Prentki refers to the metaphor of 'dropping a boulder in a stagnant pond',[2] thus initiating some kind of change. This metaphor suggests that in actively intervening, not only might there be immediate change, but such an intervention might have longer-lasting impact. However, Prentki is also acutely aware of the problem of the idea of intervention, in that it is 'implicated in issues of power and the right to speak on behalf of others'.[3] Investigating theatre and science as social intervention suggests that such work is often about voicing unheard stories, countering dominant narratives (often in the media), instigating action, or simply informing.

While theatre and science as social intervention suggests a wide spectrum of practices, this chapter focuses on three selected aspects from parts of that spectrum as examples: (1) exhibitions, lectures, and demonstrations; (2) sci-art through the collaborations of artists and scientists; and (3) theatre and global intervention around climate change.

---

[2] Tim Prentki, 'Introduction to Intervention', in *The Applied Theatre Reader*, ed. Tim Prentki and Sheila Preston (London, 2008), 181.
[3] Ibid.

Exhibitions, Lectures, and Demonstrations

Contemporary interest in 'public engagement' and 'science communication' has dovetailed with what might be termed a turn to the performative. The use of performance and theatricality becomes an interventionary strategy with the intention of contributing to a more scientifically literate public and of sharing the joy of discovery. Two historical examples serve to highlight this: Michael Faraday and the Royal Institution's Christmas Lectures, and public autopsies in the early modern era and contemporary resonances.

Performing Experiments: Michael Faraday and the Christmas Lectures for Children

Faraday, the influential nineteenth-century scientist whose work contributed to understandings of electromagnetism and electrochemistry, amongst other things, sought to encourage members of the general public to engage with science, introducing the Royal Institution Friday Evening Discourses for the public in 1825 and the Christmas Lectures for Children in 1826, the latter still running today, presented each year by different scientists. In his time, Faraday presented nineteen of these lectures himself. In his biography of Faraday, John Meurig Thomas, director of the Royal Institution from 1986 to 1991, quotes Faraday's view that the lectures 'should amuse and entertain as well as educate, edify and, above all, inspire'.[4]

Faraday's best-known lecture was his 1860 Christmas Lecture for Children, on the 'Chemical History of a Candle'. In two *British Medical Journal* issues of January 1861, the anonymous author, described only as 'one who is himself a well known chemical lecturer', reviews the 1860 series: 'Not only is Dr. Faraday's matter always of the best, but his style and delivery are so superior as to rank him as the first lecturer, as indeed he is the first philosopher of Great Britain. It is a pleasant thing to find so great a man addressing himself year after year to the young.'[5] The review details the range of experiments that Faraday presented over five lectures, and what emerges is a sense of a theatrical experience in which the audience is informed, delighted, and enthralled.

The reviewer describes one of the experiments thus: 'The expansion of water in the formation of ice was so beautifully illustrated. Small bottles made of iron one-eighth of an inch in thickness, were filled with water, and

---

[4] John Meurig Thomas, *Michael Faraday and the Royal Institution* (Bristol, 1991), 192.
[5] 'Dr. Faraday's Lectures at the Royal Institution', *British Medical Journal* (5 January 1861): 18.

the iron stopper screwed in. On immersing them in a freezing mixture, they burst with a loud rapport, scattering the freezing mixture high in the air.'[6] He also describes Faraday's explanations of the nature and properties of hydrogen using soap bubbles and collodion balloons, which was met with 'universal acclamation on the part of the juveniles'. At the end of the five lectures, which included a range of different experiments, Faraday is reported as stating: 'I could detain you for hours ...; but all things must come to an end. All I can say is, may your lives shine as the light from a candle; may you prove useful in your generation; may your acts be of a character to shed a lustre upon your time. / And so, amidst well deserved applause and the usual rush of children to the table, closed the lectures on the Chemical History of the Candle.'[7]

What is clear from reading reviews and reports of Faraday's lecture-demonstrations, and from viewing the drawings, paintings, and lithographs of these events (such as those by Alexander Blaikley), is their overt theatricality. There is a palpable impression of an audience delighting in the scenes being enacted before them, a sense of occasion, and a feeling of Faraday himself embodying the scientist as performer. Today, these lectures are still presented live and, since 1966, have been televised every year. The broadcasts now reach approximately two million viewers and are also available online and as a classroom resource. Viewing the 2018 lecture series 'Who Am I?', presented by Alice Roberts and with a guest lecture by Aoife McLysaght, it is clear that the sense of theatre, of audience engagement, and of visual stimulation still underpins these events in the presentation of complex ideas and information.[8] The use, in this series, of projection, lighting, music, striking scenography, beautifully designed props, and clear attention to an aesthetic, as well as intellectual, experience is a profound example of the performance of science in the spirit of Faraday's vision. The applause and cries of joy as thousands of multicoloured leaves fall from above to the floor at the end of the first of the 2018 lectures is reminiscent of the reports of excitement of the children at Faraday's lectures more than 150 years ago.

Faraday's lectures were part of a broader culture of scientific performance at the time. Tiffany Watt-Smith's fascinating study *On Flinching: Theatricality and Scientific Looking from Darwin to Shell Shock* (2014), for

---

[6] Ibid., 19.
[7] 'Dr. Faraday's Lectures at the Royal Institution', *British Medical Journal* (12 January 1861): 51.
[8] To view recordings of the 2018 lectures, see www.rigb.org/christmas-lectures/watch/2018/who-am-i (Royal Institution website).

example, highlights the relationship between theatre and science during the years 1872–1918. She argues that

> the worlds of Victorian science and theatre were even more intimately entwined than existing scholarship credits. In the nineteenth and early twentieth centuries, science did not only inform theatrical innovations, and theatre did not only emerge when scientists made spectacles of themselves and their discoveries, but more surprisingly, theatricality was deep within scientific experiment and a key part of the emergence of objective looking itself.[9]

Focusing on flinching, cringing, and recoiling as self-consciously enacted responses rather than involuntary reflexes, Watt Smith's study, which includes focus on Darwin, Ferrier, and Head and references to Faraday himself, shows how spectatorship blurred the boundaries between theatre and science as emotional and embodied forms of participation. Watt Smith argues that theatrical looking was not confined to the playhouse and that 'the idea of a passionately performing spectator wandered beyond the auditorium, to emerge in lecture halls and law courts, laboratories and museums of medical curiosities. Perhaps most surprisingly, it found its way into the heart of human experiment too'.[10] We can perhaps get a sense of the roots of this, and a different perspective on scientific performance as social intervention, if we go back further beyond the Victorians to the anatomy theatres of early modern Europe.

Dissections and Autopsies

Well documented in terms of theatre scholarship,[11] public dissections, reconsidered here as social intervention, reveal the profound shift of world views as layers of the body were opened to public inspection.[12] Under dissection,

---

[9] Tiffany Watt Smith, *On Flinching: Theatricality and Scientific Looking from Darwin to Shell Shock* (Oxford, 2014), 6.

[10] Ibid., 8.

[11] See, for example, Jonathan Sawday, *The Body Emblazoned: Art, Dissection and the Human Body in Renaissance Culture* (London, 1995); Maaike Bleeker (ed.), *Anatomy Live: Performance and the Operating Theatre* (Amsterdam, 2008); Karen Ingham, 'Art and the Theatre of Mind and Body: How Contemporary Arts Practice Is Re-framing the Anatomo-Clinical Theatre', *Journal of Anatomy* 216, no. 2 (February 2010): 251–63; Cynthia Klestinec, *Theatres of Anatomy: Students, Teachers, and Traditions of Dissection in Renaissance Venice* (Baltimore, 2011); and Rafael Mandressi, 'Of the Eye and of the Hand: Performance in Early Modern Anatomy', *TDR/The Drama Review* 59, no. 3 (2015): 60–76.

[12] These shifting world views resulted from what has been called the Scientific Revolution. See, for example, David Wootton, ed., *The Invention of Science: A New History of the Scientific Revolution* (London, 2015).

the human body was both a 'site of performance' and an agent of action. In the seventeenth-century anatomy theatres of Uppsala and Padua, the body took centre stage: the cadaver taken to pieces while new conceptions of the living body were being simultaneously constructed.

Commenting on the 'rituals of dissection', Martin Kemp and Marina Wallace highlight how we might understand this intersection of science and performance:

> Dissection of the human body – always a fraught business in any society – was for much of its history not primarily a technical process conducted for teaching, research or autopsies. Nor were dissections most commonly undertaken in the privacy of dissecting rooms in medical institutions. Rather, the opening up of the body was a ritual act, a performance staged for particular audiences within carefully monitored frameworks of legal and religious regulation. The most prominent dissections were staged as public or semi-public performances in specially constructed 'theatres' (the term still used for the room in which operations are conducted in modern hospitals). The audience was as likely to consist of curious non-specialists as aspiring or actual members of the medical profession, and the interior wonders of the body were rendered open to view in sequence according to a pre-determined choreography.[13]

Jonathan Sawday points out that crowds flocked to anatomy theatres in Bologna, Padua, Marburg, Leiden, Amsterdam, and London to see with their own eyes how bodies were dissected. At Bologna, for example, where representatives of the civil authorities, the papal power, and the church would gather to witness dissections, public notices were posted indicating the day and time at which dissections would take place.[14] Sawday suggests that examining contemporary images allows us to understand the ritualistic drama of the Renaissance anatomy demonstration: the hierarchical seating according to rank, the playing of music during dissection (as at Leiden and Padua), the procession that heralded the entrance of the anatomists, and the formulaic words that often began the anatomy lesson. In the theatre space, he argues, various 'confrontations' took place: the living faced the dead, knowledge faced ignorance, civic virtue faced criminality, judicial power confronted the individual.[15] We can understand the interventionary nature of this performance if we consider that these public events aimed to put on display a changing conception of the world and, in so doing, to destabilize prevailing ontologies and moralities.

---

[13] Martin Kemp and Marina Wallace, *Spectacular Bodies: The Art and Science of the Human Body from Leonardo to Now* (London, 2000), 23.
[14] Sawday, The Body Emblazoned, 42.   [15] Ibid., 75–6.

It is notable that these public autopsies also had an impact on the formal theatre itself; for example, Sawday points to public fascination with dissection in Edward Ravenscroft's play *The Anatomist, or The Sham Doctor*, first performed in 1696 in the New Theatre in Lincoln's Inn Fields in London. The play was so successful that it was rarely absent from the London stage until its popularity began to decline in the 1790s.[16] Sawday argues that it was not the play's wit nor comic invention that guaranteed its popularity throughout the eighteenth century, but 'the presence of a macabre corpse on stage which comes to life and protests against its own anatomization'.[17] Closer to our own time, Shelagh Stephenson's play *An Experiment with an Air Pump* (1998) brings this complex fascination with the dissection of human anatomy into focus by interweaving stories across two time periods, juxtaposing the ethics of illegal eighteenth-century medical dissections of grave-robbed bodies with the ethics of contemporary genetics and biotechnology. This juxtaposition is theatrically underscored by the doubling of actors from the two time periods, a kind of body-snatching built into the theatrical metaphor. Here again theatre might be understood as intervening, the playwright challenging audiences to consider the ethics of genetic experimentation.

There is a further example of dissection as theatrical spectacle if we consider the televised autopsy, filmed in front of a live audience, undertaken by Gunther von Hagens (nicknamed 'Dr Death') in 2002, the first public autopsy in Britain since 1830.[18] Von Hagens is perhaps best known for his Body Worlds exhibitions displaying a range of real human specimens that have been 'plastinated'. Touring around the world since 1995, the exhibition opened in a new, prominent position in London's Piccadilly Circus in 2019. It was his controversial autopsy, however, which we might consider a particular kind of intervention – Von Hagens emphasized the educational nature of the endeavour, yet the sense of showmanship arguably created different kinds of ripples with questions being asked about the ethical implications of the event. Like the dissection demonstrations of the eighteenth century, this autopsy was primarily for a lay audience. The audience purchased tickets for the performance and there was a queue around the block from the venue in East London's Brick Lane as people waited to get in. Reasons for being there (given by the audience to the television presenter who interviewed them while they queued) included curiosity, a desire to be educated, or because it was 'a freak show'. Once inside, the audience sat

---

[16] Ibid., 44.   [17] Ibid., 45.
[18] *The Autopsy*, Channel 4 Television (21 November 2002), presented by Krishnan Guru-Murthy.

round three sides of the performance area on raked seating. The atmosphere was clearly one of nervous anticipation, undoubtedly heightened by the television presenter walking around followed by cameras, interviewing members of the audience and telling viewers numerous times that the squeamish should not watch. A number of audience members expressed anxiety and even fear about watching the cadaver (at that point under a sheet) being cut up. When the actual autopsy started, audience reactions ranged from a mixture of wide-eyed repulsion and fascination to a very strong feeling of tension, palpably broken the first time the audience applauded.

The first applause highlighted the theatricality of the event. One of the audience members asked the professor why he was wearing his hat and if it wouldn't be more respectful to the dead man to take it off. Von Hagens stated that it was 'in respect of the people in which tradition I see myself', pointing to one of the large illustrations on the wall of a Rembrandt painting, *The Anatomy Lesson of Dr Tulp* (1632), in which the anatomist wears a similar hat.[19] The audience cheered and applauded. The applause wasn't only for this kind of banter, however – the removal of the heart and lungs, a very heavy mass deposited on a large tray for the audience to inspect later, drew another round of applause, presumably acknowledging the effort, skill, and perhaps showmanship of Von Hagens and his assistants. Again, at the announcement of a half-hour interval in the performance, the audience applauded – the end of Act 1.

Viewing the autopsy, the audience was acutely aware of its theatricality. Indeed, Von Hagens describes this kind of autopsy as 'event anatomy': the performance is an 'event', a show, and he is referred to in the programme as a 'showman anatomist'. Nonetheless, this was a real autopsy that he was performing on a real body, as he confronted the live audience and the television audience with a sense of their own mortality and challenged contemporary social norms, including taboos, particularly in Western society, around discussing death openly and performing autopsies in public.

Sci-Art: Collaborations between Artists and Scientists

A different kind of provocative theatre-science intervention can be found in the twenty-first-century rise of 'Sci-Art': collaborations between artists and scientists intended to have mutual benefit for both, while engaging public audiences and allowing collaborators to explore their own respective practices and understandings through new lenses. In the UK, this was spurred on

[19] Ibid.

particularly by the funding programmes of the Wellcome Trust, including, in the first decade of the century, its influential 'Pulse programme'. A review of the range of work supported by the Pulse programme highlights not simply an engagement with a variety of scientific issues but a real willingness to explore and push artistic or aesthetic boundaries, as exemplified by the combination of dance and visual imagery in *Skin Deep* (All Change Arts), the botanical garden site-specific improvisation and performance of *The Rainforest Pharmacy*, the visually fascinating and fragmentary hospital performance of *Visiting Time* (Sir John Colfox School and Dorset County Hospital), and the performance installation using grains of rice to visually represent human statistics focusing on infectious disease and vaccination, *Plague Nation* (Stan's Cafe), to mention just a few. In addition, larger-scale programmes of theatres such as at the Theatre Royal Plymouth and the Birmingham Rep, and the experimental, interactive work of such groups as SymbioticA and Critical Arts Ensemble – often brought to public attention by the likes of the boundary-crossing organization Arts Catalyst – have contributed to an eclectic range of theatre and performance making geared around science, medicine, and technology.

Plays about science are not new, of course, and in recent decades, Michael Frayn's *Copenhagen*, Stephen Poliakoff's *Blinded by the Sun*, Timberlake Wertenbaker's *After Darwin*, and Anna Ziegler's *Photograph 51* have all received mainstream production and attracted critical attention. More noticeable in the last twenty years, however, has been the commissioning of plays for young people as part of theatres' broader education programmes. A leading example is the Theatre Royal Plymouth's 'Theatre of Science' programmes, which commissioned plays such as *Seeing without Light* and *Still Life* as part of a broader series of workshops, school projects, and public events; and the Birmingham Rep's commissioning of *Rosalind: A Question of Life*, also part of a wider season of activities including a public symposium and workshop programme entitled 'It Ain't Rocket Science'. These examples show a multifaceted approach that engages a range of audiences through a variety of participation opportunities.

Funded partly by the Wellcome Trust and Creative Partnerships, 'Theatre of Science' began in 2003 with the Theatre Royal Plymouth in collaboration with the Peninsular Medical School. Its stated aims included, amongst others:

- to enhance awareness and provoke debate surrounding the ethics and practice in biomedical science
- to examine and evaluate innovative ways of bringing dramatists, theatre practitioners and scientists together to shape biomedical theatre, community and education projects

- to extend access to theatre and science across schools and the local community and for people of all ages and backgrounds
- to experiment with methods of public engagement with science, through large- and small-scale performances, festivals, play readings and public events.[20]

Under the direction of Rebecca Gould and Jeff Teare, 'Theatre of Science' was grounded in the view that 'the moral and ethical dilemmas involved in new science need to be debated publicly and theatre has always been about public debate'.[21] *Seeing without Light* (2005) by Simon Turley focused on HIV, including notions of genetic immunity to the virus, attitudes to the disease, and questions of scientific responsibility. It included a 'community partnership' with the Eddystone Trust in Plymouth and drama workshops in eleven local schools exploring the biomedical and ethical issues related to HIV treatment and research.[22] The second play, *Still Life* by Charles Way, explored the links between DNA and longevity and the ethics of genetic research. Particularly noteworthy is the extensive drama-based education programme that accompanied these productions, including INSET sessions with teachers, a workshop introducing dramatic approaches to biomedical science in schools, pupils devising and rehearsing their own work, and a schools festival. It also included the creation of a site-specific physical theatre performance for sixty participants of all ages supported by Gecko Theatre Company. As an intervention, what is exciting about this approach is that it was not just about participants being required to respond to the stimulus of a play or drama exercise; rather, it required them to come to terms with the material in order to make their own dramatic or theatrical statements, to create their own performances. 'Theatre of Science' developed into Theatrescience, an ongoing project of plays, workshops, performances, and festivals, including Theatrescience India, a collaboration with theatre practitioners and educators in Bangalore, Mumbai, and Kolkata.[23]

Theatre of Debate: Y Touring

Another significant example of theatre for young people is Y Touring, a touring company that ran between 1989 and 2014, developing the 'Genetic

---

[20] 'Theatre of Science: The Report', written by Laura Bowers and edited by Mel Scaffold. Theatre Royal Plymouth. Undated, p. 2.
[21] Ibid., 3.   [22] Ibid., 4.
[23] For further information on Theatrescience India, see Jeff Teare, 'Theatrescience 2002–2013', in *Knowledges in Publics*, ed. Lorraine Locke and Simon Locke (Newcastle upon Tyne, 2013), 109.

Futures' programme using what they called a 'theatre of debate'.[24] This model of theatre included performing a production followed by debate between the actors, still in character, and the audience. Their approach was cross-curricular and included the development of educational resources for teachers and youth leaders. In terms of their stated aims, Y Touring's focus was not overtly on the impact of science on the theatre itself (in the way that, say, the Theatre Royal Plymouth expressed an interest in what collaboration between theatre and science does to the kind of theatre we make), but more fully on the promotion of drama 'as a means of exploring and understanding the ethical questions arising from current and future developments in the field of biomedical science'.[25] Nonetheless, while their aim might sound somewhat instrumental, at the heart of their work was the creation of stimulating new theatre work.

Thus, again supported by the Wellcome Trust, plays include *Scenes from a Fair* by Jonathan Hall, set in 1914 and exploring the theme of eugenics; *Born of Glass* by Rhiannon Tise, focusing on IVF, surrogacy, saviour babies, and pre-implantation genetic diagnosis (PGD); *Genes 'R' Us* by Rahila Gupta, set in 2040 and imaginatively exploring the link between genes and behaviour; and *Leap of Faith* by Nicola Baldwin, looking at notions about the risks of genetically modified food. They also produced *Every Breath* and *Nobody Lives Forever*, both by Judith Johnson, the first dealing with animals in medical research, the latter with stem cell research. Of course, describing these plays in this didactic way does a disservice to the richness of the work in terms of character and dramatic action, and the way in which they specifically key into the contemporary worlds of young people.

Nobody Lives Forever provides an illuminating example of young people's theatre that engages them with scientific ideas. Aimed at Key Stage 4 children (aged fourteen and older), the play focuses on Tracey, a DJ, who has two children: Riv, in his early twenties, conceived during an ecstasy-fuelled night in the late 1980s, and Phee, born in the mid-1990s, in this case with an anonymous sperm-bank donor, a talented violinist, we are told, who climbs mountains in his spare time.[26] The play focuses on a variety of character relationships including between Riv and church-goer Cassie, and Phee and stem cell specialist Dr Khaled. Tracey is also diagnosed with the debilitating Huntington's disease, raising issues for Cassie and Riv, who have been trying for a baby; should they take their chances or go for pre-implantation genetic diagnosis? As is clear, the play is filled with a variety of complex issues and perspectives that underpin the theatre-of-debate model.

[24] www.ytouring.org.uk/science/index.html.   [25] Ibid.
[26] Y Touring, 'Preparatory Lessons' resource pack, vi.

Nobody Lives Forever was developed in partnership with the Association of Medical Research Charities and supported by the Medical Research Council, King's College London, Action Medical Research, the Department of Health, and the Royal Albert Hall. Each performance was followed by a live debate using electronic voting technology. In addition, schools were invited to make short digital films to further explore the debate on stem cell research.[27] The resource materials for teachers included 'discussion triggers' that raised some key questions such as 'When does human life begin?' and 'If stem cell research were to result in therapies and cures, who would have access to this treatment?', and provided short extracts from the play as stimulus material with follow-up prompts and questions.[28] Other resource packs included preparatory material that encompassed a synopsis of the play, character information, and preparatory lesson plans; and lessons focusing on Initial Responses, PSHE (Personal, Social, and Health Education)/Citizenship classes, Science, Drama, English, and Religious Studies.

Theatre and Global Intervention on Climate Change

Arguably, if there is one aspect of science that has gained increasing urgency in the twenty-first century, it is the environmental sciences. At the time of writing, young people around the world have been taking time off from school to protest about the lack of government action on climate change, and what was once a 'fringe' concern has become core to mainstream politics, creating explicit ideological divisions. In this context there is clear potential for theatre and performance to make creative interventions. Already there have been various performance practices in this vein – from plays about climate change, such as Mike Bartlett's *Earthquakes in London* and Moira Buffini, Penelope Skinner, Matt Charman, and Jack Thorne's *Greenland* to the work of activist-artists such as Liberate Tate, the performance art of US antigasoline ensemble Coltura, the Under the Sal Tree Festival in India, the Amazing Stars Arts Academy climate change advocacy performances in Zimbabwe, and street performances that form part of demonstrations across the world such as those by Extinction Rebellion.

To take one specific example: Climate Change Theatre Action (CCTA) is a form of global intervention, attempting to raise awareness and mobilize communities through the use of performance. In their networking approach,

---

[27] www.ytouring.org.uk/science/production.html.
[28] Y Touring 'Discussion Triggers' resource pack for *Nobody Lives Forever*.

participants across the world sign up and organize their own local events, drawing on a shared resource of short plays by commissioned playwrights. Founded in 2015 by Elaine Ávila, Chantal Bilodeau, Roberta Levitow, and Caridad Svich, CCTA is a global participatory series of short play readings and performances that coincide every two years with the United Nations' Conference of the Parties (COP) meetings, which focus on progress in dealing with climate change globally in line with agreed targets.[29] This initiative is a collaboration between three US-based organisations: the Arctic Cycle, the Center for Sustainable Practice in the Arts, and Theatre without Borders.

The Arctic Cycle, which is led by Bilodeau, the New York–based Canadian playwright and translator, focuses on the intersection of theatre, science, and policy. The company states that it

> uses theatre to foster dialogue about our global climate crisis, create an empowering vision of the future, and inspire people to take action. Operating on the principle that complex problems must be addressed through collaborative efforts, we work with artists across disciplines and geographic borders, solicit input from earth and social scientists, and actively seek community and educational partners.[30]

Their collaboration with the Center for Sustainable Practice in the Arts, which is a US and Canadian think tank that 'focuses on the intersection of environmental balance, social equity, economic stability and a strengthened cultural infrastructure',[31] and with Theatre without Borders, a volunteer network using a virtual platform that '*shares information* and *builds connections* between individuals and institutions interested in international theatre and performance exchange',[32] allows for a wide-reaching, cross-sector intervention.

The organizers of Climate Change Theatre Action commission fifty professional playwrights every two years to write five-minute plays that focus on climate change. It is clearly important to the CCTA that playwrights come from all continents and represent various cultures and indigenous nations as well. This collection of plays is then available free to any collaborators across the world, who select from the plays on offer and arrange events during an approximately six-week window coinciding with COP. A review of the different international projects that were part of CCTA

---

[29] www.climatechangetheatreaction.com/about/.   [30] www.thearcticcycle.org/initiatives.
[31] www.sustainablepractice.org/about-us/the-cspa/.
[32] www.theatrewithoutborders.com/home/about-us/ (original emphasis).

2015 and CCTA 2017 shows a breadth of approaches ranging from rehearsed readings to full productions. Participants included professional theatres, community groups, amateur drama groups, school pupils, library staff, and university students.

For example, Climate Change Theatre Action 2017 took place in October and November 2017 coinciding with the United Nations 23rd Conference of the Parties. There were almost 140 events in 23 countries. According to the organizers, plays were read and performed 'live and on radio, and presented in a variety of settings including: theatres, high schools, middle schools, universities, yoga studios, community centres, libraries, churches, museums, cafes, bars, people's living rooms, and outdoors'.[33] Alongside the presentation of the plays, collaborators are also encouraged to incorporate additional 'action' into their events, which could include collaborating across departments, working with social justice organizations, writing letters to government representatives, and sharing tools for local sustainability.

Back in my home city of Cardiff, we had a taste of this type of intervention at the University of South Wales when students and staff participated in CCTA 2017, in a project of public play readings at Chapter Arts Centre convened by Professor Márta Minier (drama) and Professor Giuliano Premier (low carbon systems engineering and senior member of the Sustainable Environment Research Centre). On speaking to student participants about their experience, two key themes emerged: excitement at the sense of being part of something bigger through an awareness of the global interconnection, and the feeling that theatre provided a voice of some kind, that it was a means to impact meaningfully on society in some way, whether large or small. The five-minute-play model was also felt to be good because it enabled participants to explore a range of theatrical responses to climate change and offered the opportunity to involve a large number of people in a way that was manageable.

Whether at a global scale or a micro level, there are numerous examples and models of how we might think about theatre and science as social intervention. While there is clearly a broad spectrum of practice, what these examples highlight is the desire and potential for social impact of some kind – raising awareness, mobilizing for action, educating, provoking thinking, engaging the public. At the heart of all this work is an aspiration for social transformation, and it is the boundaries and intersections of theatre and science that offer such a rich catalyst for intervention and change.

---

[33] www.climatechangetheatreaction.com/about/ccta-2017/.

Suggested Reading

The Autopsy. Channel 4 (UK television). Performed by Gunter von Hagens, presented by Krishnan Guru-Murthy, directed by David Coleman. Mentorn/Channel 4, London. Broadcast 21 November 2002.

Bleeker, Maaike, ed. *Anatomy Live: Performance and the Operating Theatre*. Amsterdam, 2008.

'Dr. Faraday's Lectures at the Royal Institution', *British Medical Journal* (5 January 1861): 18–19.

British Medical Journal (12 January 1861): 49–51.

Ingham, Karen. 'Art and the Theatre of Mind and Body: How Contemporary Arts Practice Is Re-framing the Anatomo-Clinical Theatre'. *Journal of Anatomy* 216, no. 2 (February 2010): 251–63.

Kemp, Martin, and Marina Wallace. *Spectacular Bodies: The Art and Science of the Human Body from Leonardo to Now*. London, 2000.

Klestinec, Cynthia. *Theatres of Anatomy: Students, Teachers, and Traditions of Dissection in Renaissance Venice*. Baltimore, 2011.

Mandressi, Rafael. 'Of the Eye and of the Hand: Performance in Early Modern Anatomy'. *TDR/The Drama Review* 59, no. 3 (2015): 60–76.

Prentki, Tim, and Sheila Preston, eds. *The Applied Theatre Reader*. London, 2009.

Sawday, Jonathan. *The Body Emblazoned: Art, Dissection and the Human Body in Renaissance Culture*. London, 1995.

Stephenson, Shelagh. *An Experiment with an Air Pump*. London, 1998.

Teare, Jeff. 'Theatrescience 2002–2013'. In *Knowledges in Publics*, ed. Lorraine Locke and Simon Locke. Newcastle upon Tyne, 2013, 105–18.

Thomas, John Meurig. *Michael Faraday and the Royal Institution*. Bristol,1991.

Watt Smith, Tiffany. *On Flinching: Theatricality and Scientific Looking from Darwin to Shell Shock*. Oxford, 2014.

Wootton, David, ed. *The Invention of Science: A New History of the Scientific Revolution*. London, 2015.

RHONDA BLAIR

Acting and Science

This chapter focuses on late twentieth- and early twenty-first-century cognitive science and neurosciences, which provide insight into imagination,
intellect, emotion, memory, language, and body as parts of a complex
process. It illuminates how we are inextricably intertwined with each other
and our environments and how these pertain to the actor, primarily within a
Western context.[1]

Debating the Power of Imitation

Since the ancient Greeks, science and philosophy have been used to define
the actor's process. In the fifth century BCE, Plato wrote of embodiment's
power to shape behaviour and consciousness, linking acting, science, and
morality. Critiquing the power of imitation and empathy to change both
orator and audience, he asked whether there is a place for imitation (i.e.,
acting) in society at all. Since imitation had the power to become habituated,
he asserted that it was morally dangerous and should not be allowed or, if
allowed, only as an imitation of virtue; thus, he paradoxically viewed imitation as both weakening and powerfully corrupting. In the fourth century
BCE, Aristotle agreed imitation was powerful, but he asserted that imitating
is a basic human drive and that humans naturally learn our earliest lessons
through it. Anticipating recent research in action and imagination, in the
Poetics, Aristotle defined the imitation of an *action* as the core of drama. In
On the Soul, Book III, Part 7, he asserted the soul never thinks without a
mental image, and that, when mental pictures are strongly present, the soul
is as moved as if the actual objects were present to the senses. These insights
have been borne out by scientific research and in modern acting techniques
that link imagination and action (e.g., Stanislavsky's active analysis,

---

[1] A definitive overview of acting and science from the Greeks through the mid-twentieth
century is found in Joseph Roach's *The Player's Passion: Studies in the Science of Acting.*

discussed in *An Actor's Work*; Michael Chekhov's psychological gesture, discussed in *To the Actor: On the Technique of Acting*; and Declan Donellan's 'actor and target' in the book of the same name).

From the first century CE until about 1750, the rhetoric of the passions, which combined classical rhetoric and the current scientific thinking, dominated. Much of this was derived from the Roman Quintilian, who asserted that actors had protean powers to transform themselves, the space around them, and spectators, by transferring their spirits, or *pneuma*, into them through the air, or *aether*. These inspiring *pneuma*, imbibed from the *aether*, permeated the actor's blood as spirits, then radiated outward, and manifested in motion. The actor thus acted in three ways: on his own body, on the physical space around him, and on spectators' bodies. Views of body, imagination, and feeling as integrated, as seen here, were subsequently built upon by others, including John Bulwer, who, in the seventeenth century, asserted that gestures are universal because they proceed naturally from the way the body works, that is, 'the tongue, without the hand, can utter nothing but what will come forth lame and impotent'.[2] The physiology and rhetoric of the passions followed Aristotle's view that internal images activate the body.

New Theories about the Self

In the eighteenth century, a machine model became dominant as inventions of new machines provided a new metaphor for the human. Humans were thought to be similar to machines in which, according to Descartes's dualism, the body (the 'machine') was driven by an inhabiting soul. In acting the greatest example of this was David Garrick, who embraced a machine view of the human, influenced by Descartes's 'I think, therefore I am' and by the invention of machines such as sophisticated automata. An actor was seen as a moving statue (*res extensa*) guided by the rational soul (*res cogitans*, firmly centred in the brain). Pumps and puppets became models for the actor's process. 'Man as machine' was taken one step further by Julien de la Mettrie, who, in 1747, described humans as being machines much like clocks, the soul resulting from how our physical matter was organized. Writing on acting, playwright Aaron Hill stated that imagination came first, affecting facial expression, and then the will compelled animal spirits to stimulate muscles into the appropriate position. By 1750 arguments about internal versus external approaches to acting appeared. Philosopher-playwright

[2] John Bulwer, *Chirologia, or the Natural Language of the Hand and Chironomia or the Art of Manual Rhetoric* (1644), ed. James W. Cleary (Carbondale, 1974), 156–7.

Gotthold Ephraim von Lessing rejected imagination as the starting point and foreshadowed modern psychophysical views when he described actors who generate internal passions by first engaging in external activity, that is, the physical (body) leads to the emotional (feeling). At this time there was no concept of the subconscious or unconscious, only of conscious mind and palpable matter.

In the latter part of the century, views that saw bodies as being moved by nervous 'vibrations' and souls as a function of physical organization began to surpass machine-based ones; scientific work such as Pierre Polinière's 1709 experiments with frog hearts and Luigi Galvani's 1780 discovery that the muscles of dead frogs' legs twitched when struck by an electrical spark presaged later studies on electrical signals from nerves and muscles. These went along with philosopher David Hartley's associationism, which held that sensations or movements induce the sensations or movements with which they were earlier connected – a precursor of sorts to what is today called *habituation*. Taking the Greeks' view of imitation's power further, associationism held that each person's flesh had an innate capacity for responsiveness; that is, soul is a function of the physical capacity to respond to sensation. Hartley was the first to use the term 'psychology' in its modern sense in 1749; marrying the idea of vibrations to associationism, he explained psychological phenomena with physiological principles, using the concept of stimulus-response. For example, we see something that frightens us (a nearby bear, the stimulus) and our heart beats faster (the response).

The distinguishing between mind and body in acting theories was taken further by French philosopher Denis Diderot. *Paradoxe sur le comedien (The Paradox of Acting*, 1773) is the paradigmatic text in modern Western acting theory. It asserts that the actor should have an absence of 'sensibility'; rather than feel what he is portraying, the actor should be in control of their performance in order to make the audience feel emotion. Diderot presages Russian directors Meyerhold and Stanislavsky; both of their approaches would involve the actor developing and creating a specific physical score to embody character and action consistently, in the service of the audience's experience. The *Paradoxe* originated concepts of 'emotion memory, imagination, creative unconsciousness, ensemble playing, double consciousness, concentration, public solitude, character body, the score of the role, spontaneity',[3] which are defined and developed in Stanislavsky's books and have become fundamental terms in contemporary Western actor training.

[3] Joseph Roach, *The Player's Passion: Studies in the Science of Acting* (Ann Arbor, 1993), 117.

Diderot's view of the individual as a flow of experiences connected through memory is echoed today in neuroscientist Joseph Ledoux's 'synaptic self'; he asserts we are a product of the workings and habituations of our synapses. Diderot's theory of sensibility anticipated terms in biology relevant to acting, including monism and the 'unconscious'. The term 'monism' was introduced by philosopher Christian von Wolff (*Logic*, 1728), who viewed the entire universe as manifestations of a single substance and specifically argued against dualistic views of body and mind.

Finding Character: Psychology, Biology, Emotion

Psychology, neuroscience, and a more modern biological science emerged in the nineteenth century (the word 'biology' first appeared in 1801–2), launching arguments between mechanists and biological vitalists, and preparing the way for the *Paradoxe*'s publication in 1830. 'Organism' replaced 'machine' as the dominant model for the human, reinforcing a monistic view. This influenced scientist, dramatist, and actor George Henry Lewes, who studied the 'organism' model's implication for acting; he introduced the term 'psychology' into dramatic criticism. He connected emotional states with biological conditions and defined a more modern view of double consciousness and attention (there is a chapter on this in Lewes's *Problems of Life and Mind*). Meanwhile, Russian physiologist Ivan Sechenov established what would become reflexology (a precursor of behaviourism), using a material approach to emotion through neurophysiology.

These new views of organisms and the unconscious affected how imagination, action, and feeling were perceived, giving rise in acting to the idea of a character having a life beyond the script; the actor began to think about 'who the character is' as a being, rather than a role to be played, a set of choices to be performed. One significant example of this is Eleonora Duse (1858–1924), whose goal was to 'eliminate the self'; noted for performances in Ibsen's plays (including Nora in *A Doll House* and the title role in *Hedda Gabler*), she was praised for the realism and emotional power of her acting.[4] By the 1870s the terms 'unconscious' and 'subconscious' provided a meeting ground for biology and speculative psychology. These developments were key to the thinking of critic William Archer, who asserted that actors work on feelings indirectly; they do not will them into existence consciously but create the psychological conditions in which they might arise. This presages Stanislavsky's 'getting to the unconscious through conscious means'

---

[4] For further discussion, see Kirsten Shepherd-Barr, *Theatre and Evolution from Ibsen to Beckett* (New York, 2015), 53–62.

(i.e., conscious means such as textual analysis, research, and exploration of physical scores are used to work on a role) and the 'magic if' (the actor imagines, 'What would I do if I were in the character's situation?') to free up imagination and creativity.

Into the Twentieth Century: Precursors of Cognitive Science

Two primary paths of research developed in neuroscience and psychology, which came to be included under the umbrella term 'cognitive sciences'. Neuroscience's beginnings can be traced to Paul Broca's 1861 discovery of the link between a particular brain area and the capacity for speech. In psychology, two contesting views were laid out early on. Sigmund Freud, initially a doctor, neurologist, and research psychologist, left to pursue psychoanalysis, publishing *The Interpretation of Dreams* in 1899; his vocabulary of the unconscious was dominant for decades in the US, profoundly influencing many acting teachers.

Conversely, philosopher-psychologists William James and Carl Lange defined the body, rather than the psyche, as the ground for emotion. Following Lewes, they separately developed the James–Lange theory (1884–5) that emotions do not lead to physical responses, but rather are the *result* of physical processes and behaviours: not 'I see the bear, I feel frightened, I run,' but 'I see the bear, I run, I feel terrified' (for more on this, see James's *Principles of Psychology*). Russian physiologist Ivan Pavlov built on this and Sechenov's work, publishing findings in 1906 that further supported physiologically based approaches to psychology. This research was foundational to Meyerhold's biomechanics and Stanislavsky's methods of physical actions and active analysis, with their emphasis on the materiality of the body and on repetition in the creative process. Stanislavsky's later work was grounded in reflexology's central idea that behaviours are reflex reactions in psychophysical chains: 'Mind you, only physical actions, physical truths, and physical belief in them! Nothing more!'[5] His goal was the creation of a habitual, replicable score that the actor could repeat and *live* in 'reflexively', and that would move the audience. Stanislavsky influenced, among others, three members of the Moscow Art Theatre company: Meyerhold, Michael Chekhov, and Richard Boleslavsky. The latter two became influential acting teachers, Chekhov in Western Europe and then in the US, and Boleslavsky in the US. Boleslavsky founded the American Laboratory Theatre in 1923; his students included three artists who would

[5] Konstantin Stanislavsky, *An Actor Prepares*, trans. E. R. Hapgood (London, 1936), 142.

be founding members of the Group Theatre and major acting teachers: Stella Adler, Harold Clurman, and Lee Strasberg. Strasberg is said to be primarily 'psychological' in his approach; yet, while he did emphasize the actor's emotional life, he said that 'the emotional thing is not Freud, ... it is Pavlov'.[6] The science influenced them all.

Mid- and Late Twentieth Century: Cognitive Sciences, from Neuroscience to Cognitive Linguistics and Beyond

During these decades it became clearer that, in the practice of the actor, body, mind, feeling, and language could not be separated; the actor is a holistic organism functioning as part of a dynamic system. The umbrella term 'cognitive science', which came to the fore in the mid-twentieth century, encompasses fields that address this, including cognitive psychology, cognitive linguistics, neuroscience, neurolinguistics, and cognitive anthropology. At its inception, cognitive science was influenced by other fields, including linguistics and computer science. Developments in computer science (the first freely programmable computer was invented in 1936) led to the hypothesis that binary processes were analogous to those of our brains. In the latter 1950s, linguists (notably, Noam Chomsky), computer scientists interested in artificial intelligence, psychologists, and philosophers founded the field of cognitive science to study the acquisition and processing of knowledge. This first generation, which lasted roughly from 1950 to 1980, marginalized physical aspects of the brain's workings. This became the purview of neuroscience.

Neuroscientists were identifying physical sources of cognition, discovering more locations in the brain for select functions and learning how experience alters brain anatomy. By 1970 they had discovered a neurological basis for memory, marked by alterations in neural structures. A decade later, positron emission tomography scans photographed activity in the brain. In 1990 functional magnetic resonance imagery provided images of dynamic neural processes. In the same year, the Human Genome Project was initiated, further exploring what it means to be human through studying organic aspects of existence. Many discoveries revealed that neural operations are too complex to be accounted for by binary codes, and more complex images of cognition were developed. This 'second generation' is attempting to identify, among other things, how consciousness arises as an embodied process.

---

[6] Lee Strasberg, "Working with Live Material," in *Stanislavski and America*, ed. Erika Munk (New York, 1967), 198.

Though humans cannot work consciously on the neural level, it helps to know how brains function and how we are materially connected to others and to our environments. For example, Iacomo Rizzolatti's 1996 publication of the discovery of mirror neurons in macaque monkeys energized research in neural simulation systems in humans and generated new questions about the nature of the self, imitation, empathy, and action. Rizzolatti found the monkeys' brains contained a class of neurons

> that respond to a particular kind of gesture, no matter who is making the gesture – the monkey whose brain activity is being recorded, or another monkey. If the monkey being recorded reaches for a grape, areas in the animal's prefrontal lobes discharge. If another monkey, or even a human, reaches for the grape, the neurons of the monkey observing the action also discharge. In short, the neurons mirror both activities of the self and activities of others directed at the same goal.[7]

For macaques, watching something can neurally be the same as doing something – the same neurons fire. This does not mean that humans have mirror neurons in the same way or that they function identically; as of 2016 only one study by Mukamel et al. had found neurons in humans similar to those in macaques.[8] However, there is continued exploration of what human neural mirroring systems might be and mean. Hypotheses posit that these might play a role in our ability to imitate, as we convert observed action into muscle movement, and that who we are and how we function are based largely upon the development of specific neural patterns, or synaptic connections. From this perspective, the sense of self is a product of our synapses; nature (genetic make-up) and nurture (experiences) are merely different ways of doing the same thing – wiring synapses in the brain that manifest as who we are.

Into the Twenty-First Century: Cognitive Ecologies

Though we do not know all of the steps by which 'matter becomes imagination' (to quote neuroscientists Gerald Edelman and Giulio Tononi[9]), how consciousness and behaviour relate to brain function is becoming clearer.

[7] Michael Gazzaniga, *The Ethical Brain* (New York, 2005), 104.

[8] Roy, Mukamel, Arne D. Ekstrom, Jonas Kaplan, Marco Iacoboni, and Itzhak Fried, 'Single-Neuron Responses in Humans during Execution and Observation of Actions', *Current Biology* 20, no. 8 (2010): 750–8.

[9] Gerald Edelman and Giulio Tononi, *A Universe of Consciousness: How Matter Becomes Imagination* (New York, 2000).

Antonio Damasio's somatic marker hypothesis provides an entry point, describing how body-states become linked with conscious responses to or interpretations of them.[10] Echoing monistic views, body, feeling, and intellect are seen as aspects of a single process: the brain creates strings of associations that arise in the body first as an emotion (defined by Damasio as a *physiological* state), which is translated into a feeling (a conscious 'registration' of the body state), which leads to behaviour that may or may not be associated with rational thought. These markers become our repertory of responses guiding reactions to new situations. Particularly pertinent is Damasio's assertion that reason in its fullest sense grows out of and is permeated by emotion and that emotion is consistently affected by conscious cognition. This 'full organism' hypothesis supports views that physicality, feeling/impulse, and thought/reason are inseparable parts of the acting process.

These 'ecological' views of cognition also hold that the person cannot be separated from the environment (much in the way Stanislavsky viewed character as being inseparable from given circumstances). Edelman and Tononi describe how higher brain functions, including consciousness, are conditioned by and require interactions with the world and other people; that is, mind is a result of reciprocal interaction between perceptual and proprioceptive experience (which is perception connected to the position and movement of the body), between external and internal environments: what happens in one aspect influences what happens in the others. Developing along the material line of Lewes and others, they assert that only physical processes are needed to explain consciousness and that consciousness arose only because of the specific evolution of the human body in response to environmental changes in the natural world and in the organization of human communities. Rejecting computer-model concepts of closed-circuit, binary logic as the basis for understanding cognitive processes, ecological views of cognition describe cognition as open, nonlinear, and subject to perturbations from an array of different sources. Processes of creativity, imagination, and memory, among others, in the acting studio, rehearsal, or performance, operate dynamically and provisionally, grounded in material realities of the body. Acting, like all of life, is a dynamic and shifting process.

Theatre practitioners and performance studies scholars began engaging with modern cognitive and neurosciences substantially in the late 1990s. Articles were appearing by 2000, and the first monographs on acting and

[10] Antonio Damasio, *The Feeling of What Happens: Body and Emotion in the Making of Consciousness* (Boston, 2000).

cognitive science appeared in 2008. The first survey book was Bruce McConachie and F. Elizabeth Hart's *Performance and Cognition: Theatre Studies and the Cognitive Turn*. Significant monographs include McConachie's *Engaging Audiences: A Cognitive Approach to Spectating in the Theatre*; Rhonda Blair's *The Actor, Image, and Action: Acting and Cognitive Neuroscience*; Amy Cook's *Shakespearean Neuroplay: Reinvigorating the Study of Dramatic Texts and Performance through Cognitive Science* and *Building Character: The Art and Science of Casting*; John Lutterbie's *Toward a General Theory of Acting: Cognitive Science and Performance*; Rick Kemp's *Embodied Acting: What Neuroscience Tells Us about Performance*; Blair and Cook's *Theatre, Performance, and Cognition: Language, Bodies, and Ecologies*; and Maiya Murphy's *Enacting LeCoq: Movement in Theatre, Cognition, and Life*. Evelyn Tribble's *Cognition in the Globe: Attention and Memory in Shakespeare's Theatre* is an essential text describing a historical study of theatre as a 'cognitive ecology' in which the actor functions.

This work offers radically new tools and perspectives to understand what it is that we do when we act. Many who apply cognitive science to acting use concepts of cognitive ecologies and 4E cognition (described below), which are related to *situated cognition* and *embodied cognition*. These provide vocabularies that are useful in the studio or rehearsal. Performance scholars Evelyn Tribble and John Sutton define cognitive ecologies as

> the multidimensional contexts in which we remember, feel, think, sense, communicate, imagine, and act, often collaboratively, on the fly, and in rich ongoing interaction with our environments ... The idea is not that the isolated, unsullied individual first provides us with the gold standard for a cognitive agent, and that mind is then projected outward into the ecological system: but that from the start (historically and developmentally) remembering, attending, intending, and acting are distributed, co-constructed, system-level activities.[11]

Theatre spaces are paradigmatic examples of cognitive ecologies.

The terms of 4E cognition – 'embodied', 'embedded', 'extended', and 'enacted' – describe how cognition works.[12] Cognition is *embodied* – it is inseparable from our physical being. Cognition is *embedded* – it depends on off-loading cognitive work and taking advantage of affordances, or potentials, in the environment, as when we step on a chair to reach a shelf. Cognition is *extended* – it goes beyond the individual's body–mind boundaries, and interacts dynamically with others. Cognition is *enacted* – it is

---

[11] Evelyn Tribble and John Sutton, 'Cognitive Ecology as a Framework for Shakespearean Studies', *Shakespeare Studies* 39 (2011): 94–103.
[12] For a succinct overview, see *The Cambridge Handbook of Situated Cognition*, ed. Philip Robbins and Murat Aydede (Cambridge, 2009), 3–13.

inseparable from action and is often an attribute or a result of action; theorists such as Alva Noë argue that perception is in fact inseparable from action.[13] This understanding of the inseparability of doing and perceiving is, again presciently, reflected in the last stages of Stanislavsky's work, his methods of physical actions and active analysis.

Extended cognition, referring to the cognitive links between us and others, involves things such as neural and kinaesthetic mirroring systems and mind-reading. Aspects of extended cognition involve 'theory of other minds' (TOM), namely, that we respond based on 'reading' the intentions of others, consciously and preconsciously. We perceive not just the action of an other, but the intention of the action; a *part* of this may be connected to mirror neurons, which, in macaque monkeys, 'respond strongest to the goal of the action, not to the action itself' – it is not just the hand reaching, but the hand reaching for a piece of food to eat.[14] This is connected to the TOM-related hypothesis that '"I" may have begun with "you"': our sense of an other may have arisen *before* we had a sense of self. Neuroscientist V. S. Ramachandran hypothesizes that TOM 'evolved *first* in response to social needs and then later, as an unexpected bonus, came the ability to introspect on your own thoughts and intentions'.[15] This resonates with acting techniques that focus on a target in the environment. Stanislavsky emphasized the actor focusing on her character's *zadacha*, more accurately translated into English as 'problem' or 'task', rather than 'objective', as it was originally by Elizabeth Reynolds Hapgood. Rather than 'what are you feeling', the questions should be: 'What do you want from the other character?' 'What are you trying to change or avoid?' and 'If you got what you wanted, what would the other character *do*?' For example, Hamlet's major problem in the play's first half is to find out if the ghost is telling the truth, and in the second half to figure out what to *do* about it.

The idea of cognition as enacted is arguably the most obviously applicable of the 4Es to acting. Because the body's capacities and actions determine and constrain what we perceive, Noë states that perception 'is something we do ... *What we perceive* is determined by *what we do* (or what we know how to do); it is determined by what we are *ready* to do.... [W]e *enact* our perceptual experience; we act it out.'[16] Philosopher Shaun Gallagher

---

[13] See, in particular, his chapter on the enactive approach in Alva Noë, *Action in Perception* (Boston, 2004).

[14] Lawrence W. Barsalou, 'Grounded Cognition', *Annual Review of Psychology* 59 (2008): 617–45 (623).

[15] V. S. Ramachandran, 'The Neurology of Self-Awareness', *Edge* 201, 22 January 2006, www.edge.org/documents/archive/edge201.html#rama.

[16] Noë, Action in Perception, 1–2.

connects this action–perception view to space and time, holding that space is first about our activities within it; spatiality is not about position, but about situation,[17] constrained by the particular possibilities of our bodies, which are 'primarily designed for action ... The brain attunes itself to what the body and the environment affords.'[18] Stanislavsky's later work presciently demonstrates applications of this principle of doing as the path to knowing and understanding.

The concept of perception-in-action can illuminate the place of mental representations, or images, in the actor's process. In some 'psychologically' or psychoanalytically based approaches, such as Strasberg's, the actor holds an image in mind and then responds based on that image; in other words, perceive first and then act. This can be useful and effective. However, Noë argues that taking action 'can be a form of representing':[19] to have a representation *is* to act. As Noë asks, if a person is *in* the world, why do they need to produce 'internal representations good enough to enable [the person], so to speak, to act as if the world were not immediately present?'[20] No '"translation" or transfer is necessary because it is already accomplished in the embodied perception itself'.[21] Or perhaps 'to visualize is to do, and to do is to visualize'. This view of representation and action as being not just integrated but inseparable requires rethinking the phases of the actor's work. Rather than thinking/'seeing' the actor's planned interpretation of a moment and then using that to inform doing, the actor, having done the necessary preparation, responds in the moment to the moment. The concept of perception-in-action, permeated by representation/image, opens up what the term 'act on impulse' can mean. This can validate reducing 'table work' time (sitting and discussing meanings and interpretations in early rehearsals) to move more quickly into the space, with actors on their feet, using their bodies in physical relation to each other to help them discover possible meanings and interpretations.

Language is a component of both action and representation. Cognitive linguistics studies how language arises and how images and structures in language shape our engagement with the world. Linguist George Lakoff and philosopher Mark Johnson argue that our sense of our bodies – the fact of *being* a body – is the source for our major metaphors of thought, meaning, and values, such that 'much of conceptual inference is, therefore,

---

[17] Shaun Gallagher, 'Philosophical Antecedents of Situated Cognition', in *The Cambridge Handbook of Situated Cognition*, ed. Robbins and Aydede, 35–52 (41–2).
[18] Shaun Gallagher, 'Invasion of the Body Snatchers: How Embodied Cognition Is Being Disembodied', *The Philosopher's Magazine* 68 (2015): 96–102 (100).
[19] Noë, *Action in Perception*, 130–1.   [20] Ibid., 22.   [21] Ibid., 80.

sensorimotor inference' (as when we say, 'I felt as light as a feather,' 'It came down on me like a ton of bricks,' or 'Time flew by'). Cognitive linguists Gilles Fauconnier and Mark Turner similarly give prominence to embodied metaphor and image. Holding that imagination is the engine of meaning and that metaphor is central to cognition, they describe how different mental spaces – small conceptual packets constructed as we think and talk – are integrated in novel ways to help us negotiate our lives. Disparate 'inputs' are combined to create new knowledge, insight, or experience that goes beyond that contained in the initial inputs, creating blended conceptual spaces; for example, when learning to ski, one might find it helpful to imagine being a waiter carrying a tray, blending these 'inputs' kinaesthetically even though they are physically radically different. In short, 'language does not represent meaning directly; instead, it systematically prompts the construction of meaning'.[22] The state of the body is both an input into and an output of language interpretation. The language – the image – that the actor uses is central to constructing meaning, thereby constraining or facilitating her engagement with a role.

Language production, language comprehension, and perception of intent are neurally inseparable; some of the same brain areas are crucial to language production *and* to language comprehension *and* to perceiving the intention of physical actions such as grasping and manipulation;[23] in fact, language may have evolved from a neurally grounded, pre-conscious perception of gestural intention. Studies have shown that 'the *sensorimotor* cortices are crucial to *semantic* understanding of bodily action terms and sentences'.[24] Some brain areas initially assumed to be solely about spatial orientation are also activated by language: the neural activation when one picks up a box is largely isomorphic with the activation stimulated when one hears the command 'Pick up that box.' Perception, image, and action are objectively, neurally connected to language. Amy Cook suggests that 'language is less a system of *communicating* experience than actually *being* experience; we do not translate words into perceptions, we perceive in order to understand'.[25] Actors should think of language as action and consider

---

[22] Gilles Fauconnier and Mark Turner, *The Way We Think: Conceptual Blending and the Mind's Hidden Complexities* (New York, 2008), 142.

[23] See Luciano Fadiga, Laila Craighero, Maddalena Fabbri Destro, Livio Finos, Nathalie Cotilon-Williams, Andrew T. Smith, and Umberto Castiello, 'Language in Shadow', *Social Neuroscience* 1, no. 2 (2006): 77–89.

[24] John Kaag, 'The Neurological Dynamics of the Imagination', *Phenomenology and the Cognitive Sciences* 8, no. 2 (2009): 183–204 (186) (emphasis mine).

[25] Amy Cook, 'Interplay: The Method and Potential of a Cognitive Scientific Approach to Theatre', *Theatre Journal* 59, no. 4 (2007): 579–94 (589).

how linguistic choices actually *create* their perceptions of and engagement with the work at hand.

Current cognitive science dislocates a number of things, among these, familiar constructs of identity, feeling, and selfhood and any sense that culture and biology are separable; these areas are, of course, fundamental to understanding acting. Though the sciences increasingly illuminate what happens when actors act, it is important to keep in mind the difference between *doing* science and *using* science; most of the applications of cognitive science to acting by practitioners and scholars are 'using science'. Different kinds of scientific evidence are useful for different aspects of performance practice, but this cannot be applied whole cloth. One must discern between data and conjecture. One must be sensitive to scientists' disagreements about research, evidence, and interpretations and to the fact that science's findings change over time as new evidence is found. Some performance practitioners are re-envisioning the science–performance interchange; the relatively young field of performance-as-research uses performance practice to investigate questions, including those related to acting and science.[26]

While theatre artists and scholars draw on science, our goals are rarely 'scientific' – typically, we use scientific findings to create a more powerful performance, to understand how a performance event works, or to teach better. This can involve a good degree of subjectivity, since the actor's job is to embody their role and be imaginative and creative, not necessarily factually 'accurate'. That said, science provides the actor with concrete information about how body, brain, feeling, and language materially work, helping the actor to be as creative as possible. The science can also be used 'poetically' and playfully, giving us new ways of acting and of playfully imagining that aren't 'scientific' at all.

Suggested Reading

Blair, Rhonda. *The Actor, Image, and Action: Acting and Cognitive Neuroscience*. London, 2008.

Blair, Rhonda, and Amy Cook, eds. *Theatre, Performance, and Cognition: Language, Bodies, and Ecologies*. London, 2016.

Blair, Rhonda, and John Lutterbie, eds. Special Section on Cognitive Science, Theatre and Performance. *Journal of Dramatic Theory and Criticism* 26, no. 2 (Fall 2011).

[26] See, for example, Annette Arlander, Bruce Barton, Melanie Dreyer-Lude, and Ben Spatz, eds., *Performance as Research: Knowledge, Methods, Impact* (London, 2017).

Cook, Amy. *Shakespearean Neuroplay: Reinvigorating the Study of Dramatic Texts and Performance through Cognitive Science.* London, 2010.

—— *Building Character: The Art and Science of Casting.* Ann Arbor, 2018.

Kemp, Rick. *Embodied Acting: What Neuroscience Tells Us about Performance.* London, 2012.

Lutterbie, John. *Toward a General Theory of Acting: Cognitive Science and Performance.* London, 2011.

McConachie, Bruce. *Engaging Audiences: A Cognitive Approach to Spectating in the Theatre.* London, 2008.

McConachie, Bruce, and F. Elizabeth Hart, eds. *Performance and Cognition: Theatre Studies and the Cognitive Turn.* London, 2006.

Murphy, Maiya. *Enacting LeCoq: Movement in Theatre, Cognition, and Life.* London, 2019.

Pitches, Jonathan. *Science and the Stanislavsky Tradition of Acting.* London, 2006.

Roach, Joseph. *The Player's Passion: Studies in the Science of Acting.* Ann Arbor, 1993.

Strasberg, Lee. 'Working with Live Material'. In *Stanislavski and America*, ed. Erika Munk. New York, 1967, 183–200.

Tribble, Evelyn. *Cognition in the Globe: Attention and Memory in Shakespeare's Theatre.* London, 2011.

Tribble, Evelyn, and John Sutton. 'Cognitive Ecology as a Framework for *Shakespearean Studies*'. *Shakespeare Studies* 39 (2011): 94–103.

12

AMY COOK

Staging Cognition

How Performance Shows Us How We Think

'Staging cognition' does not mean that a play or performance talks about the brain or science but rather that the theatricalization of the story demonstrates the ideas of science. For example, in Tom Stoppard's *Arcadia*, characters talk about chaos and complexity and through them we hear about patterns and iteration, fractals and energy. One character is tracking the grouse population on the estate and another, in another century but in the same location, is learning about Newtonian physics. The play culminates with four characters, across time and in time, dancing a waltz on the same stage. There is pattern, iteration, energy, staged as the two couples waltz and shift their trajectories to avoid colliding into a different century or off the stage. We are watching characters move together, motivated by desire, and actors navigate choreography, motivated by avoiding the other dancers and the edge of the stage. Spectators might not have understood all the physics, math, and philosophy discussed throughout the play, and they may not have seen the dance as connected to those themes, but they saw the enactment – through dance and desire, anticipation and prediction – of chaos and complexity. These are the moments I am interested in. In this chapter, I argue that theatrical innovations around personation, or the taking on of a character, in the cycle dramas of the medieval period and the off-off-Broadway theatre of today, display a changing notion of the self.

Thinking and speaking are creative and metaphoric. We do not use language as a code with which we translate what is out there; we organize what is out there around metaphors, image schemas, and mental spaces that come from embodied and embedded experience in the world. Most of what we think of as literal and not creative is in fact understood metaphorically. An abstract idea such as 'knowledge' is understood via a concrete experience of sight, for example, such that we speak of 'seeing' someone's point. The verb 'to know' does not correlate with an action we can perform or contain in a category of experience unless we understand it through our understanding of the visual system. We think the way we speak, and we speak how we think. George Lakoff and Mark Johnson argue that metaphors define what can be viewed as truth: 'In a culture where the myth of objectivism is very much alive and truth is always absolute truth, the people who get to impose their metaphors on the culture get to define what we consider to be true – absolutely and objectively true.'[1] Seeing might be a very good way of conceiving of knowing, but other basic metaphors used to understand the abstract through reference to the concrete (argument is war, time is money) might be ideologically, as well as cognitively, constraining.

To say that cognition is embodied means more than that the brain is part of the body and thus impossible to separate fully. The brain is not a computer operating 'off-site' and then sending messages to the body. Thinking is what happens when I am in my body. Imagining an eagle and seeing an eagle are activities that use many of the same cells. The meaning carried by the shape my mouth takes in saying the word is part of my experience of the word, so that most people will share similar guesses as to what 'kiki' and 'bouba' mean because of what it feels like to say the made-up words. To say that cognition is embodied means that, as Raymond Gibbs says, 'people's understandings of linguistic meanings are not divorced from their embodied experiences, but rather are fundamentally constrained by them in predictable ways'. He articulates the 'embodiment premise' in the following way:

> People's subjective felt experiences of their bodies in action provide part of the fundamental grounding for language and thought. Cognition is what occurs when the body engages the physical, cultural world and must be studied in terms of the dynamical interactions between people and the environment. Human language and thought emerge from recurring patterns of embodied activity that constrain ongoing intelligent behavior. We must not assume cognition to be purely internal, symbolic, computational, and disembodied, but seek out the gross and detailed ways that language and thought are inextricably shaped by embodied action.[2]

Comprehending language and performance is a full-bodied affair.

There are many books, this volume being one of them, providing an analysis of theatre and literature in light of new research in the cognitive sciences or in the context of contemporary scientific discoveries. Mary Crane's *Losing Touch with Nature* is about 'the period of ferment, confusion, and angst between around 1530 and 1610 in England, when the settled Aristotelian, Galenic, and Ptolemaic accounts of how the universe worked began to fall apart and the new ideas that would replace them were inchoate and in flux'.[3]

---

[1] George Lakoff and Mark Johnson, *Metaphors We Live By* (Chicago, 1980), 160.
[2] Raymond Gibbs, Jr., *Embodiment and Cognitive Science* (New York, 2005), 9.
[3] Crane, *Losing Touch with Nature*, 2.

Her argument is that certain central literary works of the period 'were crucially shaped by the mingled elation and horror occasioned by the changes their authors were living through – elation at the new power afforded by abstraction and a newly malleable universe; horror at the idea that lived experience of the world did not reliably provide access to truth about it'.[4] The detailed historical context she paints renders vibrant the intellectual discord of the time, while her articulation of the linguistic power of the metaphors that shape thinking, not just speaking, strengthens the importance of theatre at that moment. To these arguments I add the centrality of the theatricalization of the ideas expressed in the poetry.

Bruce Bartlett has pointed out the critical polysemy in Shakespeare's use of 'waight' and argues that time and matter are being connected through this word in the poetry. In *King Lear*, for example, both time and matter are evoked in the line 'The waight of this sad time we must obey.' Shakespeare's poetry sets up this connection, but it is in the performance of Lear carrying his dead daughter that this relationship can be experienced by the audience. The Quarto and the Folio edition of the play contain the stage direction '*Enter Lear with Cordelia in his armes.*' When, several lines earlier, the dead bodies of Regan and Goneril are brought on, it is not stipulated that they are carried or by whom; the Quarto and Folio state, '*the bodies of Goneril and Regan are brought in*'. The specificity of Lear carrying Cordelia in his arms is important as a theatricalization of the play's interest in linking weight and wait, space and matter. It is never easy to have the actor playing Lear carry Cordelia, and many productions must find ways of avoiding it, as few men old enough to play the part are capable of this physical feat at the end of a physically demanding three-hour performance. Yet this entrance allows the audience to see what happens when wait becomes weight. We can hear this polysemy in the words, we can see it as we read through the text, but it is only when one actor carries another actor that the audience *knows* it. This stunningly moving Pietà of a father cradling his grown daughter the way he would have cradled her as a baby breaks our hearts because we know it, we do not just perceive it. *Lear* offers its viewers a way to rethink an issue, as Crane shows, of critical concern to Shakespeare's contemporaries. Like the waltz at the end of *Arcadia*, Lear carrying his daughter is the theatricalization of the play's struggle to understand time and matter.

Medieval Performance of the Other

The theatre of the medieval period presented the spectators with numerous opportunities to think about character and personation. Imagine, for

---

[4] Ibid.

example, the first time a story was told by one person pretending to be a character. We are told by theatre historians that Thespis was the first actor, the first person to step forward from the Chorus and tell the story as if he were a character within it.[5] Imagine, hundreds of years later, when the Easter service included the *Quem quaeritis* and Mary and the Angels dialogued about Jesus' resurrection. Rather than tell the story about Jesus rising from the grave, they decided to act it out. During this same time period in Western Europe, farmers first harnessed horses for use on the farm. This is not difficult to see as a profound technological advance: imagine what you can do, faster, when you add the strength of a horse to field work. Someone had to have the idea first, but once the tool was created, it spread because it was useful. The *Quem quaeritis* provided a similar cognitive tool: seeing one person as capable of 'playing' another enables a kind of thinking about our thinking, seeing ourselves as this and not that, and understanding the miracle of a far-off land and time as something that is happening here and now.

Between the fall of Rome and about 1600, people came together in church, not in theatres. Church provided ceremony, symbolism, mimetic action, and, as E. K. Chambers notes, 'dialogued speech', which is 'latent in the practice of antiphonal singing'.[6] Starting in the tenth century, there are records of written tropes, brief sections of dialogue to be sung by the choir. The *Quem quaeritis* enacts the moment the Marys come to the tomb of Jesus and are told by the Angels that he has risen. There is evidence of this early liturgical drama (in slightly different versions and lengths) in different churches and monasteries in England and France, indicating its popularity and usefulness.[7] Chambers quotes an account of the *Quem quaeritis* from the second half of the tenth century, which describes an elaborate theatrical event, with costumes, misdirection ('Let one of these [brethren], vested in an alb, enter as though to take part in the service, and let him approach the sepulcher without attracting attention and sit there quietly with a palm in his hand'), dramatic reveals ('let him rise, and lift the veil, and show them the place bare of the cross, but only the cloths laid there in which the cross was wrapped'), singing, and bells ('this begun, all the bells chime out together').[8] As Chambers puts it: 'Dialogued chant and mimetic action have come together and the first liturgical drama is, in all its essentials, complete.'[9] The 'essential' here is the taking-on of another role: pretending to be some-one else for the purpose of storytelling.

---

[5] For reference to Thespis, one can start with Horace in 'The Art of Poetry', in Daniel Gerould, *Theatre/Theory/Theatre: The Major Critical Texts* (New York, 2000), 78.
[6] E. K. Chambers, *The Medieval Stage*, vol. 2 (London, 1903), 6.   [7] Ibid., 11–14.
[8] Ibid., 14–15.   [9] Ibid., 15.

When members of the community sing from the perspective of Mary or personate Angels, the far away and abstract idea of Jesus rising from the tomb becomes a local story of grief and redemption; the idea of these figures suddenly has a local habitation and a name. Biblical tropes told in church services developed into cycle dramas, Bible stories told on pageant wagons throughout town during a yearly festival. The story was told largely through tableaux vivant, with local guilds taking responsibility for certain scenes: the three wise men, the crucifixion, the annunciation, and so on. There were no professional actors, of course, so local guildsmen took on the part of Jesus, or Pontius, or an angel, and other guildsmen would walk alongside the wagon, telling the story – partially in character and partially out. Current theatregoers might experience this as 'breaking the fourth wall', but of course this did not exist until the nineteenth century; the story world and the audience world were barely separated at all. Jill Stevenson demonstrates how 'the medieval spectator's unique visual, and therefore physical, encounter with a play may have impacted the ways in which he or she derived ongoing religious meaning and value from the performance event'.[10] These performances offered a tool through which to reimagine the role of the Bible in people's lives.

Stevenson points out how central the perspective taking is to the construction of the religious efficacy and affective piety of the event:

> Over the course of the cycle, or even a single pageant, viewers slipped into and out of various viewing positions (I am witness at the crucifixion; I am before an image of the crucifixion; I am before a dramatic version of the crucifixion; I am a spectator at a play; I am standing on my street; I am a citizen of York; I am a member of the Christian community). A collage of social and sacred identities remained present within the spectator's visual and experiential fields.[11]

Perspective taking allows us a kind of augmented reality device whereby we learn to operate on what is in front of us based on supplemental knowledge: how it may be perceived from another angle. Jody Enders connects the personation and persuasion of medieval theatre to the development of the legal system. Quintilian argued for the role taking and perspective shifting that would grant the lawyer an understanding of suffering of their client. This kind of 'counterfeiting' ensures the persuader will have the requisite emotion necessary to persuade: 'Consequently, no proof ... will ever be so secure as not to lose its force if the speaker fails to produce it in tones that

---

[10] Jill Stevenson, *Performance, Cognitive Theory, and Devotional Culture: Sensual Piety in Late Medieval York* (New York, 2010), 2.
[11] Ibid., 77.

drive it home. All emotional appeals will inevitably fall flat, unless they are given the fire that voice, look, and the whole carriage of the body can give them' (Quintilian, XI, 3.2).[12] The emotions come from the body in relationship to other bodies. When one's butcher or blacksmith is playing Judas or Jesus, the biblical narrative moves into the present moment and gains emotional relevance. Like the conflation and separation of the characters and actors at work in medieval cycle plays, the location of present performance and past event also come together. Stevenson argues that the York mystery cycle relies on the presence of York to make sense of the past: 'The York cycle's tendency to conflate dramatic space and audience space may have privileged visceral experience and affective engagement over objective analysis.'[13] Spectators are not meant to believe they are swept away to historic Jerusalem; they are always reminded that they are both there and here, then and now.

Here and Now

When the conventions of viewing art change, there can be confusion and discomfort at first – theatre history is filled with stories of riots and displays of displeasure – but learning to consume art or stories in a new way helps us understand our own processes of cognition and perception. It is not hard to imagine what happened when Naturalism took hold in France and spectators saw actors in shabby garb, feeding chickens on stage with their backs to the audience. Philosopher Alva Noë says that 'art aims at the disclosure of ourselves to ourselves and so it aims at giving us opportunities to catch ourselves in the act of achieving perceptual consciousness – including aesthetic consciousness – of the world around us. Art investigates the aesthetic.'[14] For Noë, theatre, indeed all art, should help us reorganize ourselves to better fit the world around us. Through engaging with this strange experience, this moment in the theatre, we are charged to find new ways of picking up and exploring the ideas involved. Noë reconceives perception as a 'skillful engagement'[15] and argues for the value of honing our 'sensorimotor understanding'[16] of the world around us through a continual adjustment of our concepts:

> Don't think of a concept as a label you can slap on a thing; think of it as a pair
> of calipers with which you can pick the thing up. Seeing something is picking it

---

[12] Cited in Jody Enders, *Rhetoric and the Origins of Medieval Drama* (Ithaca, NY, 1992), 21.
[13] Stevenson, *Performance, Cognitive Theory, and Devotional Culture*, 102.
[14] Alva Noë, *Strange Tools: Art and Human Nature* (New York, 2015), 71.
[15] Alva Noë, *Varieties of Presence* (Cambridge, MA, 2012), 2.   [16] Ibid., 20.

up using one sort of caliper. Thinking about its absence requires that we pick it up, or at least try to, in a different way. If there is a difference between seeing something and thinking about it, it is because of differences in our calipers. Insofar as there are overlapping similarities and kinship between thought and experience, this is because we use some of the same tools in both cases.[17]

This means the history of the arts is also a kind of cognitive archaeology. Through the artefacts that remain – scraps of anonymous scripts, contemporary descriptions – we can hypothesize the cognitive hunger that called for this performance shift or that convention change. Further, if it is true for theatre history, it is true for theatre in the present. We can historicize the theatre changes we see now to ask: What kind of need or conceptual gap is this shift meant to aid? Many of the theatre experiences that I am having now are inviting me to think differently about how I make sense of and tell stories that weave into truth.

Target Margin Theatre, for example, is providing spectators with new ways to envision the self:

> About our process: The company created this play. Over the past three years we held meetings, readings, discussions and workshops to explore the collection of stories known as The One Thousand and One Nights. We generated language, stagings, styles, design ideas. We explored various translations, secondary material, personal responses. All of that work resulted in the event itself, and the text that is its trace.[18]

In 2018, David Herskovits, director and founder of Target Margin Theatre, began a multiyear exploration of *1001 Nights*, creating two collaborative productions as a result. *Pay No Attention to the Girl*, first performed in 2018, and *Marjana and the Forty Thieves*, which premiered in 2019, take as their jumping-off point the epic tale of Scheherazade and the tales of adultery, rape, and murder that she tells to stay alive. These are stories we know, or think we know, not unlike the biblical tales told in the cycle dramas in the medieval period. The staging innovation here is not that actors take on the roles of characters, but rather that there is no stable relationship between character and actor. *Pay No Attention to the Girl* began with one of the female actresses taking the microphone for the pre-show announcement and saying, 'I am David Herskovits.' What this announced – in addition to the start of the show and the need to turn off cell phones – was that suspending disbelief was not going to be a part of the evening. We were not 'blind' to her not being David Herskovits just as we were not going to be expected to

---

[17] Ibid., 36.
[18] Production script, *Marjana and the Forty Thieves*, Target Margin Theatre, 2019.

Fig. 12.1 *Marjana and the Forty Thieves* stages an evolution in our conceptual system from thinking about individuals telling stories to stories generating individuals. Anish Roy, with a black microphone visible on his forehead, tells a version of the story to a small group of spectators (Target Margin Theatre, 2019; directed by David Herskovits). By permission of Gaia Squarci.

ignore the ways in which the actors were playing characters, not being people. By starting the play with this impersonation, Herskovits establishes that, far from collapsing, the division between character and actor is the real site of interest.

In *Marjana and the Forty Thieves*, spectators are invited into a large tent and told to sit where they want; some lounge on bean bags, others drink wine on couches, and some sit in bright yellow chairs. The actors and the spectators all share the same space and the same light. An actor grabs a microphone, hanging from the ceiling, and begins (see Fig. 12.1). The first thing that happens is that the story stops, backs up, starts again:

CAITLIN : In the middle of the night, King Shahzaman AS he started his journey he remembered he forgot his lucky thing, he had to return home to retrieve it. When he got home there was no lucky thing, no lucky thing at all. Instead there was a

SOPHIE : All was as it had been for some time.

ANTHONY : One day, a sudden urge hit King Shahriyar – he wanted to see his brother. So he sent a messenger to go get his brother and this messenger very respectfully obeyed the orders. The messenger got to the brother King Shahzaman's palace and greeted him. Shahzaman said 'Absolutely come whenever you want brother!' and started packing for the trip. The King left with his Wazir and entourage to visit his brother. He forgot something and upon returning discovered his wife in bed with a slave. He was upset.[19]

Caitlin, who starts the play as narrator but also plays one of the Marjanas and many other characters, is the name of the actor playing the storyteller. The reviewer for the *New York Times* said, 'They spend the first part of the show retelling, at considerable, convoluted length, the premise tying together the old fables.'[20] It is true that this telling and retelling is time-consuming and lengthy, but it critically sets up the interpretive calipers necessary for understanding the rest of the play. By repeating the convention multiple times – these are actors telling a story; the story can be told in different ways; actor and character will not be aligned with stability or consistency – Herskovits stages the centrality of the parables to the construction and pliability of the self. The body that 'played' the king the first time does not need to be the same body that plays it the second, and the body that plays Marjana can be one or three bodies. We are not trapped in one character, and the role of the king or the slave or the thief can be played by many bodies. The *Theatre Times* reviewer said, 'You never feel like you're struggling to remember who's who because it really doesn't matter.' While it is true that I didn't struggle, it is not true that it doesn't matter.

The content and the form here are related, of course; the story being told about the story of *1001 Nights* is partially about how the story about the power of stories was co-opted by Antoine Galland, the Westerner who translated the stories and also added to them (Aladdin, for example, is not part of the Arabic original). Many of these stories – like the 'Bull and the Donkey' – are parables, which cognitive scientist Mark Turner describes as

> a laboratory where great things are condensed in a small space ... The essence of parable is its intricate combining of two of our basic forms of knowledge – story and projection. This classic combination produces one of our keenest mental processes for constructing meaning. The evolution of the genre of parable is thus neither accidental nor exclusively literary: it follows inevitably from the nature of our conceptual systems.[21]

[19] Ibid.
[20] Elisabeth Vincentelli, 'Review: "Marjana and the Forty Thieves" Gives a Lesson in Storytelling', *New York Times* (8 April 2019).
[21] Mark Turner, *The Literary Mind: The Origins of Thought and Language* (London, 1997), 5.

Marjana and the Forty Thieves stages an evolution in our conceptual system from thinking about individuals telling stories to stories generating individuals. The individuals, however, seem to inhere not in the bodies but in the ecology of the room: the tent, the design team, the story, the spectators. Each actor has a black microphone taped conspicuously to his or her forehead. The technology is not required to hear the actors, but rather to alter their performance: while the microphones remain off most of the time, occasionally the (visible) sound designer/operator will turn on an actor's mic so that the spoken line becomes a kind of whisper, with the sound not coming from the actor's lips but from a speaker. Just as the characters are played by different bodies, the expression of the character is dispersed from the singular body of the actor to the whole room via the designer.

Theatrical characters – at least since the rise of Realism – have also tended to be strongly delineated individuals. In other words, the dramaturgy attends to the singular human being and their challenges, psychology, triumph, or fall. When, in *Death of a Salesman*, Linda insists at Willy Loman's funeral that 'attention must be paid', Arthur Miller, through Linda, is arguing that despite the challenges of the family and changes in economic/social structure of society, the work and value of the *individual* man must be respected. Characters have been important in theatre because they were singular. Characters in theatre more recently, however, are not as singular, as evidenced in Target Margin's shows as well as other contemporary productions.[22] Theatre gives us a way to stage and reimagine categories like the self during moments when they are placed into flux. The psychological realism of Arthur Miller or Tennessee Williams, a dramaturgy of the internal causes that motivate the individual, is giving way to a theatre that shifts our perspective from the 'insides' of characters (wherein one finds their history or backstory) to the networks that connect us, that make us enact the event together.

Steven Johnson's 2001 book *Emergence* argued that the metaphor of the twenty-first century will be the 'swarm logic' of bees, ants, brains, and software, places where meaning and identity take shape from the actions of the whole: 'Just like the clock maker metaphors of the Enlightenment, or the dialectical logic of the nineteenth century, the emergent worldview belongs to this moment in time, shaping our thought habits and coloring

---

[22] For more on the idea of character in contemporary theatre, see Elinor Fuchs, *The Death of Character: Perspectives on Theater after Modernism* (Bloomington, IN, 2000); Christina Delgado-García, *Rethinking Character in Contemporary British Theatre* (Berlin, 2015); and Amy Cook, *Building Character: The Art and Science of Casting* (Ann Arbor, MI, 2018).

our perception of the world.'[23] I started and ended *Building Character* with the image of the murmuration of starlings, individual birds that fly together creating a seeming whole, and I did so to invite us to think not about individuals but of a whole. The research on extended cognition, as well as the crucial well-being of the planet and our species, calls on us to challenge the science of the individual body, the individual self.

As I write this, the Amazon rain forest is burning. If countries think about this as Brazil's problem, they do not need to get involved; if they understand the Amazon as the 'lungs of the world', they might be able to see the limits of 'America First'. In the same way, if I think about myself as extending into my community – as being a part of the story and a part of the storyteller, as we see in *Marjana* – then more matters than just my story, my safety, my life. There is a species-saving value to challenging the story of my bounded, discrete self. And this story is being told in innovative theatre productions as well as scientific philosophy. Extended cognition is the theory that thinking expands beyond the 'skin and skull'.[24] Thinking is what happens between humans and their environmental tools, connecting seemingly discrete units (brain, hand, smartphone) into a cognizing system. If our environment becomes part of the cognitive act, we must extend what and where we imagine as the 'mind'. Distributed cognition, on the other hand, is a way of thinking about all cognition. According to Edwin Hutchins, 'distributed cognition begins with the assumption that all instances of cognition can be seen as emerging from distributed processes'.[25] This networked self is plastic, changeable, more like the current research on the brain than the idea of individual, semi-permeable cells that was so popular in medical and literary research of the nineteenth century. Our theatre is staging an experience of emergence, extended cognition, and the kind of swarm logic that just might save our species.

If the history of theatre can be seen as a kind of cognitive archaeology, where new conventions evidence new cognitive leaps or conceptual tools, what might we say about where we are going based on where we are in Target Margin's tent, listening to actors tell stories? We certainly are not interested in the internal psychology that dominated much of theatre in the twentieth century. The theatre that detaches character from actor, like *Marjana and the Forty Thieves*, demands that we reimagine what it can

---

[23] Steven Johnson, *Emergence: The Connected Lives of Ants, Brains, Cities, and Software* (New York, 2001), 66.

[24] Andy Clark, *Supersizing the Mind: Embodiment, Action, and Cognitive Extension* (New York, 2008), 78.

[25] Edwin Hutchins, 'The Cultural Ecosystem of Human Cognition', *Philosophical Philosophy* 27, no. 1 (2014): 36.

mean to create art, to find solutions, and to feel and think as a group, rather than as individuals. It privileges the environment of the work's presentation rather than the backstory of its characters. This is a world where characters and ecology are one. This theatre asks us to care about ourselves as mutually dependent *organisms* with the miraculous ability to communicate, rather than independent, communicating *individuals*. Perhaps today's theatrical innovators are inspired by the research on climate change, our microbiome, or black holes. Or perhaps they are just artists, teaching us to see anew as they always have.

Suggested Reading

Clark, Andy. *Supersizing the Mind: Embodiment, Action, and Cognitive Extension.* New York, 2008.

Cook, Amy. *Shakespearean Neuroplay: Reinvigorating the Study of Dramatic Texts and Performance through Cognitive Science.* New York, 2010.

'Bodied Forth: A Cognitive Scientific Approach to Performance Analysis'. In *The Oxford Handbook of Dance and Theater*, ed. Nadine George-Graves. Oxford, 2015.

Building Character: The Art and Science of Casting. Ann Arbor, MI, 2018.

Crane, Mary Thomas. *Shakespeare's Brain: Reading with Cognitive Theory.* Princeton, 2001.

Losing Touch with Nature: Literature and the New Science in 16th-Century England. Baltimore, MD, 2014.

Dancygier, Barbara. *The Language of Stories.* Cambridge, 2012.

Hutchins, Edwin. 'The Cultural Ecosystem of Human Cognition'. *Philosophical Philosophy* 27, no. 1 (2014): 36.

Johnson, Steven. *Emergence: The Connected Lives of Ants, Brains, Cities, and Software.* New York, 2001.

Lakoff, George, and Mark Johnson. *Metaphors We Live By.* Chicago, 1980.

Noë, Alva. *Varieties of Presence.* Cambridge, MA, 2012.

Strange Tools: Art and Human Nature. New York, 2015.

Spolsky, Ellen. 'The Biology of Failure, the Forms of Rage, and the Equity of Revenge'. In *The Oxford Handbook of Cognitive Literary Studies*, ed. Lisa Zunshine. New York, 2015.

Stevenson, Jill. *Performance, Cognitive Theory, and Devotional Culture: Sensual Piety in Late Medieval York.* New York, 2010.

Turner, Mark. *The Literary Mind: The Origins of Thought and Language.* London, 1997.

13

FREDERIQUE AIT-TOUATI

Clouds and Meteors

Recreating Wonder on the Early Modern Stage

In the second half of the sixteenth century, a literary and encyclopaedic genre developed: the *theatrum naturae,* or theatre of nature. In this sense, the 'theatre' was a book considered as a theatrical, visual, and literary space. It was linked to the tradition of 'theatres of memory', the most famous of which is that of Giulio Camillo (ca. 1480–1544), which aimed at classifying the objects and knowledges of the world. Camillo, a renowned master of rhetoric in Venice, developed in the 1530s the project of a universal mnemonic system in order to bring together all the human concepts and all the things that exist in the world.[1] In his book *L'Idea del Teatro [The Idea of the Theatre],* published posthumously in Venice and Florence in 1550, he used the theatre as a mental operation that consists in creating a totalizing and visible world. But this ideal theatre also existed as a material, wooden theatre built in honour of the French King François I as an exquisite machine theatre, which would never be completed and whose operation would remain secret. This back and forth movement between the *idea* of the theatre and its material embodiment will be one of the main interests in this chapter.

It is essential at the outset to underline the difference between this tradition of *theatrum naturae* and the well-studied *topos* of the *theatrum mundi* figuring humankind as actor on the world stage. Rather than the vanity of a tragic-comic human existence, the metaphor of the theatre of nature emphasizes the beauty and order of the world as a divine creation.[2] However, because their interest lies in the materiality of the world, theatres of nature are not limited to metaphors. Most often they become real objects, places, machines, or buildings, like Camillo's theatre. This vogue for the

---

[1] The classic study on this topic is Frances Yates, *The Art of Memory* (Chicago, 1966).
[2] See Ann Blair, *The Theater of Nature: Jean Bodin and Renaissance Science* (Princeton, 1997).

encyclopaedic theatre is an important stage in the long history of the relationship between theatre and knowledge. It points to a need to model the
world through order and taxonomy, trying to capture with a single glance
what we cannot grasp – the whole globe, which is not at our scale. Maps,
encyclopaedias, globes, and wooden theatres built at the time belong to this
effort to put the world, nature, or knowledge in a limited and enclosed
space.[3] This chapter explores the theatre as a device and a technology that
allows us to grasp and show things that are too distant and vast: the cosmos,
the stars, the sun, and other mysterious, remote, natural phenomena. The
theatre is this paradoxical optical device that makes it possible to see what is
not seen. This explains why theatre becomes one of the essential paradigms
of science and knowledge not only in the seventeenth century, but for
understanding nature more generally.

A man of both science and the theatre, in 1686 Bernard Le Bovier de
Fontenelle published the *Conversations on the Plurality of Worlds [Entre-
tiens sur la pluralité des mondes]*,[4] which featured a philosopher and a
marchioness discussing the world system and recent discoveries made by
astronomers. In this founding text of popular astronomy, the cosmos is
presented as a huge machine theatre whose functioning is explained by the
philosopher. This conception of the cosmos is in line with Cartesian mechanism, which states that the universe is made of a single continuous matter,
in which each movement causes a further movement, according to the laws
of motion.[5] The cosmos is like a huge clock, explains Descartes. It is akin to
theatrical machinery, Fontenelle expands in the *Conversations*, one generation later. The dramaturgy of the book is well known: bucolic and gallant
staging in a garden, new actors on the cosmic stage (comets, Jupiter's
satellites, Saturn's rings, imagined other worlds and their inhabitants),
description of the world as an opera, explanation of its workings – the
theatrical metaphor plays to the full here. In fact, in the famous illustration
of the original edition of the *Conversations* representing the Copernican
system (Fig. 13.1), the draperies on either side of the engraving leave no
doubt: we are in a theatre, and Fontenelle gives us the opportunity to see the
spectacle of the universe. At the threshold of the text, between the preface
and the first chapter, the engraving – which had to be unfolded in the

---

[3] See Frances Yates, *Theatre of the World* (Chicago, 1969).

[4] Fontenelle, *Entretiens sur la pluralité des mondes*, ed. Christophe Martin (1686; Paris,
1998). For the English edition, see Fontenelle, *Conversations on the Plurality of Worlds*,
trans. E. Gunning (London, 1803). All quotations are from this edition.

[5] See, for instance, Daniel Garber, 'Descartes' Physics', in *The Cambridge Companion to
Descartes* (Cambridge, 1992), 286–334.

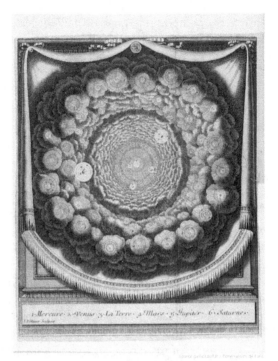

Fig. 13.1 Fontenelle, *Conversations on the Plurality of Worlds*. By permission from Bibliothèque Nationale de France, gallica.bnf.fr.

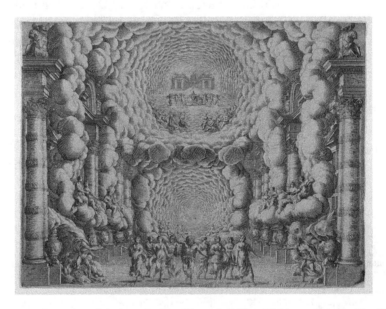

Fig. 13.2 Engraving of the last act of *Les Noces de Pélée et Thétis*, set design by Torelli.

original edition – spectacularly reveals the world's vast machine. It reveals it, but says nothing about it: you have to read the *Conversations* to understand how it works. This flamboyant metaphor of the world as theatre, first visual, then explained at length in the text, should be understood in the context of the theatrical culture so prevalent during the reign of Louis XIV. In what follows, I will trace a parallel genealogy, scenographic and technical, of this central metaphor, relying on the materiality of the scenic work and making full use of the illustrations of the text.

Fontenelle and Torelli's Clouds

Let's take a closer look at the engraving. The sun is in the centre; around it the planets are scattered in a whirl of clouds. These clouds might surprise us: What are such atmospheric, terrestrial manifestations doing in a cosmic space? The stage design solves the puzzle by indicating that it is less a representation of natural phenomena than of theatrical clouds. By their arrangement and shape, these clouds are clearly depicted as staging accessories, or props. The obvious theatrical reference indicates that this element of the drawing must be interpreted as a cultural sign already constituted, a representation of a representation. What is striking here is the combination of heterogeneous graphic and pictorial codes: cosmological diagrams are borrowed from the learned and astronomical tradition, and multiply the famous system of the Copernican world to illustrate the 'plurality of worlds'; the optical rays around each star evoke solar representations linked to Louis XIV; and finally, since the clouds are theatrical machines, their stylized depiction clearly evokes cardboard or cut and painted wood. In fact, to understand the origin of this image, it is necessary to go back to one of the most famous shows of the century, *Les Noces de Pélée et Thétis*, described in the subtitle as an Italian comedy in music intertwined with a ballet on the same subject given in Paris in 1654, with a libretto by Isaac de Benserade and Francesco Buti, music by Carlo Caproli, and set design by Giacomo Torelli.

Shortly after the civil wars known as the Fronde (1648–53), during which the aristocracy and parliament rebelled against royal power, several festivities and grandiose spectacles were organized by Mazarin to celebrate the sovereign's return to glory. Following the success of *Le Ballet de la Nuit*, performed on 23 February 1653, Mazarin initiated this new production, combining French court ballet and Italian-style musical comedy, in order to celebrate the renewed harmony of the kingdom of France. *Les Noces de Pélée et Thétis* includes some of the elements that made *Le Ballet de la Nuit* a success: the young king dances Apollo again (alongside Lully), the libretto, again written by Benserade, gives the same political message of harmony found after the Fronde ('Discord had come, but it would have been ashamed to appear in the theatre after being driven out of France; it was not appropriate that it should disturb this pleasant celebration'[6]), and the machines are the work, once again, of Torelli. The challenge for Mazarin was to get this mixture of French court ballet and Italian opera accepted; to accomplish this he was relying on the sumptuous machines and set design by Torelli, known as the 'Italian magician'.[7] Performed at Le Petit-Bourbon in April and May 1654 (just before Louis XIV's coronation), the show was a triumph. The memory of its beautiful decorations and machines is preserved in a booklet signed by Torelli with engravings by Israel Silvestre based on François Francart's drawings, addressed to his protector and benefactor Mazarin.[8] The booklet gives a central place to machines. Torelli offers a kind of ekphrasis of the show, trying to capture the visual experience of the dazzled spectators. The 'Regular Description of the Machines, Changes in the Theatre, and Incidents in this Book' tells the story of the piece by describing its successive paintings and sets. The aim is to preserve the memory of the show, to praise the work of the 'inventor' of machines, but also to allow those not present to get an idea of the magnificence of the performance. The printed booklet is thus the intermediary between the performance and its political role as an institutionalization of power, of which it is a trace.

Torelli's sets and engravings were widely known, distributed, quoted, and used throughout the second half of the century. Did Fontenelle know about these engravings? This is most likely, because he chose precisely the story of Thétis and Pélée for his first libretto, which he composed in 1689, three years after the publication of the *Conversations*. It will therefore come as no surprise to find the famous Torelli cloud, this whirl of circular clouds opening onto a luminous perspective, in the engraving of the world system at the opening of the *Conversations*. If the clouds of Fontenelle resemble

---

[6] *Les Noces de Pelée et Thétis, comédie italienne en Musique entremêlée d'un Ballet sur le même sujet, dansé par sa Majesté*, Prologue (Paris, 1654).

[7] Marie-Françoise Christout, 'Les Noces de Pélée et Thétis, an Italian Comedy with Music Intertwined with a Ballet Danced by the King (1654)', Baroque (online), May 1972, online since 4 October 2012, accessed 16 July 2017, http://baroque.revues.org/375.

[8] The description of the sets was printed in Italian and French, accompanied by ten engravings by Israel Silvestre (1621–91), after François Francart (1622–72), under the title *Décorations et machines aprestées aux Noces de Tétis, ballet royal; représentées en la salle du Petit-Bourbon, par Jacques Torelli, inventeur (Scene e Machine preparate alle Nozze di Teti. Balletto Reale representato nella sala del piccolo Borbone)*. Caproli's score is lost, but the ballet's dance tunes have been preserved, and Bensérade's verses for the same ballet were published, with Buti's Italian poem, under the title *Les Noces de Pelée et Thétis, an Italian Musical Comedy Intertwined with a Ballet on the Same Subject*.

theatre sets, it is because they are in fact a direct invocation of one of the most important theatrical productions of seventeenth-century France. To stage the heliocentric theory, Fontenelle chose one of the greatest theatre men of his time; to reveal the mechanics of the world, he borrowed one of his most extraordinary machines from Torelli (Fig. 13.2).

We must pause for a few moments on this double perspective of clouds. Clouds are indeed an essential element of the baroque decor: the famous Italian engineer Nicola Sabbattini devotes eleven of the fifty-seven chapters of his *Pratica di fabricar scene e machine ne' teatri [Manual for Constructing Theatrical Scenes and Machines]*[9] to clouds, and the German architect Joseph Furttenbach studies them in many engravings. Clouds are the machines par excellence, those that make the sky literally 'praticable' by allowing actors representing the gods to appear and fly. Clouds are a pictorial *topos* before being a scenic *topos* and are part of a classical and mythological iconography linking the terrestrial world and the divine world.[10] But gradually, with Sabbattini and even more so with Furttenbach and Torelli, clouds move from the status of machines linked to the function of *deus ex machina*, used in this case as an ornament concealing the machinery that carries the actors, to the status of autonomous and central elements of the set. Aesthetics and cloud mechanics developed in *'pièces à machines'* and operas in the first decades of the seventeenth century.[11] They were organized as 'paradises' and 'glories' capable of carrying many actors or singers and offering sophisticated stage movements that give the impression that the sky is opening up. It is just such a complex machine that Torelli deploys for the climax of *Les Noces de Pélée et Thétis*, allowing the Gods of Heaven and the Gods of Earth to be united in the final ballet. The engraving gives only a weak idea of the technical prowess of this last scene, described here by Torelli himself:

> At the end there comes Hercules with Prometheus delivered [with] the liberal arts, which also dance, while eighteen people descend from Heaven in six clouds, which partially cover the architecture of the Palace: then its perspective changes into clouds; and there seems to be a great depth with many Gods

---

[9] Nicola Sabbattini, *Pratica di fabricar scene e machine ne' teatri (Manual for Constructing Theatrical Scenes and Machines)* (Ravenna, 1638).

[10] See Hubert Damisch, *A Theory of /Cloud/: Toward a History of Painting* (Stanford, 2002) (*Théorie du nuage: pour une histoire de la peinture* [Paris, 1972]).

[11] On machine tragedy, see Christian Delmas, *Mythe et mythologie dans le théâtre français, 1650–1676* (Droz, 1985); on Torelli, see Per Bjurstrom, *Giacomo Torelli and Baroque Stage Designs* (Stockholm, 1961). On the history of glories and flying machines in the theatre, see Viktoria Tkaczyk, *Himmels-Falten, zur Theatralität des Fliegens in der Frühen Neuzeit* (Munich, 2011).

below: ... when the other clouds slowly opening at the back discover a Palace all in gold and crystal of various colours; and this view is all the more wonderful, as Juno and Hymenaeus dancing, there comes out from between the clouds and in front of the Palace a Choir of Love, who dance on them, with much grace and thus end such a superb representation.[12]

The description of the movements of the machines ('changes', in the technical vocabulary of the time, 'mutazioni' in the Italian text) gives a sense of the constant metamorphoses that take place before the eyes of the spectators. According to the rules of the genre, each scene starts by a spectacular change of scenery. But the technical talent of 'Torelli, inventor' is also deployed within each scene: a mountain sinks to give way to dancers (Act 1); clouds gradually cover the columns of a palace, then open to reveal dazzling perspectives, a celestial palace, or dancing and singing cupids (Act 3). It should be emphasized that the theatre sets resemble cut-out paper, paintings, or engravings arranged in space. There is thus a form of circulation from the page to the stage.

Descartes's Clouds: Staging Meteors

At the time of the publication of Sabbattini's *Pratica* (1638), Descartes published *Meteorology [Les Météores]* (1637) in which he proposed to transform clouds into a subject of study. The text begins with these lines:

It is natural for us to have more admiration for things that are above us than for those that are on the same level or below us. And although the clouds are scarcely higher than the summits of some mountains, and often it is even possible to see some that are lower than the pinnacles of our steeples, nevertheless, because we must turn our eyes towards the sky to look at them, we imagine them to be so high that poets and painters even make them into God's throne, and picture Him there, using His own hands to open and close the doors of the winds, to sprinkle the dew upon the flowers, and to hurl lightning against the rocks. This leads me to hope that if I explain the nature of the clouds here, in such a way that we will no longer wonder at anything that we see of them, or that descends from them, we will find it easy to believe that it is likewise possible to find the causes of everything that is most admirable above the earth.[13]

---

[12] Giacomo Torelli, *Décorations et machines aprestées aux Nopces de Tetis, ballet royal, représentées en la salle du petit Bourbon par Iacques Torelle inventeur* (Paris, 1660).

[13] René Descartes, *Les Météores*, in *Œuvres*, tome VI (Paris, 1996), AT VI, p. 231 (trans. Stephen Gaukroger).

Why are meteors so central, among all the phenomena of nature? Because they are the source of the human feeling of wonder when we experience phenomena that we do not understand. Wonder ('admiration') is, according to Descartes's *Passions of the Soul*, 'the first of all passions': 'When our first encounter with some object takes us by surprise, and we judge it to be new, or very different from what we have previously experienced or from what we expected it to be, this causes us to wonder at it and be astonished.'[14] Wonder is useful, but it can become excessive if it makes us crave novelty for its own sake. Meteors are the wonders par excellence: they arouse amazement, fear, and faith. They are the foundation of religious iconography, natural magic, and royal entertainment.[15] It is understandably these very meteors that Descartes will first and foremost interpret, explain, mechanize, and, in short, de-animate. Descartes proposes nothing less than to demystify clouds by explaining their machinery. If he is able to explain the nature of the clouds, he hopes, the reader will probably want to accept the idea that all the wonders of the world have a logical explanation, a physical 'cause', and stop seeing miracles in natural phenomena (and engineers as magicians).

> After that, driving the vapours through the air, I will examine where the winds come from. And having them assembled in a few places, I will describe the nature of the clouds. And by dissolving these clouds, I will explain what causes rain, hail and snow.... I will not forget the storms, the thunder, the lightning and the various fires that light up in the air, or the lights that are seen there.[16]

Vapours, winds, rain, hail, snow, storms, thunder, lightning, fires, and the colours of the rainbow: this enumeration recapitulates the catalogue of effects of scenography treaties. 'How all of a sudden can the sky be covered with clouds'; 'Ways to bring forth the dawn'; 'How to fake a river with a continuous stream'; 'How to make the sea suddenly rise, swell, shake and change colour'; 'How to colour the sky': these are some headings in the table of contents of Sabbattini's *Pratica*. The first pages of the *Meteorology* set in motion this whole arsenal of scenography from the baroque stage in order to reverse it and make it the tool of a demonstration, and this in a double movement: literalizing the metaphor of theatre of nature (which becomes a *pièce à machines*) and, simultaneously, unveiling the scenographic techniques of this theatre. The machines of nature, made

---

[14] René Descartes, *The Passions of the Soul*, article 53 (Paris, 1649).
[15] See, for instance, Simon Werrett, *Fireworks: Pyrotechnic Arts and Sciences in European History* (Chicago, 2010).
[16] Descartes, *Les Météores*, 232.

equivalent to the machines of man, are emptied of any mystical or theological significance and mechanized.

What is striking here is the strength of the 'I', the affirmation of a sovereign body that not only describes but literally organizes the elements around it. The philosopher depicts himself here as master of the heavens, capable of 'assembling the winds in a few places' or 'dissolving the clouds': Is Descartes playing some kind of demiurge, a god of mythology? He is, rather, a machinist, capable of mastering meteors and producing the same phenomena as the 'masters of illusions' of his time. However, unlike 'the great Sorcerer' Torelli, Descartes advocates a theatre of the elements whose functioning can be fully elucidated by means of a simple and mechanical explanation. The opening paragraph of the *Meteorology* can therefore be construed as a response to the tradition of natural magic,[17] as if Descartes were reversing Giambattista della Porta's advice to create wonder: 'if you would have your work appear more wonderful, you must not let the cause be known: for it is a wonder to us, which we see to be done, and yet know not the cause of it. For he that knows the causes of a thing done, doth not admire the doing of it; and nothing is counted unusual and rare, but only so far forth as the causes thereof are not known.'[18] On the contrary, Descartes's aim is 'to find the causes of all that is most admirable on earth'[19] and to expose them. In Baroque scenography, clouds are both the mythological home of the gods and the machines that make it possible to travel through the sky in all directions. They are exactly at the junction of two representations of the universe: one mythographic, the other scientific. Therefore, they represented for Descartes a major philosophical challenge. Far from being the vehicles of myth, they constituted for the philosopher the tools of a mechanistic pedagogy. In order to rebuild on new foundations, Descartes undertook to empty the phenomena of nature of any magical character.

However, as Koen Vermeir, in particular, has clearly shown, not all mechanization automatically means mechanistic reductionism; for the Jesuit polymath Athanasius Kircher, for example, magnetic instruments celebrated

divine love and faith, attracted and linked to each other.[20] Far from being the means of simplification, demystification, or reduction, Kircher's

---

[17] Giambattista della Porta, *Magia Naturalis* (Naples, 1589) (French translation: *La Magie Naturelle, ou Les Secrets et Miracles de la Nature* (Lyon, 1631). On Descartes and della Porta, see Stephen Gaukroger, *Descartes, an Intellectual Biography* (Oxford, 1995), 59.

[18] Giambattista della Porta, *Natural Magick* (New York, 1957), iv.

[19] Descartes, Les Météores, AT VI, p. 231.

machines have a profound metaphysical and apostolic role: it is the human emulation of the divine *ingenium* that helps us to understand nature. One of Kircher's 'axiomata' at the beginning of the *Ars Magna* (and derived from Plato and Maimonides) states: 'what technique is for humans, nature is for God'.[21] We must be attentive therefore to the scope of this theatrical metaphor in the Cartesian context: it not only serves to mechanize the spectacle of the elements; it also points towards an apostolic tradition of machine shows. It could be argued that Descartes first targets clouds because, at least since Aristophanes' *Clouds*, they had been the vehicles of the gods and part of the long history of religious spectacle. The religious performances organized in Florentine churches for the Ascension, Annunciation, and Pentecost at the beginning of the fifteenth century are the probable origins of Baroque air machinery. The first machine that allowed 'a man representing Christ to rise to the roof of the church', built for the Ascension show, then developed into the different *nuvole* (clouds) that influenced both the iconography of paradise and the subsequent sceno-technical developments of the European theatre.[22] If Descartes contributes to 'reducing' natural phenomena to simple causes at the beginning of the *Meteorology*, the fact that he does so through an extended scenographic metaphor therefore signals that he works on two levels, demystifying and explaining the wonders of nature but, in so doing, reducing clouds, lightning, and other 'clouds' and 'paradises' of the spectacles to stage techniques. Compared with Kircher's theological machines, which bear witness to a divine *ingenium*, Cartesian machines bring about a profound shift of meaning. Descartes thus not only achieved a secularization of natural phenomena by revealing the theatrical machines; he also radically transformed the meaning and scope of the machines themselves.

The effects invented in the fifteenth century[23] to impress and arouse faith work exactly backwards in seventeenth-century *théâtre à machines*. What has changed is the location: 'paradises' no longer appear in a church but in a theatre, a dedicated, closed place, which immediately signals that everything

---

[20] Koen Vermeir, 'Athanasius Kircher's Magical Instruments: An Essay on Science, Religion and Applied Metaphysics (1602–1680)', *Studies in History and Philosophy of Science* 38, no. 2 (2007): 363–400.

[21] Quoted by Vermeir, in ibid.

[22] Paola Ventrone, '*Nuvole* et Paradis merveilleux dans la scéno-technique florentine du XVe siècle', in *Revue d'Histoire du Théâtre, no. 278, Mécanique de la représentation. Machines et effets spéciaux sur les scènes européennes (XVᵉ–XVIIIᵉ siècles*, ed. Marie Bouhaïk-Gironès, Olivier Spina, and Mélanie Traversier (2018), 23–38. See also Joslin McKinney and Philip Butterworth, *The Cambridge Introduction to Scenography* (Cambridge, 2009).

[23] See especially Hubert Damisch, *A Theory of /Cloud/: Toward a History of Painting* (Stanford, CA, 2002).

we see there is artifice and fiction. The aim is no longer to impress the faithful flock but to seduce the public with the splendour of the machines. Special effects lose their liturgical status and become technical and optical wonders for the pleasure and amazement of the spectators. The agents that animated Renaissance earth became, in Descartes, a set of mechanical phenomena that could be explained because they could be reproduced. The marvel of the spectacle of nature became the wonder of the human mind capable of understanding this machinery of nature.

If it seems relevant to explain the Cartesian mechanism by means of theatrical machines, it is not only because Descartes himself seems to play the machinist at the beginning of the *Meteorology*. It is also, as Simon Werrett has shown, because Descartes 'reconfigured traditional boundaries of art and nature, wonder and skill ... In doing so, traditional distinctions between art and nature were broken down – art ... became the source of descriptions of nature.'[24] Free of its last vestiges of magic and occultism, machine theatre became the means of showing the power of physical and mechanistic explanation: an admirable philosophical theatre.

Fontenelle's Opera

A generation later, Fontenelle too likened the philosopher to the 'machinist hidden in the ground'.[25] In mythology as in the plot of *Les Noces*, the one who assembles and dissolves the clouds is Jupiter; on stage, in the 1654 play, it is Louis himself. Backstage, it is Torelli. And in the physics treatises, it is Descartes. The 'inventor' of stage machines seems to have perfectly accomplished this Cartesian program, subsequently developed by Fontenelle: you can be amazed by this cosmic machinery, but then you must be amazed by the physical and mechanical ingenuity of nature, mimicked by the technical ingenuity of men. For the educated man, says Fontenelle after Descartes, there is no miracle and magic, only artifice, in the first sense of art and industry. The aim of secularization is clearly stated, as Fontenelle made clear when he explained to the marchioness of the *Conversations* the revolution Descartes brought to the understanding of natural phenomena: 'After all Descartes and some other moderns appear: they tell you that *Phaeton rises in consequence of being drawn by cords, fastened to a descending weight, which is heavier than himself*. It is no longer believed that a body can have

---

[24] Simon Werrett, 'Wonders Never Cease: Descartes's "Météores" and the Rainbow Fountain', *The British Journal for the History of Sciences* (2001): 129–47 (131).
[25] Fontenelle, *Entretiens sur la pluralité des mondes*, 17.

motion, unless acted upon by another body; that it can rise and descend without a counterbalancing weight; this, whoever examined the mechanism of nature is only going behind the scenes of a theatre.'[26] In the *Conversations*, Descartes appears as the philosopher who disillusioned the audience (of the opera as much as the theatre of nature). The spectacle of nature, like the spectacle of the opera, is made of machines that dazzle and deceive. Most people 'are affected only by the obscure and marvellous. They admire nature merely because they consider it a sort of magic [*un faux merveilleux*]; something too occult for the understanding to reach: to them a thing appears contemptible as soon as they find the possibility of explaining its nature'.[27] In Fontenelle as in Descartes, we find the idea that *admiration* of the audience is generally misplaced.

The metaphor of opera highlights both the wonder of the show and its simplicity, even its triviality: 'Confess the truth, have you not hitherto entertained a more exalted idea of the works of nature? Have you not considered them with more veneration than they deserve?'[28] A rhetorical question, of course, and a strategic one, inviting the Marchioness to articulate the principle of the true wonder by herself: 'I contemplate the universe with more awful delight now I find that such wonderful order is produced by principles so simple.'[29] The criticism of the 'false wonder' leads to the reintroduction of a new type of wonder, one that is stripped of its occult content: the wonder of the world's machine, made up of pulleys and springs. Because it makes it possible to clear the cosmology of its occult associations while retaining its inherent wonder, the metaphor of opera is particularly operative. But it is a new genre of wonder, which no longer provokes the loss of the faculties of intellectual and moral judgment described by philosophers, but a philosophical wonder. This new wonder can be found, Fontenelle explains, in the craftsman's shop: 'In short, the universe is but a watch on a larger scale; all its motions depending on determined laws and the mutual relation of its parts.'[30] The true wonder, says Fontenelle, is not on the side of the fable and the occult but offstage, where technical ingenuity unfolds in all its virtuosity.

Thus, Fontenelle inherited both Cartesian physics and the tradition of Torelli's machine theatre. Torelli's theatre of machines reinterpreted through the prism of Descartes's theatre of meteors: this is the dual origin, both philosophical and scenographic, of one of the most important

---

[26] Fontenelle, *Conversations on the Plurality of Worlds*, trans. E. Gunning (London, 1803), 10.
[27] Ibid., 11. [28] Ibid., 10. [29] Ibid., 11. [30] Ibid., 10.

astronomical texts of the late seventeenth century – one that will have a lasting influence on the popular understanding and representations of the new Copernican cosmology. The changing signification of clouds over the century, from the marvellous atmospheric phenomena to the simple machines whose workings are observed, confirms the central role of theatrical culture, not only as an echo or illustration of the ongoing Copernican revolution but also as its iconographic and intellectual matrix: What better way to show the infinity of Copernican space than through Torelli's infinite perspectives?

Theatre of Power

Shortly after the publishing success of the *Conversations*, Fontenelle chose for his first opera libretto (in his name) to repeat *Thétis et Pélée*. When he started writing the libretto, Fontenelle was already experienced in writing for the stage, but his first attempts were far from conclusive: he claimed authorship of the verses of *Bellérophon*, Lully's opera on verses first attributed to his uncle Thomas Corneille, created in 1679. As for the first tragedy he wrote in 1680, *Aspar*, it went down in theatre history for having caused whistles. The choice to write for opera can therefore be interpreted as a fortuitous return to the stage at a moment of many advantages and few risks: the genre is in vogue; Lully's recent death leaves room for the young composer Collasse and a young man of letters just crowned with the success of the *Conversations*; above all, the argument is taken from one of the most impressive shows of the century. In fact, Fontenelle explicitly refers to the two founding shows of Louis XIV's personal reign: *Le Ballet de la Nuit*, mentioned in the prologue (where the Night, the Victory, and the Sun are presented), and *Les Noces de Pélée and Thétis*, which together provide the argument for his own opera. *Thétis et Pelée*, an opera with music by Collasse and a libretto by Fontenelle, was premiered at the Royal Academy of Music on 11 January 1689. Did this show political ability or a literary strategy to establish his reputation as a theatre man? It is difficult to say, but the production certainly provides firm proof of the importance of Torelli's machines in his scientific and dramatic work. Indeed, Jean Berain's sets include the stylistic and iconographic matrix of Torelli's clouds, although he retains only the celestial part.

The story of the revival and transformation of these theatrical clouds, from Torelli's set to the successive illustrations of the *Conversations*, shows how literal as well as metaphorical Fontenelle's idea of a theatre of the world is, and that it is based on a deep knowledge of stage techniques as well as a taste for the stage machines invented by the great set designers of the time, notably Torelli himself. In doing so, Fontenelle profoundly transformed the meaning of the mythological wonder that was at the heart of the theatrical culture of his time. It is not so much the actions of the gods as the machines of the world that arouse his interest. The philosopher presents himself as an informed spectator, capable of appreciating the beauty of the work of machines like that of the cosmological factory of the world. An essential iconographic matrix, the theatre ideally serves the philosopher's purpose in that it gives a charming spectacle offered to all (a starry night) and a mechanism whose mysteries must be understood (the physical laws of the universe). Does this mean that Baroque opera participated, through Fontenelle, in the profound upheaval in performances brought about by the Copernican revolution? He offered, at least, visual codes that were both effective and elegant in representing simultaneously the triumph of heliocentrism and of the absolute monarchy. When Fontenelle cites Torelli's emblematic setting in the engraving in *Conversations*, he makes a reference, transparent to the public of the time, to the performance that had celebrated the restoration of the monarchy. This is a way of reaffirming the centrality of the absolute monarch even in heaven. Thirty-five years after its creation in Paris in 1654, Fontenelle's takeover of *Thétis et Pelée* in 1689 celebrated the glory and triumph of the young Apollo who had become Jupiter, master of Heaven and Earth. The metaphor of the opera that runs through the text of the *Conversations* must then be understood not only as a gallant, philosophical, mechanistic reference but also as a political symbol. The gods of Olympus are a pretext for a double celebration: that of the power of the Sun King and that of the ingenuity of the machinists. The force of the image created by Fontenelle lies in synthesizing, in a single striking picture, political, scientific, and mechanical power: the king, the philosopher, and the engineer reign, each in their own way, over the clouds.

Suggested Reading

Blair, Ann. *The Theater of Nature: Jean Bodin and Renaissance Science*. Princeton, 1997.

Damisch, Hubert. *A Theory of /Cloud/: Toward a History of Painting*. Stanford, 2002.

Descartes, René. *Les Météores*, in *Œuvres*, tome VI. Paris, 1996.

Fontenelle. *Entretiens sur la pluralité des mondes*, ed. Christophe Martin (1686; Paris, 1998). For the English edition, see Fontenelle, *Conversations on the Plurality of Worlds*, trans. E. Gunning. London, 1803.

McKinney, Joslin, and Philip Butterworth, eds. *The Cambridge Introduction to Scenography*. Cambridge, 2009.

Tkaczyk, Viktoria. *Himmels-Falten, zur Theatralität des Fliegens in der Frühen Neuzeit.* Munich, 2011.

Werrett, Simon. *Fireworks: Pyrotechnic Arts and Sciences in European History.* Chicago, 2010.

Yates, Frances. *The Art of Memory.* Chicago, 1966.

   Theatre of the World. Chicago, 1969.

14

KIRSTEN E. SHEPHERD-BARR

'The Stage Hand's Lament'

Scenography, Technology, and Off-Stage Labour

My starting point is the ephemerality of performance and the challenge of knowing what went on during a theatrical event from the past. Theatre scholars have used a range of metaphors to describe this challenge: reconstructing performance is like excavating fossils (Joseph Roach), 'catching the wind in a net' (Jure Gantar), 'freezing the snowman' (Emma Smith), or even sorting out the buttons in mother's button box (Christopher Baugh).[1] Naturally, we tend to focus on what the audience actually saw, but we can only ever achieve a partial, imperfect version of past performance, and we rely on the text and what evidence there is from theatre reviews, prompt books, actors' memoirs, and the like. I believe we can achieve a more holistic picture of past performances by understanding the theatrical ecologies of which they were a part and by combining theatre history and performance analysis with science and technology. I take as a case study the extraordinarily vibrant and diverse theatre culture of the nineteenth century, a period when – as Baugh puts it – 'the products of technology ... could as easily take on the role of protagonist as offer illustrations of the scenes of the drama'.[2]

The field of theatre and science has overwhelmingly centred on how theatre has engaged with scientific ideas, with plays being the primary objects of inquiry – the texts left behind once the performance is long over. Indeed, we often speak of 'science plays' as shorthand for 'theatre and science' or 'science on stage'. But there is another 'science on stage' and that is the science of *doing* theatre. This is an applied and technological science,

---

[1] Joseph R. Roach, 'Darwin's Passion: The Language of Expression on Nature's Stage,' *Discourse* 13, no. 1 (1990–1): 41; Jure Gantar, 'Catching the Wind in a Net: The Shortcomings of Existing Methods for the Analysis of Performance', *Modern Drama* 39, no. 4 (1996): 537–46; Emma Smith, '"Freezing the Snowman": (How) Can We Do Performance Criticism?,' in *How to Do Things with Shakespeare: New Approaches, New Essays*, ed. Laurie Maguire (Malden, MA, 2008), 280–7; and Christopher Baugh, *Theatre, Performance and Technology* (London, 2013), xiv.

[2] Baugh, *Theatre, Performance and Technology*, 5.

not a history-of-ideas science, and it usually gets completely overlooked because it was never meant to be seen in the first place. Prising open this facet of the theatrical past to see how science, technology, and theatre merged in practical terms raises some interesting questions that are relevant to the field of 'theatre and science' as a whole.

Lighting Innovations

A good example of the influence of technology in the theatre and on artistic ingenuity is the history of stage lighting. By the mid-twentieth century, theatres were becoming too clean; there was not enough dust and smoke in the air for the sorts of lighting techniques that had been pioneered by Adolphie Appia and others just after the turn of the twentieth century, one of which was to project light onto the air in ways that created the illusion of three-dimensional objects like pillars. This effect was possible because the air was heavy with smoke, dust, and other particles. So Joseph Svoboda, the great Czech scenographer, invented a way to thicken the air. As Karen Freeze explains in her discussion of Czech stage technology, 'to utilize light as a material substance he and his technical team invented the low-voltage lighting ramps whose twelve-volt units emitted very intense and focused white light that appeared as a three-dimensional pillar of light', and in order for this to work in the too-thin air they sprayed 'an aerosol mixture of ionized water droplets [i.e., electrostatically charged water vapour], which revealed low-voltage luminaries'. The technology was proprietary and was sold across the world.[3]

Svoboda's ingenuity with light underscores how theatre and science are both grounded in in-the-moment experimentation: you have a hypothesis, you test it by putting a bunch of things together and seeing what happens, and you have to repeat the experiment many times to get a reliable result. In both cases, an *idea* shapes the experiment, but the emphasis is on the practical work of *doing*. Baugh's account of Svoboda's working life emphasizes the role of experimentation and the conception of theatre as a laboratory:

> Scientific investigation, and its ability to generate new technologies, was a consistent feature of Svoboda's artistic process and therefore of the internal

---

[3] Karen Freeze, 'Czechoslovak Theater Technology under Communism: Ambassador to the West', *Technology and Culture* 53, no. 2 (April 2012): 449. For examples of Svoboda's lighting innovations, see Jarka Burian, *The Scenography of Josef Svoboda* (Middletown, CT, 1971), and Josef Svoboda, *The Secret of Theatrical Space: The Memoirs of Josef Svoboda*, ed. and trans. J. M. Burian (New York, 1993); see also Joslin McKinney and Philip Butterworth, *The Cambridge Introduction to Scenography* (Cambridge, 2009); and Arnold Aronson, ed., *The Routledge Companion to Scenography* (London, 2017).

organization of the theatre. The scenic department of the National Theatre in Prague was structured as a collection of research laboratories that examined optical, mechanical, and electrical qualities of stage equipment, and the material qualities of fabrics and plastics in Svoboda's ceaseless experiment with surfaces for receiving, reflecting, and transmitting light. When the theatre could not provide the expertise, Svoboda developed relationships with academic and commercial scientific research.[4]

Svoboda's innovations can be traced back to the conditions of the nineteenth-century stage, as his own efforts to recreate that environment attest. That century saw a succession of revolutions in lighting the stage: gas light, which was first used as the sole means of stage illumination in a production of *Aladdin* at the Opera in Paris in February 1822; then limelight, which was an improvement on this in terms of precision, brilliance, and safety, though it still had very real hazards; and finally electricity, which was introduced in theatres in 1880 but by no means universally adopted right away. Indeed, these technologies often coexisted, and limelight was used to illuminate the stage well into the twentieth century.

But behind limelight's brilliant effects on stage lay an extraordinary physical effort, described in detail by the anonymous author of a series of articles on theatrical work behind the scenes published in 1883 in *The Stage*:

> The first machine used in the manufacture of lime-light is a retort into which chlorate of potass [*sic*] and black oxide of manganese, in the proportions of four to one respectively, is put. The retort is then placed over a fire, by the heat of which the chemicals are decomposed. This decomposition should be allowed to take place only very slowly, and the gas emanating from this decomposition is oxygen. This then passes by means of a tube into a vessel containing water, through which the gas passes for purposes of cooling and purifying; this vessel is made exactly on the principles of the Hubble-bubble, or Turkish pipe, and from it the gas flows through another tube directly into the gas bag, which varies in size according to requirements, and is made of many thicknesses of india-rubber twill, and filled with a brass tap, to which a lock is sometimes added to prevent the tap being turned on accidentally. Then a similar bag is filled with hydrogen gas – ordinary coal-gas, carburetted hydrogen, is generally used, but where this is not to be obtained easily then sulphuric acid is poured on iron or zinc filings, and the result is the pure hydrogen gas, which is given off into a receiver, and passes thence into the bag. Here we have a bag of oxygen and another of hydrogen ready for use.[5]

---

[4] Baugh, *Theatre, Performance and Technology*, 135.
[5] Anonymous, 'Limelight', *The Stage* (21 December 1883), reprinted in Michael R. Booth, ed., *Victorian Theatrical Trades* (London, 1981), 42.

Several sentences later the author gets to the actual light box and burner:

> The light-box is about 9 inches by 11 in size, is on a double swing bracket to
> enable it to be moved in any direction, and is made of wood lined with iron and
> fitted with grooves for the coloured glasses or mediums, and with the lens fixed
> behind these grooves.... Inside the box, and of course behind the lens, is the
> lime-light burner itself. This is called the oxy-hydrogen jet ... [and it] is made
> so that the admixture of the gases from the different bags does not take place
> until the moment of ignition.[6]

After all this we still have not reached the lime itself, which, we finally learn,
consists of a lime cylinder that has to be moved constantly up and down,
right and left to expose a fresh part of the surface of the lime to the gas jet – a
movement usually done by hand. It is essential to have this constant motion
or the regularity of the light is arrested. The lime cylinder must be made of
pure lime; there cannot be any silica in it, and 'the purest lime is found in and
near Nottingham'.[7]

This rare first-hand account gives a vivid sense not just of the complex
chemical processes required for stage lighting but also of the labour and skill
involved. It comes as a shock to learn that the lime cylinders were tiny – a
mere 7/8 inch in diameter and 1¾ inch in length – yet the constant turning
that is required 'is attended with much inconvenience to the workmen, as the
lime dust is inhaled into the nostrils and throat, and sets up a severe inflam-
matory irritation and almost unquenchable thirst. Workmen engaged in this
lime turning generally wear wet cloths over the mouth and nose to avoid the
effect of the lime-dust as much as possible.'[8]

Technology and Backstage Labour

Who were these thirsty workers? Where did they come from, what other jobs
did they do in order to make ends meet, since so much of theatrical labour
was piecework and hourly? This passage is remarkable not just for its wealth
of information about how lighting effects were created at this time but also
for its illustration of the interweaving of different levels of knowledge and
modes of understanding. A theatre technician of the twenty-first century may
have advanced knowledge of applied electronic principles and computerized
operating procedures, but 'science' involves more conceptual and theoretical
approaches to knowledge and its applications. Perhaps this passage on
limelight in the Victorian theatre shows how these levels of knowledge

[6] Ibid., 42–3.   [7] Ibid., 43.   [8] Ibid., 44.

integrally relate to one another and suggests a radically different epistemology at the core of science in the theatre from that of today.

The fact that the lime came all the way from Nottingham is intriguing, too. Who were the people who quarried it, conveyed it, distributed it to the theatres? What was their relationship to the end product they were serving and indeed co-creating? Such thoughts dog the anonymous writer of those articles for *The Stage*, who notices the same disconnection between labourer and product. A startling example is given in a piece on tailors and seamstresses, which describes an elaborate pilgrimage to see the weavers of the gold and silver fringe that adorns many pantomime and burlesque costumes. The weavers work in their own homes, so the journey to find one takes the reporter and their crew finally to a pastry shop in Blythe Street, Bethnal-Green Road, above which in a small, dingy room they find Mr Tutton, a weaver, 'seated in a corner, plying his unwearying shuttle through a glistening, gorgeous sheen of silver plate weft ... Yet, strange to say, neither the hard-working weaver nor his wife had seen a pantomime for the past quarter of a century, and had never had an opportunity of witnessing the impression – the stage effect – of their contribution.'[9] Hosiery and costumes worn in burlesques, extravaganzas, and pantomimes were usually made 'in some little out-of-the-way country village, or have endured the chimney atmosphere of a smoky provincial town'.[10] The hair for wigs made for theatre on the Continent was 'collected by travellers' across Europe, 'who visit the different villages, and who pay about two marks for a head of average length and thickness'.[11] Think of the vast network of human hair collecting that this suggests. Back in the workrooms in London, teams of girls make the wigs; one workroom contained thirteen girls, and another 'some score of females' thus employed. They 'display considerable aptitude, and as they are paid by piece work turn out in the course of nine and a half hours working day a large amount of completed material'.[12] But since the proprietor, Mr Clarkson, 'gets a considerable quantity of his work done by out-door labour, the number [of girls] present during our visit gave but a faint idea of the employment afforded by a solitary branch of the "Theatrical Trades"'.[13]

This series of articles suggests a wide scattering of theatre workers on whom productions relied, in addition to those working on site. Theatre

---

[9] Anonymous, 'Fringes, Foil Paper, Spangles, Jewellery', *The Stage* (9 November 1883), reprinted in Booth, *Victorian Theatrical Trades*, 16.

[10] Anonymous, 'Hosiery,' *The Stage* (12 October 1883), reprinted in Booth, *Victorian Theatrical Trades*, 1.

[11] Anonymous, 'Wigs,' *The Stage* (19 October 1883), reprinted in Booth, *Victorian Theatrical Trades*, 6.

[12] Ibid., 8.   [13] Ibid., 9–10.

workers were doubly invisible because of their part-time work patterns, often supplementing their income through nontheatrical jobs, and had no union until well into the twentieth century. The fact that the workers were often women is especially interesting and worth pursuing, building on studies of the actress by Gail Marshall, Tracy Davis, Maggie Gale, and others to encompass other forms of work by women in the theatre.[14] Most behind-the-scenes theatre workers belonged to the working classes, whose rise was so thoroughly charted by E. P. Thompson in his 1963 book *The Making of the English Working Class*. We still know relatively little about their daily lives and culture of work, especially how they made a living from such poorly paid, peripatetic, and often seasonal labour (creating the costumes and scenery for Christmas pantomimes, for instance). There is, however, growing scholarly interest in stage labour, such as Baugh's *Theatre, Performance, and Technology* and the collection *Working in the Wings: New Perspectives on Theatre History and Labor*, edited by Elizabeth Osborne and Christine Woodworth.[15] As with Thompson's ground-breaking methodology, which explored sources usually ignored by historians (such as orally transmitted stories, folk art, sports and games, songs and ballads) and sought to understand how artisan workers engaged with new technologies, the aim of this recent body of research is to uncover the culture of work these theatre laborers created and lived, and to grasp how they – from the limelight men to the wig makers to the seamstresses – related to *their* technologies.[16]

There is rich contemporary material still to be mined, for example, in long-forgotten music hall songs and sketches such as 'The Property Man: The Stage Hand's Lament', which the music hall star Alfred Lester performed in 1911 and later adapted into a sketch called 'The Scene Shifter's Lament' in 1921.[17] The song celebrates 'a clawss wot's been neglected'; the theatregoer owes a 'debt o' gratitoode' to 'the man as does the limelight, "noises orf",

---

[14] See especially Tracy C. Davis, *Actresses as Working Women: Their Social Identity in Victorian Culture* (New York, 1991), 20ff. Davis also gives the numbers of women working in theatre and in what kinds of capacities (mainly backstage labour) (30).

[15] See, for example, Elizabeth A. Osborne and Christine Woodworth, eds., *Working in the Wings: New Perspectives on Theatre History and Labor* (Carbondale, IL, 2015), and Christin Essin, 'An Aesthetic of Backstage Labor', *Theatre Topics* 21, no. 1 (March 2011): 33–48.

[16] E. P. Thompson, *The Making of the English Working Class* (London, 1980; first published 1963); see especially chapters 8 and 9 on artisans and weavers in the Industrial Revolution. I am grateful to Jane R. Goodall for drawing my attention to this connection.

[17] Arthur Wood and Harold E. Melvin, 'The Property Man: The Stage Hand's Lament' (London, 1911); and Alfred Lester, 'The Scene Shifter's Lament' (London, 1921); Weston Stack, Bodleian Library, Oxford, Music N12567126.

and works the drop, / An' all for twenty bob a week, wich ain't no special cop'. The chorus is a lyrical ode to such hard work behind the scenes:

> For I am the h'elements, the sunshine and the breeze, ...
> It's me that works the thunder-clap, the lightning, and the rain
> An' then I rolls the clouds away and lights 'em up again.[18]

'The Property Man' was just one of many songs celebrating lowly workers of all kinds. Music hall did tend to recognize the underdog and make fun of the pretentious 'swell' – there are songs about the billboard man (in one version, 'the sandwich man's lament'), the 'birdcatcher', and the 'cable car gripman' (composed by Hugh Morton and Gustave Kerker, who also wrote another 'The Property Man' song).

There have been some key critical shifts in recent years that can help us frame investigations into stage work. One is a greater valuing of material culture, which has been productive for theatre studies as well as other disciplines; for instance, the new journal *Performance Matters*, about the *materiality* and the *consequentiality* of performance, recently had a special issue on Science and Performance. Rita Felski's questioning of the 'uses' of literature and her emphasis on the 'everydayness' of literary and artistic work is also helpful here.[19] A third development is the anthropologically driven investigation of 'intangible' or 'invisible' cultures, derived from Eric Wolf's ground-breaking study *Europe and the People without History*, which laid some foundations that are applicable here. Wolf treated 'peoples' as 'dynamic systems, with fuzzy boundaries, inherently susceptible to change'.[20] Perhaps the sorts of 'theatrical ecologies' I have been describing are varieties of such 'dynamic systems'. In addition, as Thomas Hylland Eriksen notes, Wolf wanted to challenge 'the immanent ideological dimension of "culture" conceptualized as "webs of significance" spun by humans (Geertz 1973), where only a few in fact do the weaving and the majority are simply caught (Scholte 1986)'.[21] This interfaces well with theatre's working cultures: just looking at what it took to illuminate the stage in the nineteenth century, it becomes clear how diffuse the labour is and how wide its 'webs of significance'.

I am proposing not a wholesale adoption of Wolf's methodology that overlooks its ethnographic roots but, rather, the application of certain of his

---

[18] Wood and Melvin, 'The Property Man'.
[19] Rita Felski, *Uses of Literature* (Oxford, 2008), 13–17.
[20] Eric R. Wolf, *Europe and the People without History* (Berkeley, CA, 2010; originally published 1982), preface by Thomas Hylland Eriksen, x.
[21] Ibid., xi.

principles to the analogous cultures of theatre work. Much of this has to do with agency. One of Wolf's aims was to challenge what he called 'some unexamined romantic notions about the nature of human action in the world':

> One notion portrays humans as inherently creative and ever ready to reinvent who they are and who they want to be. Another is that humans will instinctively resist domination and that 'resistance' can be thought of and studied as a unitary category. I believe that here the wish has become father and mother to the thought. People do not always resist the constraints in which they find themselves, nor can they reinvent themselves freely in cultural constructions of their own choosing.[22]

While the obvious reason workers of the theatre have been overlooked or ignored is that they have been literally behind the scenes and therefore invisible to scholars focusing on the finished theatrical product, another subtler reason may lie in this caution about resistance; Wolf suggests that we may wishfully foist it onto those we are investigating, as unconsciously as we search for the subversive in literature, as Felski argues. Theatre workers were part of 'cultural constructions' that they may have chafed against, certainly, but may not have known how to alter. Yet, as Wolf concludes, 'common people were as much agents in the historical process as they were its victims and silent witnesses. We thus need to uncover the history of "the people without history" – the active histories of "primitives", peasantries, laborers, immigrants, and besieged minorities.'[23]

The interest in invisible cultures is turning increasingly to work.[24] At the same time, a similar reconfiguration of interests is occurring in the field of literature and science with regard to technology. In the 2017 special issue of *Journal of Literature and Science* on 'the state of the field', Jennifer L. Lieberman called for a formalization of technology's place in the field, in terms of not just subject matter but also methodologies. She asks if we are analyzing technology and culture 'in the same way that we analyse the arts and artifacts of literature and science'. Especially striking is her observation that of the few articles that deal with technology within the larger field of publications relating to literature and science, even fewer deal with technological history (as opposed to present or futurist work in new media or posthumanism).[25] Lieberman gives a fascinating account of the frosty stand-off

---

[22] Ibid., xiii.   [23] Ibid., xxvi.

[24] For example, recent conferences include 'Working Life' (University of Reading in 2018) and 'Invisible Hands: Reassessing the History of Work' (University of Glasgow in 2018).

[25] Jennifer L. Lieberman, 'Finding a Place for Technology', *Journal of Literature and Science* (2017): 26.

between the history of science and the history of technology and their respective scholarly organs. She also proposes that science has been studied with literature more frequently than technology has 'because it is associated with discursive practices, while technology is associated with material culture'.[26] She concludes that literature and science's 'historical emphasis on textuality may have also rendered technology a more difficult concept to grapple with than science'.[27] Arguably, this applies as well to historical approaches to theatre that have privileged the dramatic text.

Already in 1959 Roger Burlingame used the phrase 'the hardware of culture' in an article in the launch issue of the journal *Technology and Culture*,[28] and though 'hardware' has now taken on a different meaning I think it is still a potent way to think of how cultural forms like theatre are generated with tools and technologies as much as with words and bodies. A radical decentring of the text becomes possible if we think about theatre in this way – the text is the mere residue of performance, the bones of the 'fossil' being dug up.

Theatrical Patents

As Baugh points out, 'there has always been an important link between scientific discoveries, technical developments and their presentation and use within the theatre', from Bernardo Buontalenti in the Renaissance to Inigo Jones and the court of Charles I and later to the nineteenth-century theatre's flamboyant showcasing of new industrial technologies. In fact, during this period, some of the technological advances that would benefit society at large were *first experienced* in the theatre, such as hydraulic power and electric lighting.[29] Conversely, many inventions that became revolutionary in the theatre, including limelight and folding seats, were originally intended for other uses (e.g., military or public conveyance). But the latest technologies were often put to use in 'low' performance forms like pantomime, spectacle, and sensation melodrama – the kind of theatre that modern drama as well as theatre scholarship initially turned its back on – so this dynamic intersection of performance, science, and technology has not yet been fully explored beyond the realm of theatre studies.

This trail of invention leads us straight back to ideas and to the engineers, chemists, and others who came up with technological innovations for the

---

[26] Ibid., 27.   [27] Ibid.
[28] Roger Burlingame, 'The Hardware of Culture,' *Technology and Culture* 1, no. 1 (1959): 11–19.
[29] Baugh, *Theatre, Performance and Technology*, 2–3.

stage. Each idea is a response to a practical problem, and in contrast to the ephemerality of performance, there is a detailed and complete record of ideas put into practice, in the form of theatrical patents. These range from 'the truly ingenious through the solidly serious to the plainly daft', as John Earl puts it in his foreword to a collection of nineteenth-century theatrical patents;[30] the editors of the collection include any patents that mention theatres as potential utilizers of the invention, which casts the net wonderfully wide and shows the intersection of different cultural, scientific, and social areas in single inventions. For example, an 1879 patent relates to the creation of 'light-absorbing powders and their use at night for buoys, sea compasses, barometers, sheet plate signboards, theatrical scenery, pictures, and artificial flowers'.[31] The patents collectively cover 'most of the physical aspects' of nineteenth-century theatre at least once, some with considerable influence.[32] They provide a snapshot of theatrical evolution, most of it concentrated on the making of illusion, a display of creativity not despite but *because* of the physical constraints of the theatre. Inventors figured out how to make an elephant turn a somersault; how to stage a race with live, galloping horses; how to make people fly, or a ghost appear to be walking out of the floor (the Corsican Trap).

Inventors sought ever more elaborate ways to conjure illusions of all kinds on stage, and took advantage of the availability of new materials such as large sheets of glass. 'Pepper's Ghost' relied on these, and its inventor, professor of chemistry John Henry Pepper, submitted no fewer than seven patents perfecting this illusion between 1863 and 1879. There are also patents for artificial rainbows and for ways to make someone look engulfed in fire. A particularly gruesome patent from 1874 'comprises an arrangement of mirrors for producing illusions in theatrical and other entertainments, the object being to produce the illusion of a human being or other body being apparently taken to pieces or put together again'; this is apparently done by two sets of vertically-fitted glass mirrors (sadly, there is no accompanying illustration of the dismemberment).

As with those parched and sweaty limelight men described earlier, nineteenth-century theatre was a health and safety nightmare. Stages and their machinery were mostly made of wood; 'there was little concern for

---

[30] John Earl, 'Foreword,' in *British Theatrical Patents, 1801–1900*, ed. David Wilmore and Terence Rees (Irthlingborough, 1996), vi.

[31] No. 5255 of 1879, Patentee: W. Morgan-Brown acting for J. Peiffer MacCarty, W. F. C. Périgord de Sagan, and T. Prince. *British Theatrical Patents*, p. 42.

[32] Wilmore and Rees, eds., *British Theatrical Patents*, vii.

personal safety'; and 'the average life of a theatre was about seven years'.[33] The constant danger of fire yielded many patents for fireproof materials, and they usually came in clusters in the wake of a serious, often fatal, theatre fire. The patent record also reveals the ongoing problems of ventilation and heating, how to keep theatres illuminated while removing 'foul air' quietly and efficiently.

Who generated all of these ideas? Who were the workers on this end of the spectrum of theatrical labour? Professions of patent applicants span dozens of different fields. There are the expected ones – the chemists, engineers, electrical engineers, mechanical engineers, civil engineers, 'scientific engineers', many gas engineers, a 'Yorkshire dyer', photographers, opticians, 'scientific instrument makers', a 'physician', and a 'homeopathic surgeon'. Academics are everywhere, with professors of chemistry, maths, and physics having a go at some theatrical invention or other; in 1892, for instance, a professor of physics named Charles Vernon Boys came up with a way to make words and images appear to be moving, akin to the effect achieved when you flip at speed through a series of drawings and it looks like a moving image. This was then used for large-scale advertising at theatres.[34]

The list of names, while overwhelmingly male, does include some women (whose profession is often given as 'spinster'). One of these was the dancer Loie Fuller, who lodged several patents relating to her famous serpentine dance; one shows clearly how the dance worked, with its elaborate positioning of hidden electric lights, coloured lighting gels, and use of glass and reflection (see Fig. 14.1). Another patent (from 1899) describes Fuller's ideas for 'simulating fire on the stage' (Fig. 14.2).

Yet a few years earlier a patent had been filed for using real flame, safely housed in a space beneath the stage and reflected via glass and mirrors so that it could be projected realistically onto the stage. It is interesting that Fuller goes for a stylized, simulated version of fire rather than availing herself of the more realistic techniques available; while the prohibitive cost of fire insurance would have been a consideration, this is wholly consistent with her avant-garde aesthetic.

Rethinking Parameters and Methodologies

This record of theatrical patents, teeming with ingenious devices for fooling the public (and for ensuring its safety), is not just valuable evidence of theatrical work and its harnessing of science and technology; it also

---

[33] Ibid., x.   [34] Ibid., 91.

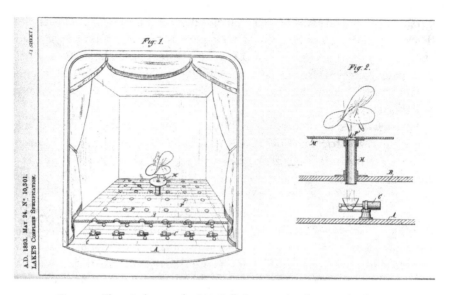

Fig. 14.1 Theatrical patent for Loie Fuller's serpentine dance mechanisms.
Source: **theat**research archives.

underscores the complex interrelationship of aesthetic innovation and technological change. It raises questions about how we tell the story of movements like Realism or Modernism – what role we assign to the scientific and
mechanical factors that enabled and perhaps caused artistic or literary
change. Take as one example the narrative of stage realism, which conventionally goes something like this: playwrights like Ibsen got tired of the
fakery and shallowness of spectacle and melodrama, and started writing
plays that delved more deeply into human psychology and revealed domestic
problems. In this narrative, the playwright is the brave, visionary hero
leading the way to Realism. But the fact is that realism on stage was largely
driven by technological advances, specifically developments in lighting technology. Terence Rees writes in his study of theatre lighting:

> It was the nineteenth century ... that saw the greatest technological revolution
> in history, from candlelight and oil lamps to electric light in the space of three
> generations. In the theatre most of this period was dominated by gaslight,
> which passed from the rudimentary and primitive to the extremes of sophisti-
> cation in an even shorter space. Naturally, methods of production and styles of
> performance were entirely altered by these developments, which aroused much
> public interest in their own time but attract very little scholarly attention in
> ours.[35]

---

[35] Terence Rees, *Theatre Lighting in the Age of Gas* (London, 1978), 7.

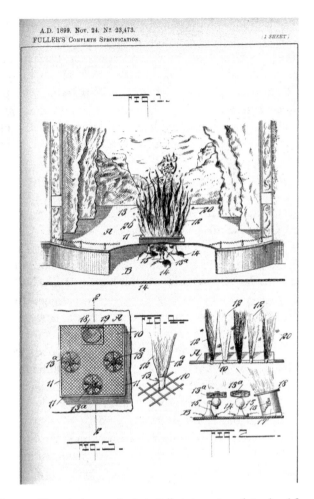

Fig. 14.2 Theatrical patent for Loie Fuller's invention of simulated flames.
Source: **theatresearch** archives.

Equally important was the theatrical art of scene painting, a whole industry in itself. Yet it could not keep pace with the advances in lighting. Some scene painters regarded the developments in stage lighting as a threat, and a power struggle emerged between them and the lamp men.[36] One might assume that the scene painters would win hands-down: they had much more prestige, some of them, like Clarkson Stanfield, becoming members of the Royal Academy. But scene-painting lagged behind lighting innovations; the

[36] Jean-Pierre Moynet, *Backstage in the Theatre: Scenes and Machines*, trans. Christopher Baugh (London, 2015), xx.

introduction of electricity made stage lighting *too* brilliant, so that it was incompatible with the kind of painting that prevailed on stage because it revealed too much detail, was too harsh, and ruined the effects that relied on softer light and produced suggestiveness rather than photographic realism. Bram Stoker (Henry Irving's stage manager) credits Irving with pioneering 'how to produce soft effects with various coloured lights thrown one through the other; to use together gaslight and limelight, both "open" and concentrated lights; to produce silhouette effects by turning down or up certain portions of the footlights, and so leaving the edges of the stage in comparatively dimmer light'.[37] We see here that experimentation is still going on late in the nineteenth century, and by an actor, to reconcile the new lighting technologies with existing resources of the stage.

As the avant-garde theatre practitioner Edward Gordon Craig wrote in 1908, 'after the practice the theory'.[38] How differently might we read and teach plays of the past, in light of such examples of practice? Rather than understanding what happens in a Boucicault melodrama, a Wilde comedy, or an Ibsen play primarily by reading the text and perhaps studying what reviews are available, could we factor in a greater awareness of backstage labour, and of theatre's interaction with science and technology at the time, thinking about how the piece might have been illuminated, what kind of scenery might have been used and how and when it was shifted, the presence of people in the wings making it happen, and how all of this activity might have affected and shaped the atmosphere in the theatre, the texture of the piece, the acting, and the audience response? This might require a more selective approach, perhaps focusing more on contextual objects, images, and archives than textual analysis. It might be something along the lines of how Mark Sandberg in *Ibsen's Houses* describes the field of 'new reception studies', which samples a range of material relating to the given play but 'does not seek to reconstitute an entire horizon of discourse'.[39] Ironically, part of the problem is in the way drama and theatre studies developed out of the domain of literature nearly a hundred years ago to become separate departments of theatre and performance studies, reflecting a sharp divide that has since softened between dramatic theory and practice. This was not such a problem until interdisciplinarity took off and fields such as literature and science formed themselves around textual, discursive practices, focusing

---

[37] *The Forgotten Writings of Bram Stoker*, ed. John Edgar Browning (London, 2012), 152.

[38] Olga Taxidou, *The Mask: A Periodical Performance by Edward Gordon Craig* (London, 1998), 2.

[39] Mark Sandberg, *Ibsen's Houses: Architectural Metaphor and the Modern Uncanny* (Cambridge, 2015), 13.

on narrative and poetry much more than theatre and performance (and on scientific ideas rather than technology and the applied sciences).[40]

It is legitimate to ask whether stage machinery and engineering, however innovative and technical, are actually forms of 'science'. Can we broaden our definition of this 'science' sufficiently to encompass theatrical technology and labour, or does it threaten to become meaningless by being too diffuse? One way of answering this question is to note that in that compendium of theatre patents, the terms 'apparatus' and 'contraption' appear in almost every entry; in other words, theatre unites, or should unite, the 'ideas' side with the 'practical' side. Literary scholars have been thinking about this union for years. Invoking Jonathan Swift's advocacy of knowledge that 'usefully assists in everyday experience', Alan Rauch enjoins us to take greater account of 'the miscellaneous cultural material that lies outside our analytic scope. It is that outlying material, when identified, that ironically warrants a new analysis altogether.'[41] In many ways, theatre workers and innovators constitute such 'miscellaneous cultural material' by being invisible both then and now. Looking into nineteenth-century theatrical patents reveals just how much that invisible world behind the scenes matters to the end result – the cultural objects and events that receive our scholarly and critical attention.

In her book *Literature and Science*, Charlotte Sleigh points to two trends that have opened up the field to fresh perspectives: a much broader definition of 'culture' (modelled by historians of science such as Bernard Lightman and by biographer Paul White) and a new interest in 'history of the book' studies. Sleigh argues for a synthesis of these two trends, combining 'an historical appreciation of metaphor with an understanding of the cultural processes by which books are written and read'.[42] We can take 'history of the book' more broadly to encompass the mechanisms of production and the conditions of materiality across all genres and modes, including theatre. In addition, in his own book on literature and science, Martin Willis points out that performance has become central to the field through work that investigates 'links between the display of science and modes of theatrical representation more commonly associated with the dramatic arts' – essentially pointing to a 'performance turn' in the field.[43]

---

40 Lieberman, 'Finding a Place for Technology', 27.
41 Alan Rauch, *Useful Knowledge: The Victorians, Morality, and the March of Intellect* (Durham, 2001), 9.
42 Charlotte Sleigh, *Literature and Science* (London, 2010), 17.
43 Martin Willis, *Literature and Science* (London, 2014), 15.

Beyond such disciplinary considerations, recuperating past theatrical ecologies might ultimately enhance our understanding of nineteenth-century theatre's role in the wider culture, 'a milieu where art and learning mingled with theatre and circus', as Rosemary Hill puts it in her book on the illustrious architect and scene designer Auguste Pugin.[44] For every Pugin, there were dozens of the 'men [and women] wot is'nt seen'. I hope I have brought them a bit into the limelight and suggested how their work is worthy of our attention not only in and of itself, but because it provides an entirely different and relatively neglected way of understanding 'science on stage'.

Suggested Reading

Aronson, Arnold, ed. *The Routledge Companion to Scenography*. New York, 2017.

Baugh, Christopher. *Theatre, Performance and Technology*. London, 2013.

Booth, Michael R., ed. *Victorian Theatrical Trades*. London, 1981.

Burian, Jarka. *The Scenography of Josef Svoboda*. Middletown, CT, 1971.

Davis, Tracy C. *Actresses as Working Women: Their Social Identity in Victorian Culture*. New York, 1991.

Essin, Christin. 'An Aesthetic of Backstage Labor'. *Theatre Topics* 21, no. 1 (March 2011): 33–48.

Freeze, Karen. 'Czechoslovak Theater Technology under Communism: Ambassador to the West'. *Technology and Culture* 53, no. 2 (April 2012): 449.

Hill, Rosemary. *God's Architect: Pugin and the Building of Romantic Britain*. London, 2007.

Lieberman, Jennifer L. 'Finding a Place for Technology'. *Journal of Literature and Science* 10, no. 1 (2017): 26–31.

Moynet, Jean-Pierre. *Backstage in the Theatre: Scenes and Machines*, trans. Christopher Baugh. London, 2015.

Osborne, Elizabeth A., and Christine Woodworth, eds. *Working in the Wings: New Perspectives on Theatre History and Labor*. Carbondale, IL, 2015.

Rees, Terence. *Theatre Lighting in the Age of Gas*. London, 1978.

Roach, Joseph R. 'Darwin's Passion: The Language of Expression on Nature's Stage'. *Discourse* 13, no. 1 (1990–1): 41.

Wilmore, David, and Terence Rees, eds. *British Theatrical Patents, 1801–1900*. Irthlingborough, 1996.

Wolf, Eric R. *Europe and the People without History*. Preface by Thomas Hylland Eriksen. Berkeley, CA, 2010; originally published 1982.

[44] Rosemary Hill, *God's Architect: Pugin and the Building of Romantic Britain* (London, 2007), 50.

INDEX

Abbott, Steve, 3
acting
  body and, 163–7, 184–5
  cognition and, 169–74
  history of, 15, 23, 167–75, 179–80
  personation and, 176, 178–81
  psychology and, 165, 172, 186
  science and, 167–75
actor, the, 167, 180
  character and, 102, 137, 165–6, 181–5
  humankind as, 29, 50, 55, 60, 188
  multirole casting and, 42, 47–8, 153, 184
  objectification of, 89
  scientists as, 49. See also Rapley, Chris
Adler, Stella, 167
Ahmed, Sara, 107–8
American Laboratory Theatre, 166
Anderson, William, 23
Angelaki, Vicky, 49, 127, 143
animals, 70, 74, 80–1
  Aristotle and, 82–3
  birds, 43–5, 186
  elephants, 78–80, 83, 212
  humans and, 72, 78, 81, 168
  medieval bestiaries and, 72, 74–5, 77, 81
  monkeys, 70, 76, 168, 171
  performance and, 77, 82–3
  scientific research and, 43–4, 85, 157, 168
  species loss, 55, 71–2. See also extinction
Anthropocene, the, 50, 55, 74
  climate change and, 71, 74, 79, 142
  theatre and, 56, 65, 68, 82
Antoine, André, 23
Appia, Adolphe, 204
Archer, William, 165
Arcola Theatre, 101, 105
Arctic Cycle, the, 159
Aristophanes, 1, 197

Aristotle, 15, 78–9, 82–3, 85, 162–3
Artaud, Antonin, 31, 37, 86, 113, 142
astronomy, 17, 189, 191, 200
  Copernican system, the, 189, 191, 200–1
asylum, the, 89, 120, 126, 128; See also
  'madness'
Austin, J. L., 118
autopsy, 93, 152–4. See also body, the;
  theatre architecture; von Hagens

Baartman, Saartjie, 93–4. See also Parks, Venus
Baldwin, Nicola, Leap of Faith, 157
Ballet de la Nuit, Le, 191, 200
Barthes, Roland, 23
Bartlett, Mike
  Earthquakes in London, 48, 50–3, 158
Bartlett, Neil
  Plague, The, 101, 104–5, 109–14
Baugh, Christopher, 203–4, 211
Beckett, Samuel, 64–5
  Endgame, 1, 63–7
  Happy Days, 64
  Waiting for Godot, 66
Benjamin, Walter, 61
Benserade, Isaac de, 191–2
Bentham, Jeremy, 128
Bernard, Claude, 19, 24, 85, 87
Bernhardt, Sarah, 120
Bilodeau, Chantal, 71, 159
biomechanics, 40, 166
Birmingham Rep, 155. See also Gearing,
  Rosalind
Blaikley, Alexander, 150
Blau, Herbert, 99
body, the, 67–8, 163–5. See also diagnosis
  dissection of, 45, 85, 151–4. See also
    autopsy
  hair, 207

body, the (cont.)
  objectification and, 87–93, 95–9, 128–9
  race and, 90–3
  skulls, 60–3, 65
  transhumanism and, 138–40
Body Worlds, 153. See also von Hagens
Boleslavsky, Richard, 166–7
borderline personality disorder, 118, 123–4.
  See also diagnosis
Brecht, Bertolt, 24, 36, 40, 90, 113
  epic theatre, 41, 43, 52
  Life of Galileo, 24–5, 52, 132
Brexit, 104, 106–7
Broca, Paul, 166
Büchner, Georg
  Woyzeck, 18, 36–7
Bulwer, John, 163
Buontalenti, Bernardo, 211
Burlingame, Roger, 211
Bush Theatre, the, 101, 103

Camillo, Giulio, 188
Campos, Liliane, 3, 136, 138
Camus, Albert, 104
  Plague, The, 104–5
Carklin, Michael, 1
Carson, Rachel, 64
Centre for Sustainable Practices in the Arts, 159
Chambers, E. K., 179
Charcot, Jean-Martin, 119–22, 129
Chaudhuri, Una, 142. See also climate change
Chekhov, Anton, 9, 20, 22
Chekhov, Michael, 163, 166
Chomsky, Noam, 167
city, the, 101–5, 110, 114. See also London
  gentrification and, 102–6, 111, 113
  race and, 102–3, 105–6
  theatre and, 103, 105
Civilians
  Great Immensity, The, 141
climate change, 55, 71, 79, 158
  activism and, 158–60
  science and, 50, 52, 74–5
  theatre and, 48–53, 71, 140–3, 158–60, 187
Climate Change Theatre Action (CCTA), 140,
  158–60
Clurman, Harold, 167
cognition, 37–8. See also acting; cognitive
  sciences
  audiences and, 11, 36–7, 134
  ecology and, 169–72, 186–7
  staging of, 26–7, 29–30, 34–7, 176
  theatre and, 181–2, 186

cognitive sciences, 132, 167, 177, 186. See
  also acting; cognition
  bodies and, 169–70, 174, 177, 186
  language and, 172–4, 176–7
  psychology and, 29, 133, 164, 166–7
  theatre and, 133, 169–70
Collasse, 200
Complicité, 26, 29, 35, 136–8
  Disappearing Number, A, 26, 137–8
  Encounter, The, 26
  Mnemonic, 137, 146
contagion, 103, 105, 114. See also city, the
  affect and, 109, 113–14
  fascism and, 107, 109–12
  language and, 101, 106–8
  race and, 106, 109, 114. See also race
  theatre and, 86, 101
Craig, Edward Gordon, 216
Crick, Francis, 47–8, 88

Damasio, Antonio, 169
Darwin, Erasmus, 41
Daston, Lorraine, 5, 14–15, 17–19, 21
De Landa, Manuel, 65
Deleuze, Gilles, 59, 110, 113
Della Porta, Giambattista, 196
depression, 116, 125–7. See also diagnosis;
  Prebble, Effect, The
Descartes, René, 163, 189, 194–9
diagnosis, 96, 118–19, 128
  bodies and, 97, 118–19, 128–9
  diagnostic gaze, 117, 121, 126, 128–9
  gender and, 117, 119–21
  performance and, 118–19, 122–3,
  128
  psychiatry and, 116–17, 124–6, 129. See
  also hysteria; 'madness'
  race and, 125
  theatre and, 117, 121, 123–4, 128–9
Diagnostic and Statistical Manual of Mental
  Disorders (DSM), 116
Diamond, Elin, 117
Diderot, Denis, 164–5
DNA, 46–8, 53, 88, 156
Dolan, Jill, 13
Donellan, Declan, 163
Donne, John, 1, 16, 94, 97–9
Douglas, Stan, 108
du Sautoy, Marcus, 26, 29, 38
  X&Y, 26
Dürrenmatt, Friedrich
  The Physicists, 25
Duse, Eleonora, 165

ecocriticism, 59, 142
ecology, 132. *See also* climate change; cognition
  atmosphere, 50, 52, 64
  theatre and, 55–6, 60, 62–3, 67–8
eco-performance, 55
Ecotheatre, 68, 142. *See also* eco-performance
Edelman, Gerald, 168–9
Edson, Margaret
  Wit, 1, 94–9
'Elephant Man', the, 92
Enlightenment, the, 41–2, 77, 185
eugenics, 13, 86, 157
Expressionism, 36–7, 40
extinction, 70–2, 79–80, 83. *See also* animals
Extinction Rebellion, 158

Faraday, Michael, 149–51
fascism, 104, 106–7, 110–13. *See also*
  contagion
Fauconnier, Gilles, 172–3
Feldshuh, David
  Miss Evers' Boys, 90–1, 96
Fontenelle, Bernard Le Bovier de, 192–3, 198,
  200–1
  *Conversations on the Plurality of the
    Worlds*, 189–91, 198–9, 201
  Thétis et Pélée, 200–1
Foucault, Michel, 65, 111, 116, 122, 128
  animal semantics, 74, 77, 82. *See also*
    animals
  medical gaze, the, 87, 95
Francart, François, 192. *See also* Torelli,
  Giacomo
Franklin, Rosalind, 46, 88
Frayn, Michael
  Copenhagen, 2, 25, 49, 136, 155
Freud, Sigmund, 27, 32, 110, 166
  in plays, 121–2, 129. *See also* Furse,
    Augustine
Fuller, Loie, 213
Furse, Anna
  Augustine (Big Hysteria), 117, 120–3, 126,
    128
Furttenbach, Joseph, 193
Future Bodies, 138–9
Futurists, 40

Galen, 85
Galilei, Galileo, 16. *See also* Brecht, *Life of
  Galileo*
Galison, Peter, 14–15, 17–19
Galland, Antoine, 184
Galvani, Luigi, 164

Garrick, David, 163
Gearing, Deborah
  Rosalind: A Question of Life, 46, 49, 53.
    See also Birmingham Rep
gender, *See* diagnosis; race; women
  objectivity and, 13
  psychiatry and, 117, 119–23
  transhumanism and, 138–40
Gibbs, Raymond, 177
Glaspell, Susan, 9
Glass Half Full Theatre, 141–2
  Once There Were Six Seasons, 142
Green Shakespeare, 56. *See also* eco-
  performance
Greenland, 48, 158
Group Theatre, the, 167
Guattari, Félix, 59–60, 110–13
Gunderson, Lauren
  Silent Sky, 146
Gupta, Rahila, *Genes 'R' Us*, 157

Hacking, Ian, 119
Hall, Jonathan, *Scenes from a Fair*, 157
Haraway, Donna, 71, 79
Harding, Sandra, 41–2
Hardy, G. H., 137
Hartley, David, 164
Harvey, William, 87
Headlong Theatre Company, 51. *See also*
  Bartlett, *Earthquakes*
Heidegger, Martin, 59
Herskovits, David, 182–4. *See also* Target
  Margin Theatre
Human Genome Project, the, 167
Hill, Aaron, 163
Hitler, Adolf, 111. *See also* fascism; Nazis; war
HIV, 96, 156
Hodgkin, Dorothy, 46
Hogarth, William, 30
Hugo, Victor, 18
Huntington's disease, 157
hysteria, 27–8, 32, 86, 120, 128–9. *See also*
  diagnosis; 'madness'
  gender and, 117, 119–23

Ibsen, Henrik, 9, 20, 22–3, 117, 214
  A Doll's House, 20, 165
  An Enemy of the People, 12–14
  Ghosts, 12
  Hedda Gabler, 21, 165
International Classification of Disease (ICD),
  116
Irving, Henry, 216

James, William, 29, 37, 120, 166
James–Lange theory, 166. *See also* James, William
Johnson, Judith
  Every Breath, 157
  Nobody Lives Forever, 157–8
Johnson, Mark, 172, 177
Johnson, Steven, 185–6
Jones, Inigo, 17, 19, 211
Jonson, Ben, 19

Kant, Immanuel, 18
Keats, John, 18
Kene, Arinzé
  Misty, 101–3, 105, 109–14
Kepler, Johannes, 16
Kircher, Athanasius, 196–7
Koch, Robert, 85

La Mettrie, Julien de, 163
Laing, R. D., 124–5
Lakoff, George, 172, 177
Lange, Carl, 166
Latour, Bruno, 110
Le Bon, Gustav, 110–11
Leavitt, Henrietta, 146. *See also* Gunderson, *Silent Sky*
Lessing, Gotthold Ephraim von, 164
Lester, Alfred, 208
Lewes, George Henry, 165–6, 169
Lieberman, Jennifer L., 210–11
limelight, 205–6, 208, 211. *See also* stage technology: lighting
London, 101–3, 105, 108. *See also* city, the
Lonsdale, Kathryn, 46
Lunar Society, the, 41
Lunbeck, Elizabeth, 15, 21

Macmillan, Duncan
  Lungs, 49, 51, 53
  2071, Chris Rapley, and, 49–53
'madness', 116–17, 119–20, 125–6, 129
Marlowe, Christopher
  Doctor Faustus, 40
Marsilly, Hélène Dumoustier de, 19
Maudsley, Henry, 37
McBurney, Simon, 26
  Beware of Pity, 27–8, 30–5, 37
  A Rake's Progress, 30
McLysaght, Aoife, 150
medical sciences, 86
  drug trials, 127, 129. *See also* Prebble, *Effect, The*

ethics and, 90–2, 153
hospitals, 24, 86–7, 91, 94–6, 155. *See also* Salpêtrière
in plays, 44–5, 88, 90–3, 157–8. *See also* Edson, *Wit*
objectification and, 87–99
psychiatry and, 116–18. *See also* diagnosis
race and, 90–3, 109
reproduction, 146–7, 157–8
theatre and, 2, 85–6, 88–90
women and, 44–6, 93
memento mori, 61
Meyerhold, Vsevolod, 164, 166. *See also* biomechanics
microbiology, 85–6
Miller, Arthur, 185
  Death of a Salesman, 185
Modernism, 20, 40, 214
Moi, Toril, 20
Moscow Art Theatre, the, 166
music and performance, 91, 102–3, 140, 150, 152
  music hall, 208
  musical comedy, 191
  opera, 30, 192, 199–201
Musset, Alfred de, 18
Mussolini, Benito, 111. *See also* fascism

Naturalism, 19–24, 89, 181. *See also* realism
  science and, 19–20
Nazis, 104, 107. *See also* fascism; Hitler
neuroscience, 116, 165–9. *See also* cognitive sciences
Newtonian physics, 38, 176
Nichols, Mike
  Wit (television film), 99
Noces de Pélée et Thétis, Les, 191, 193, 200
Noë, Alva, 171–2, 181–2
Nordau, Max, 37
1001 Nights, 182, 184

O'Neill, Eugene, 9

Pangea, 63
Parks, Suzan-Lori
  Venus, 93–4, 96
Parry, Lisa
  2023, 146–7
Pasteur, Louis, 85, 87–8
Pavlov, Ivan, 166
Payne, Nick
  Constellations, 25
  Incognito, 146

Penhall, Joe
  Blue/Orange, 117, 123–6, 128–9
  Some Voices, 123
Pepper, John Henry, 212. *See also* stage
  technology
Peyret, Jean-François, 136. *See also* Théâtre
  Feuilleton
Phantom Limb Company, 138, 143
photography, 21–2, 121–3
Piscator, Erwin, 35–6
Plato, 15, 64, 67, 162, 197
  metaphor of the cave, 1, 57–60, 62
  theatre and, 57–9, 66
Poliakoff, Stephen
  Blinded by the Sun, 155
Polinière, Pierre, 164
Prebble, Lucy
  Effect, The, 117, 125–9
Priestley, Joseph, 41
psychopharmacology, 116, 127. *See also*
  diagnosis; medical sciences
Pugin, Auguste, 218
puppets, 58, 80, 142–3, 163
Pushkin, Alexander, 18

Quintilian, 163, 180–1. *See also* acting

race, 13, 89, 103, 105, 107. *See also* body,
  the; city, the; contagion; diagnosis;
  medical sciences
  gender and, 93, 103
  psychiatry and, 125
radio, 24, 160
Ramanujan, Srinivasa, 137
Rapley, Chris, 49–50. *See also* Macmillan,
  Duncan
Rashdash, 140
Ravenscroft, Edward
  Anatomist, or The Sham Doctor, The, 153
realism, 23–4, 117, 165, 185, 214. *See also*
  Naturalism
Réamur, René-Antoine Ferchault de, 19
Reckless Sleepers, 143
Schrödinger's Box, 143–4
Reed, Walter, 87–8
Reich, Wilhelm, 112. *See also* fascism
religion, 75, 152
  performance and, 44, 176, 179–82, 197
Ribot, Théodule, 37
Rimini Protokoll, 138, 143
Rizzolatti, Iacomo, 168
Roach, Joseph, 2, 175, 203
Roberts, Alice, 150

Romanticism, 5, 18–19
Ronconi, Luca, 136
Rothfels, Nigel, 78–9, 81
Royal Institution Christmas Lectures, 149–50
Russell, Bertrand, 37–8

Sabbattini, Nicola, 193–5
Salpêtrière, the, 119–21
scenography, 102, 123, 137, 150, 204–5
  Baroque, 195–6
schizophrenia, 116, 123–4, 128–9. *See also*
  diagnosis
'Sci-Art', 8, 138, 148, 154
science, *See also* cognitive sciences; medical
  sciences
  art and, 18–19, 55. *See also* 'Sci-Art'
  education and, 147, 155–8
  ethics and, 43–6, 48, 52–3, 127, 157–8
  interdisciplinarity and, 131–3, 141
  literature and, 3, 19–20, 23–4, 210–11,
    216–17
  magic and, 74–5
  objectivity and, 13–15, 17–19, 21, 24
  observation and, 13–15, 17–18, 21
  performance and, 2, 73, 77, 149–52, 217
  public understanding of, 38, 134–5, 147–8,
    154–6
  technology and, 167, 203, 210–11, 217
  theatre and. *See* acting; devised theatre;
    Naturalism; theatre and science
  women and, 43–6, 48, 146. *See also* gender;
    women
'science play', the, 1–2, 4, 14, 203
  characteristics of, 26, 41, 46, 136–7
science and technology studies (STS), 134–6
scientist, the, 13, 19, 22–3, 150
  in plays, 24, 44–6, 49, 52–3, 88
Sechenov, Ivan, 165–6
Sexual Offences Act 1967, 105
Shakespeare, William, 16, 18, 64, 67
  Hamlet, 1, 17, 40, 57, 60–3, 65, 171
  King Lear, 178
  Tempest, The, 16
Shepherd-Barr, Kirsten, 26, 30, 48, 136
Showalter, Elaine, 120
Sidney, Sir Philip, 16
Silvestre, Israel, 192. *See also* Torelli, Giacomo
Simpson, Charly Evon
  Behind the Sheet, 92, 96
Sims, Marion, 92
site-specific performance, 77, 140, 155–6
Sleigh, Charlotte, 132, 217
Slutkin, Gary, 108

Smith, Matthew Wilson, 36–7
Smithson, Robert, 65
Sophocles
  Electra, 15
Spooner, Jon. *See* Unlimited Theatre
stage design, 42–3, 51–2, 191
  scenic design, 17, 192–4, 200, 215–16
stage technology, 26, 185, 203, 210–11,
    213–16
  'Pepper's Ghost', 212
  lighting, 204–6, 211, 213–16. *See also*
    limelight
  patents, 212–13, 217
  stage machines, 191–4, 197–9
Stanfield, Clarkson, 215
Stanislavsky, Konstantin, 162, 164–6, 169,
    171–2
Stein, Gertrude, 24
Stephenson, Shelagh
  An Experiment with an Air Pump, 1, 41–6,
    153
Stevenson, Jill, 180–1
Stoker, Bram, 216
Stoppard, Tom
  Arcadia, 1, 3, 25, 41, 46, 132, 176, 178
  The Hard Problem, 26, 133
Strasberg, Lee, 167, 172
Stravinsky, Igor, 30
Strindberg, August, 36–7
  A Dream Play, 34, 37
Svoboda, Joseph, 204
Swift, Jonathan, 217
syphilis, 88, 91
  Tuskegee syphilis study, 90–1

Tarde, Gabriel, 110, 112
Target Margin Theatre, 182, 185
  1001 Nights, 'Marjana and the Forty
    Thieves', 182–5
  1001 Nights, 'Pay No Attention to the
    Girl', 182–3
theatre
  applied theatre, 140, 148. *See also* devised
    theatre
  collaboration with scientists, 138–9, 141,
    147. *See also* 'Sci-Art'
  devised theatre, 4, 131, 135–7
    audiences and, 134–5, 140, 143
    climate change and, 140–3
    science and, 131–4, 138
  documentary theatre, 143
  education and, 139, 147–8, 155–8. *See also*
    applied theatre

geology and, 56–7, 63, 67–8
  material culture and, 209, 217
  metaphor and, 27–8, 30–1, 38, 56–7,
    188–91
  objectivity and, 14–16, 24–5
  observation and, 14–15, 21, 23, 25
  postdramatic theatre, 131, 136, 143
  science and, 1–3, 11, 40–1, 151, 203–5
    devised theatre, 131–4, 137
    Naturalism, 19–20
  in plays, 25–7, 40, 53, 146, 157, 160
  verbatim theatre, 131, 141
Theatre of the Absurd, 24
theatre architecture, 183
  anatomical theatres, 85, 89, 124, 152
  circus, 77
  early modern playhouse, 16, 151
  operating theatres, 85, 89, 123, 152
Théâtre Feuilleton, 133. *See also* Peyret,
    Jean-François
Theatre Royal Plymouth, 155, 157
  'Theatre of Science', 155–6
Theatre Without Borders, 159
Theatrescience, 156. *See also* Theatre Royal
    Plymouth, 'Theatre of Science'
theatrical labour, 42, 206–10, 213, 216–18
theatrum mundi, 63, 188
theatrum naturae, 188
Third Angel, 138–9
Thomas, John Meurig, 149
Thompson, E. P., 208
Tise, Rhiannon, *Born of Glass*, 157
Tononi, Giulio, 168–9
Torelli, Giacomo, 191–4, 196, 198–201
Trafalgar Studios, London, 103
tragedy, 15, 61, 71, 78–9, 85. *See also*
    Aristotle
transhumanism, 138–40
Trump, Donald, 104, 106–7
Tsing, Anna, 79, 83
Turley, Simon, *Seeing Without Light*, 155–6
Turner, Mark, 173, 184

United Nations' Conference of the Parties
    (COP), 143, 159–60. *See also* climate
    change; Climate Change Theatre
    Action (CCTA)
Unlimited Theatre, 139
  Future Bodies, 138–9

vaccines, 85
Vedral, Vlatko, 139
Verfremdungseffekt, 42. *See also* Brecht

Vienna, 27–9, 34
Vienna Circle, 37–8
Vitruvian Man, 128
von Hagens, Gunther, 153–4

Wang, Esmé Weijun, 118
war, 53. *See also* Brecht, *Life of Galileo;*
    Zweig, *Ungeduld*
  bombs and, 24, 64
  Cold War, the, 64
  Fronde, the, 191–2
  Second World War, the, 24, 46, 90
Waters, Steve
  Contingency Plan, The, 48
Watson, James, 47–8, 88
Watt-Smith, Tiffany, 2, 150–1
Way, Charles, *Still Life,* 155–6
Weaver, Deke
  Unreliable Bestiary, The, 70–7, 79–81, 83
    Bear, 72, 75, 77, 83
    Elephant, 72, 76–80
    Monkey, 70, 72, 76, 81
    Tiger, 75
    Wolf, 72–3, 77
Weber, Samuel, 62–3, 67
Wegener, Alfred, 63
Wellcome Trust, the, 155–7
  'Pulse Programme', 155
Wertenbaker, Timberlake
  After Darwin, 41, 46, 155

Williams, Tennessee, 185
Wolf, Eric, 209–10
women, 20. *See also* gender; hysteria;
    'madness'; medical sciences; science
  actress, the, 208
  African American, 90, 92
  objectification and, 92–9
  scientists, 42, 46, 146
  work and, 42, 207–8, 213. *See also*
    theatrical labour
Woolf, Virginia, 57
Wright, Joseph (of Derby), 41, 45–6
  An Experiment on a Bird in the Air Pump,
    41–4

Y Touring, 156–8
  Baldwin, Nicola, *Leap of Faith,* 157
  Gupta, Rahila, *Genes 'R' Us,* 157
  Hall, Jonathan, *Scenes from a Fair,* 157
  Johnson, Judith *Every Breath,* 157
  Johnson, Judith, *Nobody Lives Forever,*
    157–8
  Tise, Rhiannon, *Born of Glass,* 157

Ziegler, Anna
  Photograph 51, 46, 88, 132, 155
Zola, Émile, 19–24, 86, 89
Zweig, Stefan, 27, 37
  The World of Yesterday, 28, 30
  Ungeduld des herzens, 27–32, 34–9

9 781108 700986